WILLIAM SAROYAN

William Saroyan. *(Courtesy of Layle Silbert.)*

WILLIAM SAROYAN

The Man
and the Writer
Remembered

Edited by
LEO HAMALIAN

Rutherford • Madison • Teaneck
Fairleigh Dickinson University Press
London and Toronto: Associated University Presses

© 1987 by Associated University Presses, Inc.

Associated University Presses
440 Forsgate Drive
Cranbury, NJ 08512

Associated University Presses
25 Sicilian Avenue
London WC1A 2QH, England

Associated University Presses
2133 Royal Windsor Drive
Unit 1
Mississauga, Ontario
Canada L5J 1K5

The paper used in this publication meets the requirements of the American
National Standard for Permanence of Paper for Printed Library Materials
Z39.48-1984.

Library of Congress Cataloging-in-Publication Data

William Saroyan : the man and the writer remembered.

    "Selected books by William Saroyan": p.
    1. Saroyan, William, 1908–   . 2. Authors,
American—20th century—Biography. I. Hamalian, Leo.
PS3537.A826Z93   1987   818′.5209 [B]   86-45936
ISBN 0-8386-3308-0 (alk. paper)

For Aram and Lucy Saroyan
His best pieces of poetry

Contents

Preface

Everything and everybody is sooner or later identified, defined, and put in perspective . . . the truth as always is simultaneously better and worse than what the popular myth-making has it.

—"Memories of the Depression,"
The Literary Review, Fall 1983

When William Saroyan wrote these words shortly before his lonely death in 1981, he must have sensed that sooner than later his lifetime of letters would be subjected to the kind of critical assessment that it deserved but rarely received. This volume of essays, without pretending to be definitive, addresses itself mainly to that serious void in American literary criticism. Its intent is not only to identify and define whenever possible, but also to "put in perspective" a writer who has a legend to his own generations, though merely a name to the next.

Before and after World War II, Saroyan's plays were sensations (in 1942, he even established his own theater in New York), while his works of fiction, especially his short stories, were admired, studied, and often imitated by aspiring writers in search of a style (their poetic freshness of feeling and their originality of form led one critic to call them "lyric shouts"). However, as was the case with many other artists in America who swam against the changing intellectual currents or popular taste of their time, Saroyan's star sank out of sight. During the latter part of his career, he was almost forgotten. He bore this fate with enviable equanimity and no diminution of creative energy (even the uncollected stories of his last twenty-five years will one day make a minor classic), but his reputation eroded so radically that his work was denied the serious scrutiny accorded to his contemporaries of no greater talent.

How are we to account for this mystifying myopia among establishment critics who have the power to identify and define? There is no simple answer to this question—ever—but it seems reasonable to suppose that many of them regarded Saroyan as a strictly "California product" whose concerns were too regional for sophisticated eastern tastes of the time. Some critics seemed to think that the ethnic themes in much of

11

his work gave it a parochial flavor and limited its appeal. Still others thought that his prose was careless and hasty, without respect for craft. And there were those who dismissed him as a brash optimist bent on exploiting soft uncritical attitudes of audiences who wanted only affirmative and upbeat messages in their entertainment, a feeling probably fed by the somber mood of the World War II era.

Unsurprisingly, the public sense of him as a creative artist became blurred. Those who had been excited by his early promise as a fresh voice in American letters were perplexed by the perverse pleasure he appeared to derive from the attention, often derisive, paid to him by the press. Seduced into extravagant antics and self-flaunting that no more revealed his true nature than Hemingway's posturings reflected the man within, Saroyan unwittingly incited an image of himself as a jongleur, a hayseed writer hooked on publicity, an odd phenomenon whose luck was running out along with a minor talent once mistaken for major.

This collection of various opinions and impressions seeks to compose a picture that puts Saroyan in a new and different light, one that separates the solid accomplishment from the flashy myth. Toward that end we have assembled intimate portraits by family members, close and distant friends, and admirers well-positioned to know his strengths and weaknesses as a mortal. Several contributors, novelists themselves, evaluate the influence that Saroyan's fiction exerted on theirs, while others explore and interpret his work in detail as well as in perspective (as Saroyan himself said, "It's a sad work of art that needs explanation, a bad work that can't stand one"). As he predicted, the Saroyan who emerges from these observations is "simultaneously better and worse than what the popular mythmaking has it."

Though the contributors to this volume cannot be conveniently bundled into any sort of "school" or office of opinion, they do seem to hold in common certain attitudes toward Saroyan's work. First of all, they all agree that it has been undervalued by the literary establishment that fixes the standards for "serious" writings—that is, what appears in anthologies, what gets taught in college classrooms, what gets written about in critical and scholarly journals—in brief, what writing with the imprimature of "literature" is perpetuated from generation to generation of educated readers. Now, some years after Saroyan's death, these are signs that reader's tastes are changing, that critical assumptions about his work may be broadening (three books on Saroyan have been published recently, and least two more are in progress). In the future, one is tempted to predict, Saroyan will be hailed as the trailblazer for writers who have taken up his theme of the immigrant experience in America. Few writers have understood the modern tragedy of deracination and exile better than Saroyan.

Second, nearly all the contributors comment on his ability to confront and challenge the contradictions of mortality. "The test of a first-rate mind is the ability to hold two opposed ideas in the mind at the same time and still retain the ability to function," wrote F. Scott Fitzgerald. "One should, for example, be able to see that things are hopeless and yet be determined to make them otherwise." It is precisely this view of life that Saroyan shared and expressed so eloquently in his own version of how one could live creatively under the birth-sentence of doom. Nowhere did he summarize it more memorably than in a passage from *Obituaries* that recalls his early experience in the Fred Finch Orphanage: ". . . the boy on the Oakland porch goes to sleep upon the universe of ice and wakes up and remembers the death of his father and mother, and sees the sun. . . ."

It seems obvious that this childhood experience imprinted itself lastingly on his sensibility, despite his disclaimer ("ten or twenty years later [he] doesn't really know the details of his howling or rage or bereavement"). He had to reconcile himself to the outrageous reality of death, to the agonizing separation from his family, and soon thereafter to the harsh conditions of physical existence in the semiarid San Joaquin Valley, which must have been far more primitive than pictured in his recollections of it. As a kind of strategy for survival, he spent hours in the Fresno library. Books taught him, books tormented him, and books opened a vista of unlimited possibilities, which his youthful imagination began to transmute into stories soon to appear in an Armenian journal published in the East. By this time of his life, Saroyan had already come to recognize the paradox that all mortals must eventually face: the mutability of human life opposed by an enduring life-force "felt, known, and believed: . . . substance, energy, intelligence, man, motion, thought, impulse, and act" ("Two Theatres," *Theatre Arts Monthly* 22, no. 2 [November 1938]: 793). And though he did not profess to be a profound thinker, he was acutely aware of his own relationship to this scheme of things. Many of us may undergo what we take to be the experience of illumination, but we seldom make this satori central to our vision and enactment of life. Saroyan, though, was to maintain a form of fidelity to the illumination afforded by his insights. He would create his art out of this paradox of being, and he would keep his sense of wonder before a cosmos so precariously balanced between such polar forces. In whatever he wrote—and his basic themes were hunger, love, fear, truth, death, and immortality—his sense of fatality was infused with the irrepressible conviction that the sun would appear again in the universe of ice.

Once we identify the vision that sustains the seemingly jocular surface of Saroyan's work, we can follow the logic behind the statement that Saroyan is one of the most fundamentally religious writers in contemporary letters since D. H. Lawrence. As I have implied, ultimately it is this spiritual quality in Saroyan that must have appealed to many of the contributors to this volume. As Matisse once said, "All art worthy of the name is religious . . . if it is not religious, it does not exist."

In what specific respect was Saroyan religious? It was not, of course, in any conventional or traditional sense that he was religious. In fact, though he respected the Armenian Orthodox church as the keeper of the nation's cultural flame, he was indifferent to its central doctrine of salvation and the ecclesiastical traditions associated with that belief. In "The Bicycle Rider in Beverly Hills, Saroyan says of his family religion: "We weren't irreligious, but we had long preferred to keep our religion to ourselves. It is true that one of our boys had made the pilgrimage to Jerusalem in 1801, but the family has it that he was insincere, for he transacted considerable profitable business en route, and spent a rather long time in Constantinople on the way back. . . . The family had God but the attitude was that He was one of the early member of the family. The pose of Christ, his intelligence, manners and wit were examined and found wanting. If we had any Saints at all, they were members of the family about whom over the years a vast lore of lies had been invented, which in time came to be considered amusing gospel." Nor do I mean to suggest that his work attempts to beautify the ugly or purports to see a naughty world as a nice one. Even when he represents the ambiance of childhood innocence, such Pollyanna views of the world are laughed off the scene by a witticism or wisecrack.

What makes his work religious is his talent for transforming and illuminating by his own special inner radiance anything that is drawn into the sacred circle of his imagination. The mundane takes on a magical quality, and the ordinary becomes glamorous. Even when he remembers that searing experience as an orphan in the arctic reaches of his soul, he curbs, resists, and even denies some part of the spontaneous outcry against the injustice of life that took away his father, that threw him still raw and unready into the fight for survival, and creates his own fictional universe that gave meaning to the chaotic arrangement of life. He thus triumphed over his suffering. So often words are abused and degraded in the author's attempt to express the inexpressible, but in Saroyan there is a sifting and tempering that was part of a perpetual process of interior writing that engaged the great issues of existence, no matter how swiftly he registered his thoughts on paper.

From the very beginning (the young writer starving to death), Saroyan's people collide with the ruthless facts of life. They are, in a phrase of Robert Frost's, "acquainted with the night." But in dramatizing his distinctive vision of the world, they convert accident into positive energy and they take lusty pleasure from the simple acts and gestures of daily life—relaxing, musing, conversing, renewing and amazing themselves, establishing connections with each other, sacralizing the very soil of their once-strange surroundings. If, as some critics say, these people are based on idealized images of Armenians who never existed except in the imagination of an emotionally needy boy, it is equally true and more important that Saroyan created lyric characters that his readers and audiences found memorable probably because they epitomized so brilliantly what was lacking in American society of that time—spontaneity, sincerity, warmth of feeling, and unfettered expression of individual identity. In his time, Saroyan made the little city of Fresno no less mythopoetic than Joyce's Dublin, Durrell's Alexandria, Faulkner's Yoknapatawpha County, or William Kennedy's Albany.

A volume of this kind, honoring Saroyan for his achievement, is long overdue. Many of the selections first appeared in the special Saroyan issue of *Ararat* and were edited for the purposes of this book. Others were solicited, and two came in "over the transom." The contributors were invited to write about any aspect of Saroyan's life or work that appealed to them. The essays, fortunately, fell into a rather orderly arrangement reflected in the table of contents. I would like to thank Dr. Arthur Zeiger for reading the manuscript and making many useful suggestions.

Following this preface, Brian Darwent's biographical essay presents an incisive overview of Saroyan's family background and its connection to his career as a prolific writer of stories, plays, novels, and memoirs. Before Saroyan could unleash his creative powers, he had to integrate Old World values with New World urgencies, the pain of spriritual exile and deracination (according to his daughter Lucy, Saroyan secretly yearned for his father's homeland) with the necessity of regeneration. Out of this emotional crisis, the young Armenian soon forged the art through which he could redeem the past and face the future. For Saroyan, this art was a means of conquering madness and chaos, a way to resolve the conflicts of his own life as well as the eternal oppositions of human existence. The pattern of his life, Darwent implies, is the literary equivalent of the popular American myth of Horatio Alger—the penniless boy who becomes a self-made success.

In "Beginnings," Edward Foster contends that Saroyan is one way or another was writing autobiography in his most acclaimed books and that his later openly autobiographical works are "logical continuations of something he had been doing from the start," depicting the foibles of his family, ancestors, and countrymen. If his major contribution to American literature is that special Saroyan "voice" echoed in the next generation of American writers like Richard Brautigan, Jack Spicer, and Jack Kerouac, it was his Armenian heritage that made that voice "one of the richest in American literature."

Indeed, once we recognize that Saroyan's infinite variety forms a seamless web of the kind that Foster perceives, we also see that an unwavering, constant factor in the flux of his roller-coaster life and work was his powerful sense of ethnic identity, of belonging to his tribe while transcending its traditional view of life's possibilities, of speaking to and for his people. Saroyan regarded Armenians, wherever scattered in the diaspora, as kinsmen whom he accepted with a passion usually reserved for the members of one's family. This feeling was no affectation, no mere sentimental or superficial attachment to the past, nor a retreat into a safe refuge when his reputation in the wider world began to slip, but a living, electric force in his life. We may observe this early in his career, in such pieces as "Anatranik and the Spirit of Armenia" and "The Armenian and the Armenian" from *Inhale and Exhale* and in such essays as "The Armenian Mouse" and "Armenian Photographers," (available only in the special Saroyan number of *Ararat* mentioned in Clark Blaise's essay). These fraternal feelings compelled Saroyan to visit Armenia three times. These visits must have intensified the ancestral voices always within, and as a result, several interesting plays (two of them never performed professionally) were born out of this return to his roots. Dickran Kouymjian examines and evaluates these little-known dramas in "The Last of the Armenian Plays," contending that in spite of the explicitly Armenian themes and characters in them Saroyan sought to celebrate the nobility of *all* men and women, of every nation, of every social and economic class. The values that Saroyan inherited from those indomitable immigrants who made the San Joaquin Valley bloom suffused his prose in countless ways, both obvious and subtle. After reading or seeing these Armenian plays—they should be available in print soon—we may be convinced that the corner of the earth closest to Saroyan's secret heart was neither Fresno, Frisco, or New York, but the obscure town of Bitlis, the ancestral home of the Saroyan tribe.

Concentrating on Saroyan's earliest years, S. A. Robbins emphasizes the influence of the orphanage experience on the psyche and personality of the mature man. On one hand, the "universe of ice" became a dominant metaphysical force in his relationship with other people; on the other hand, the crystallization of repressed memories from orphanhood kept him in touch with a "never-ending sense of what it was like to be a child." Hence, the "consistent innocence of his fiction." If one guards against oversimplifying a very complex and creative sensibility, one may, like Edward Loomis in "The Young Saroyan and the American Dream," take this psychological insight into the realm of social consciousness. "Misery was his milieu," says Loomis of the boy who survived those Depression years. But there were also the "sunlit idylls," and Saroyan as a writer found the way to re-create some of those unforgettable moments that also belong to his boyhood in Fresno. In doing so, he affirmed the possibility that the American dream could become reality for the downtrodden, "however inadequately distributed were its benefits to the populace." Peter Sourian, who knew Saroyan personally, also believes that the source of his art was the "traumatically painful experience" of his "God-awful" Fresno boyhood, which he lived through only by transforming it into something mythical and mysterious, almost glamorous. But his later writing, even when it attempts to evoke the melancholy magic of those early years, is flawed for Sourian because it seems willfully to deny the "regenerative, sometimes bitter insights to which his personal maturity may have actually brought him."

Among the beautiful myths that Saroyan created out of his bleak boyhood days was his most beloved novel, *The Human Comedy*. For Alfred Kazin ("Ulysses in Fresno"), the mythic parallels are secondary to the struggle that develops between native innocence and the world's experience. Part of the human comedy is loneliness, and as Homer's mother says, there is no antidote for that sickness—it is part of growing up and becoming Ulysses, the lonely voyager.

Harry Keyishian, in "The Dark Side of Saroyan," thinks that these seeds of pessimism became full-blown in the fifties, starting with *The Assyrian and Other Stories*. He attributes the growingly somber mood of Saroyan's later work to his confrontation with "human failure, loss and limitation," often in his personal life. But taking issue with Sourian's judgment that Saroyan's later writing is sentimental and disorderly, Keyishian concludes that despite everything, what Saroyan "wills and compells us to understand is wholeness," which embraced even the negative.

In addition to Homer and William Blake, among the prewar influences on Saroyan was George Bernard Shaw, who, according to Daniel Leary, stood for "health, wisdom, and comedy" (and who, by the way, apparently despised Armenians for reasons that are obscure). Leary looks back on Saroyan's most prized play, *The Time of Your Life*, through the lens of Shaw, and in so doing, shows precisely how these three elements—"health, wisdom, and comedy"—were skillfully combined into a "mode of contemplating and dealing with a world that seemed unhomelike, inhuman, unpredictable, and mad," much as Shaw had blended them in his own plays.

Late in 1941, Saroyan was invited to Hollywood again to write a film script to be called *The Human Comedy* (later he converted the script into his most popular novel). When he was refused the chance to direct it himself, he produced a short called *The Good Job* in order to prove that he knew how to make a film. According to Dickran Kouymjian, the film was not a roaring success, but *The Human Comedy* starring Mickey Rooney as Homer, was. Saroyan did not live to see the novel restored to dramatic form in Wilfred Leach's musical version on Broadway.

Saroyan's career was arrested for the duration by the outbreak of World War II. On 18 October 1942, while decisive battles were raging at Guadalcanal and Stalingrad, he was inducted into the Army Signal Corps as a buck private and assigned to basic training at Camp Kohler, near Sacramento. R. C. McIntyre in a revealing vignette recalls his brief encounter with the reluctant patriot. Soon afterward, Saroyan took up duties in the Signal Corps' film center at the old Astoria Studios in Queens, New York. Jack Warner, a former army officer, describes the circumstances that brought him together with Saroyan to work on a film project considered "vital" to the American war effort. Though that project was canceled, Saroyan did write the draft script of an instruction manual called "Part I—The Basic Slit Trench."

The next section assembles a variety of personal impressions of the living, palpable, flesh-and-blood reality—not the celebrity, but the friend, the intimate, the mentor, the parent, and finally the figure who embodies for both Armenians and non-Armenians their most human aspirations: the desire, the will, and the ability to change the destiny of powerless people and to influence the course of events through words rather than violence.

If Saroyan was capable of inspiring admiration that verged on idolatry, he does not come off entirely unscathed in these fond recollections. Garig Basmadjian's uninhibited interview suggests that Saroyan's toughest critic (and some would add "worse enemy") was Saroyan himself. With characteristic candor, he confirms the suspicion that in his daily affairs he was not free of the mortal flaws of common humanity and, like so many men to whom fame has come early, was not always easy to abide. Despite the excesses that must have tried the patience of even the most loyal, James Tashjian, Edward Hagopian, Brenda Najimian-Magarity, and William Childress gave us affectionate portraits of the elderly writer.

In companion pieces his daughter Lucy and his son Aram hold up the glass to their father and show his image, warts and all. But one reflection diminishes him while the other magnifies him, as though his children were sighting him through opposite ends of a telescope.

His penchant for publicity notwithstanding, Saroyan thought of himself as a very private person, even reclusive in his later years, and it is true that few people outside of his family circle (which included his cousin Archie Minasian, a poet/house painter of Palo Alto, and his Uncle Aram) were permitted to become his intimates. Among the few exceptions were two California-based young writers whom he seems to have adopted as "surrogate sons." David Kherdian presents Saroyan in his role as an antiguru who encouraged him to write poetry as a vocation but discouraged him from becoming a disciple. A strong sense of independence and a love of laughter were always indispensable for Saroyan. The novelist Herbert Gold weighs the strengths and weaknesses of the Gifford-Lee oral biography ("it lacks the sense of Saroyan's *joie de vivre,* the language always bubbling up"), and with quiet authority, questions some of the myths that have multiplied around Saroyan's name, especially the allegation that he was a closet anti-Semite who abused his wife for not revealing that she was Jewish (Lucy dismisses these charges as arrant nonsense). Clark Blaise, a Canadian novelist, uses the oral biography as a springboard for his own ruminations over a writer whom he admired from a distance in time and space.

There are some writers who respond immediately and intuitively to other writers. When he first stumbled onto the work of Saroyan, the dramatist and critic Arthur Sainer experienced an unspoken, subterranean sense of kinship with a man he had met only in books. It was not so much Saroyan's opinions or themes that he found magical (though Sainer as a Jew could readily sympathize with Saroyan's deracinated and ravaged Armenians), as it was the tone of voice, the sincerity of style, the alternative sensibility to that of the pervasive T. S. Eliot. Though remote from Saroyan's esoteric culture, he felt an exhilarating closeness with the man and wanted to hold imaginary conversations with him as though they had been friends for years. In homage to his master, he ended up sending his own work to *Hairenik,* an Armenian publication.

Saroyan stimulated a somewhat similar reaction in the youthful Pete Hamill: "Reading Saroyan for the first time in those months in Mexico, I touched his myths, and in some stumbling uncertain ways, discovered my own. When the year was over, I no longer wanted to be a painter. I wanted to write." Hamill perceptively points out something that needs to be explored in detail by scholars: the importance of Saroyan's influence on many young writers of the following generation. And in his essay, Joel Oppenheimer describes the impact that Saroyan made on the imagination of a thirteen-year-old who was just beginning to read seriously.

Saroyan had admirers abroad as well, among them novelists like Morris Lurie in Australia, Robert Nye in Ireland and Jack Trevor Story in England. In "The Middle-aged Man on the Flying Trapeze," Story pays him the ultimate accolade: "For my money Saroyan is the greatest writer's writer that ever was, for he nourished and sustained me for twenty-six years and never never let me down. Without Saroyan I would be either an indifferent electronics engineer or a fairly efficient butcher on the point of retirement." What others (including Scott Fitzgerald) had dismissed as mere diary scribbling Story describes as "art of the highest order . . . [a] synthesis of life that is so convincing it is mistaken for life itself."

The correspondence of writers often disappoints our expectations, but a few of them, such as Ezra Pound, D. H. Lawrence, Flannery O'Connor, and Saroyan, were very much themselves in this mode. Their letters can be personal, intimate, relaxed, happily chaotic, a reflection of the complex, volatile being who composes them. In the next section, Saroyan speaks to us in his own unmistakable voice, through representative letters (it is said that he wrote more than 50,000 in his lifetime) to William Childress, Jules Archer, and James Laughlin. Because almost everything he wrote received the full force of his creative power, Saroyan's correspondence shares the color, the energy, and the great simplicity of his imaginative prose. As T. S. Eliot remarked, "Great simplicity is only won by an intense moment or by years of intelligent effort, or both. It represents one of the obvious conquests of the human spirit: the triumph of feeling and thought over the natural sins of language." Even this small sampling of his letters (others have appeared in the special Saroyan issue of *Ararat* and in the September 1981 issue of *The Armenian Review*) demonstrates that communication by post became for Saroyan an exercise in self-expression that embraced his entire being. It was deceptively casual, like so much of his fiction, but the act of corresponding seems to have enriched his own life no less than it apparently illuminated moments in the lives of the recipients, whether they were struggling young writers like Henry Miller, Jules Archer, and William Childress, or promising publishers like James Laughlin. In that remarkable letter to the yet-unknown Henry Miller, for which Laughlin provides a framework, Saroyan sounds very much like his unforgettable self: astringent, compassionate, penetrating, prophetic, arrogant, but never righteous.

In his final years, Saroyan devoted a considerable amount of time to settling matters of his estate and to putting his papers and manuscripts into some semblance of order, a process still in progress at the Saroyan Foundation (among them is an autobiographical work called *50/50*, so called because during his fiftieth year, Saroyan wrote 50 lines a day every day). Toward this end, he had to accept legal advice, though he used to say that he despised all lawyers. He may have made an exception of Fresno-Born Aram Kevorkian, whose obituary essay stands as a fitting tribute to his memory and a finale to this volume.

Leo Hamalian

WILLIAM SAROYAN

Saroyan's Life and Work: An Overview

BRIAN DARWENT

"Get the family out of here, leave this place, go anywhere else, but do not stay here any longer, go to America if you can manage."

This urgent advice Minas Saroyan gave to his family at the turn of the century as he lay dying in the ancient city of Bitlis, situated close to Lake Van in the western, Turkish-occupied sector of the historical Armenian homeland. His son-in-law Armenak Saroyan (the two sides of the family had the same family name) had already come under the influence of the Reverend William Stonehill, a fundamentalist missionary from Brooklyn, at the mission school in Bitlis. Armenak had adopted the Presbyterian faith, and was being prepared for work in America. Travelling ahead of his family, he reached New York in 1905. With his excellent English, and contacts in church circles, he was soon preaching at the Armenian Orthodox Church in Paterson, New Jersey. He sent at once for his wife and family, though he found it necessary to supplement his income with odd jobs.

The family members on arrival were not content to stay on the East Coast. Armenak found himself pressed to abandon his preaching career and travel on with them to California, where many other Armenian refugees were settling, including important relatives of his wife, Takoohi.

Their fourth child and second son William (the only one native to the New World) was born in Fresno on 31 August 1908 and named after the Reverend Stonehill. Armenak meanwhile was not adapting well to California. He had none of the entrepreneurial spirit necessary for success in the New World, having aspirations as a poet and writer as well as a talent for preaching, and his family was impatient with his unworldly preoccupations. It was said of Armenak that he was "too good for this world," and tragically he soon succumbed to peritonitis in 1908, at the age of thirty-six.

Following their father's death, William, his brother Henry, and his

Armenak Saroyan, New York, 1907. *(Courtesy of Aram Saroyan.)*

sisters Zabel and Cosette were placed in the Fred Finch Orphanage in Oakland, while Takoohi took up menial work in nearby San Francisco. For young William this meant in effect the loss of his mother as well. Six years were to pass—not entirely unhappy ones: William was to remember fondly in particular the Irish cook's wonderful meat pie— before the family was properly reunited back in Fresno, in the San Joaquin Valley. His maternal grandmother Lucy, widow of Minas Saroyan, soon joined the household. She was to be a strong influence on William, who later described her as the family's "force, authority, intelligence, wisdom and faith."

As he grew up in Fresno, an American boy who also belonged to the exiled Armenian tribe, William had an undistinguished academic career. His intelligence was recognized, however, and he was urged to go to college. But bored by the slow pace of schoolwork and irritated by the frequent reminders that he was the son of an immigrant, he left school early—though not before he had learned to touch-type at the Technical School. His mother had shown him when he was nine, what had survived of his father's unpublished writing, and the secret ambition to be a writer was born at that point. At twelve, a chance reading of Guy de Maupassant's short story "The Bell" confirmed the ambition. He began to explore the shelves of Fresno's well-stocked but underused public library. During the early days of silent movies, he lost no opportunity to gain unpaid entry into the darkened world of the Bijou theater.

In those years he sold newspapers on the streets to earn money badly needed by his family, living in what he would later describe in *My Name is Aram* as "the most amazing and comical poverty in the world." Afterward he became a messenger with a postal-telegraph company, acquiring a reputation for high-speed deliveries.

At eighteen, Saroyan was ready to seek his fortune. His first serious attempt to leave Fresno took him only—and by mistake—as far as Los Angeles, where in a moment of desperation he joined the National Guard and was subjected to two weeks' training. Soon afterward, back home, he had a story accepted by the *Overland Monthly,* a western magazine that in its day had published Jack London and Ambrose Bierce. Now he felt ready for New York, and on borrowed money made the trip by Greyhound bus in 1928. The first thing he did was to visit Mrs. William Stonehill in Brooklyn. She came to the door, looked at him a moment, then said, "You are Armenak Saroyan's son. Please come in." She then told him about his father and mother when she had known them. From then on, things went badly. His suitcase containing all his money had been sent to New Orleans. He had a cheap night at the YMCA, took a job with the postal telegraph, and found a furnished room "which stank" at the New York Hotel near Washington Market,

Mihran, Armenak, William, and Takoohi Saroyan, Fresno, 1909. (Mihran was Armenak's brother from whom he borrowed $100 for the trip from Paterson, New Jersey, to Fresno.) *(Courtesy of Aram Saroyan.)*

The Saroyan children: Zabel, Henry, William, and Cosette, Fresno, ca. 1910.
(Courtesy of Aram Saroyan.)

and spent his spare time on the streets or in the New York Public Library. His early schedule left him free to explore the city, but he got nowhere with his literary ambitions, and with the coming of winter he was soon homesick. In less than six months, the adventure was over. He returned to California wiser, more sober, embarrassed, and no longer confident that he would write something so irresistible that it would bring him instant fame.

The family had moved to San Francisco, where William worked at a variety of uninspiring jobs (the most memorable with a funeral establishment). By the time of the Great Depression he was committed to writing and gave up all pretense of seriously pursuing any other career. Occasional winnings from gambling supplemented the scant living he earned by selling vegetables in Saturday market stalls.

An Armenian journal, *Hairenik*, began to publish his work in 1933. James H. Tashjian, in his preface to his *My Name is Saroyan*, has emphasised the importance of these early publications. A more important breakthrough came, however, late in 1933, when Whit Burnett and Martha Foley of *Story* magazine accepted "The Daring Young Man on the Flying Trapeze"—a short story, part experimental, about a young writer who starves to death, with dignity—for which he was paid fifteen dollars.

Now in his middle twenties, William Saroyan informed the editors of *Story* that he would send them a new story each day for a whole month (January 1934) and, without waiting for their reaction or comment, set to work. He began with no firm ideas as to what the stories would be about, but this hardly mattered because his basic working method of choosing a starting point almost at random and taking it from there—at full speed—was already well established. Midway through the month a telegram arrived: yes, the stories were being received with great interest—keep them coming! Meanwhile, Edward J. O'Brien had selected a *Hairenik* story (written under the pseudonym "Sirak Goryan") called "The Broken Wheel" for his *Best American Stories of 1934*. William Saroyan's apprenticeship had ended.

More pieces were printed in *Story*, and as word spread of this new and exciting prodigy, stories were soon appearing in *The American Mercury, Harper's, The Yale Review, Scribner's* and *The Atlantic Monthly*. By October 1934, Random House was ready to publish *The Daring Young Man on the Flying Trapeze, and Other Stories*. Surprisingly for a collection of short stories, the book was a best seller. Saroyan had arrived on the literary scene with a bang. His work had most of the critics "dancing in the streets," though there were dissenting voices that resented this sudden rise to fame of an unschooled writer from the boondocks, who broke or disregarded the rules and had already a reputation as a self-proclaimed genius. Hemingway attacked him in *Esquire*, in petulant mood, while

Thurber was inclined in private letters to dismiss him as just another proletarian writer who couldn't write. Saroyan was unimpressed. Soon he was planning a trip to Europe, and to the land of his forebears.

This first journey to foreign parts was to remain the most meaningful and memorable of his life, though on that journey he wasn't quite able to reach his father's city, Bitlis. His travels, taking in London, Edinburgh, Paris, Vienna, and Moscow, stopped in Erivan, some two hundred miles short. In Moscow he met the Armenian poet Yeghishe Charentz, and was promised an interview with Maxim Gorky, an offer later withdrawn. Russia under Communism disappointed his hopes for the emergence of a new civilized order based on the ideals of the common man, and he couldn't conceal the fact. Passing through Finland before returning to America, he paid the composer Sibelius an unplanned visit.

Saroyan's eagerly awaited second book, *Inhale and Exhale,* published in 1936, was a truly massive collection of stories into which he seemed to want to cram everything he had so far written that hadn't gone into his first book. The book was not a great critical and commercial success, though it undoubtedly contains some of his finest stories, including a number of pieces about his roots.

Late in 1936 he went to Hollywood and briefly took a job at Budd Schulberg's studio, where he appears to have worked conscientiously, if to little effect. While there he was approached by four students who wanted to use his work to launch a publishing company (Conference Press). As a result, Saroyan's third book, *Three Times Three,* a volume as slim as its predecessor was fat, appeared by the end of the year. Among these stories was "The Man with the Heart in the Highlands," which he would later convert into his first successful play. He had written the story in a feverish condition just prior to rushing to hospital for an appendicitis operation that saved his life.

Next, in 1937, came *Little Children,* published by Harcourt Brace (Saroyan's principal publisher for many years). Up to this point, notwithstanding his commercial success, he had taken little trouble to revise or edit his stories—a practice he regarded as a kind of cheating. This new, rather more thoughtful collection, was the first in which the stories were written in a broadly consistent style, and the title reflected fairly accurately the contents of the book. *Little Children* drew heavily on Saroyan's childhood experiences in Fresno, anticipating the later and more successful *My Name Is Aram.*

Saroyan published three more collections in the thirties: *Love, Here is My Hat* (1938), *The Trouble with Tigers* (1938), and *Peace, It's Wonderful* (1939). His career as a playwright began in earnest with *My Heart's in the Highlands* (adapted from the story) in 1939. The play was well received, most importantly by George Jean Nathan, and was swiftly followed in the same year by his greatest theatrical success, *The Time of Your Life*. This earned the New York Drama Critics' Circle Award and the Pulitzer Prize (the first play to win both), though the latter he declined because of his strong feelings about commerce patronizing the arts. It also won him a further reputation for arrogance as a result of his taking personal charge of the production, against expert advice, before the play reached Broadway. *The Time of Your Life* was followed by a string of Broadway productions—*Love's Old Sweet Song, The Beautiful People, Across the Board on Tomorrow Morning, Talking to You, Hello Out There*—and for a period in 1941 he established the Saroyan Theatre at the Belasco. Suspicious of the New York theatrical establishment, he preferred to finance and direct his own work. After the tremendous success of *The Time of Your Life*, these later plays were comparative flops, providing perhaps the first glimpse of the spectacular literary fall that was soon to follow.

But in the early stages of the war in Europe, Saroyan appeared otherwise to be safely at the peak of his popularity. *My Name Is Aram* (1940), a collection of stories resembling a novel, which presented in a poetical light the Armenians of his boyhood days, was a Book of the Month choice and sold extensively. With *The Time of Your Life* playing to audiences across the nation, he moved into a suite at the prestigious Hampshire House, overlooking Central Park, and lived for a time the life of a millionaire.

And his theater activities, he took time off to assemble a collection of Armenian folk tales, which he published as *Saroyan's Fables* (a limited edition book). Then, late in the same year (1941), he went to Hollywood to write a film scenario, *The Human Comedy*. He sold the script to MGM for $60,000 but was prevented from directing the film himself, which he had believed would be the arrangement. The film was a hit, but Saroyan disliked it. He turned *The Human Comedy* into a novel (published in 1943), which became his most popular book of all—though, ironically, the one he was least happy with on later reflection because, pressed for time, he had concluded the story by suggesting that something good could come out of war.

Despite the immense success of *The Human Comedy*, Saroyan's moment as a literary hero who could do no wrong had now almost passed. In October 1942 he was drafted into the army as a private—almost at his own insistence, for he had taken steps to ensure that his family were no longer dependent on him. But a most unwilling and uncooperative recruit, he had a very hard time in consequence. With his literary and theater activities suspended, early in 1943 he married Carol Marcus, a young society girl and a friend of Oona O'Neill (who was to marry Charlie Chaplin), and was permitted to live with his wife (now pregnant) off the Astoria Army Post in his own apartment. Taking this privilege a little too much for granted on one occasion, he was obliged to spend a little time on Governors Island.

After the birth of their son Aram, Saroyan was posted to England. His time in London (with the Signal Corps) in 1944 coincided with the flying bomb offensive and the preparations for the D-Day landings. He was allowed time off to write a novel to promote Anglo-American relations. Working in the Savoy Hotel (at his own expense) he produced in just a few weeks *The Adventures of Wesley Jackson*. His reward was supposed to be a leave to visit his new family in New York; but the novel failed to please (publication was in fact delayed until after the war) and the deal was forgotten. Instead, the possibility of a court-martial was talked about, for the book was strongly antiwar at a time when such sentiments were unthinkable.

Discharged at last in 1945, he later said that he had fought the army for three years—and won. But the late 1940s were to be very difficult years for Saroyan. He had lovingly dedicated a 1944 collection of stories, *Dear Baby,* to his wife, but after the birth of daughter Lucy in 1946 the marriage began to fail. And at the same time, his literary career went into steep decline.

He had already ceased offering plays to Broadway producers because he was intensely dissatisfied with the system (in particular, he was appalled by the practice of arranging a private viewing of a play before potential backers, which put Art directly on trial before Money); and the critics disliked *Wesley Jackson* when it finally appeared in 1947. Between the writing of the novel and its publication, Hitler's death camps had come to light, making a mockery of Saroyan's invented German prison camp. One view of Saroyan's sudden decline suggests that his rhapsodic optimism couldn't survive the harsh truth about human nature uncovered at the end of the war. Himself a member of a dispossessed race upon which genocide had also been attempted, Nazi bruitality was not beyond his imagining. But the impact of the war revolutionized literary tastes, and Saroyan was suddenly almost old hat.

Responding to this challenge would be difficult enough, but he was now in earnest pursuit of the "fantasy of founding a family"—which seemed to mean satisfying the social demands of his wife and mother-in-law—and in poor condition for meeting literary challenges. These were very unproductive years indeed, and meanwhile his doomed marriage moved toward its inevitable end. When things finally came to a head in 1949, he left immediately for Europe.

In Paris, in a mood of despair, he wrote *The Assyrian,* a long story about a dying writer drawn and en route to the land of his ancestors, which formed the basis of a new collection. On his return to America after three months, he went to Reno for a divorce, spending time in Las

Vegas, gambling, while he established the necessary residence period in
Nevada. This particular gambling spree was financed in part by an
advance of $35,000 on three as yet unplanned books—an indication that
his career had not yet exactly touched rock bottom. The books were
eventually written in a single month: two novels, *Rock Wagram* and *The
Laughing Matter,* in both of which marriage breakdown is a major theme;
and a shorter fantasy work (and something of a personal favourite),
Tracy's Tiger. In 1950 he also published *The Twin Adventures*—a war-time
diary kept during the writing of *Wesley Jackson,* together with a reprint-
ing of the novel itself. None of these books was commercially successful,
but soon afterward he had a surprising worldwide hit with a pop song,
"C'mon-a My House," sung by Rosemary Clooney.

Saroyan's problems with Carol was that he could neither live with her
nor without her. They were briefly remarried in 1951, but this soon led
to fresh divorce proceedings. Carol was given custody of the children,
and once they were housed, he began looking for a place for himself,
finally settling into a modest but instantly loved house on the beach at
Malibu, where he began to try to pick up the pieces. So far as he was
concerned the marriage, especially in its final stages, had been a costly
and killing experience, and he was now deep in debt to the tax collector.
Carol married Walter Matthau, putting herself finally beyond his reach.

At Malibu in the fifties Saroyan regained his soul sufficiently to arrest
the alarming decline in his literary fortunes. In 1952 he published *The
Bicycle Rider in Beverly Hills,* the first and most poetic of his many full-
length experiments in autobiography. It reestablished his links with his
best sources: his early orphanage experience, his Armenian heritage,
and his boyhood bicycling life on the streets of Fresno. It was followed by
a warm-hearted novel of the theater (written for his daughter and
serialized in the *Saturday Evening Post*), *Mama, I Love You*; a new collection
of short stories, *The Whole Voyald;* and a book for his son, *Papa, You're
Crazy.* He had another play on Broadway for a lengthy run in 1957, *The
Cave Dwellers,* and there were a number of television productions and
adaptations of his works. Meantime he was publishing stories and articles
in the usual wide variety of magazines and newspapers. During the six
years at Malibu he earned around a quarter of a million dollars. But
these earnings did nothing to improve his tax situation; the debt remained (roughly $50,000 in 1958), and there seemed little prospect of
ever paying it off.

He left Malibu in 1958 and headed for Europe, ostensibly to make a
film in Yugoslavia, which never materialized. He was left with no clear
plan, only the vague thought that he might buy a vineyard and perhaps
even forget about writing. His typewriter stayed in its case for a time.
But gambling losses used up the vineyard money and at length he found

himself in Paris, facing once more the unwelcome prospect of trying to work himself out of debt. (His book *Not Dying* perhaps his gloomiest, most self-critical and most defensive memoir, is mainly concerned with this period.) He contacted the film producer Darryl Zanuck, who was based in Paris at that time, and agreed to write a script. In this particular case he was asked to write a film scenario, but elected instead to write a play, for which he was paid $60,000. *The Dogs, or The Paris Comedy* was a hit (in German translation) in Vienna, and later in Berlin also, and more work of the same lucrative if somewhat distasteful kind followed for a time. Typically, though, the money earned was not used to pay off debts. "I certainly didn't gamble away every penny," he wrote in a memoir, in flippant mood. "I drank some of it away, and I bought a raincoat."

Gambling was only the most uncontrollable manifestation of his compulsion to get rid of money as fast as he earned it. He was also an inveterate traveler, and as a matter of course would seek out the best and most expensive hotel in a new town or city. And in his day he had given plenty away, when he had it to give. But gambling was the worst of it; and yet he needed to gamble. It was central to his approach to writing, and to life itself. He often justified it by saying that it helped his work, and the fact is that many of his best stories and plays were written in the aftermath of a bad gambling experience. Despite having earned so much himself, he despised the whole business of money-making, and gambling provided the perfect opportunity to demonstrate his contempt for the stuff. He had always been able to earn money when he needed it; now he had to learn how to hold onto it, even if that meant according it a grudging respect. He set up home and a working base in a fifth floor walk-up apartment in Paris, and the fight back to solvency began in a serious way, if not exactly in earnest.

He was invited to write an autobiography, and, believing it would pay his debts, he produced his most detailed (except for his traumatic marriage and army experiences, which are scarcely hinted at) autobiographical work, *Here Comes, There Goes, You Know Who.* But on his own later admission, the book did rather poorly, and in any case he had made a bad deal through his customary habit of not bothering to read the small print. Among his other activities in the early sixties, he created *Sam, the Highest Jumper of Them All* with Joan Littlewood's Theatre Workshop in London after admiring its production of Brendan Behan's *The Hostage.* Back in America in 1963, he recorded a pleasant cross-country drive at the wheel of an immaculate 1941 Lincoln limousine (picked up in New York), with a cousin as traveling companion, in *Short Drive, Sweet Chariot.* Two novels followed: *Boys and Girls Together* (which had evidently been suppressed for a number of years) and *One Day in the Afternoon of the World.* Then, thirty years after the publication of his first book, he

repeated his early effort of writing a new story or piece each day for a
whole month, keeping at the same time a daily journal in which he
discussed his present life and work in relation to January 1934. This
journal was published alongside the original stories as *After Thirty Years:
The Daring Young Man on the Flying Trapeze.* Meanwhile, his plays were
being taken up with enthusiasm in Eastern Europe, notably in Czecho-
slovakia.

Gradually he brought his gambling and drinking under reasonable
control, though there were lapses. During a three-month stay in London
in 1966, for instance, he managed to go through $20,000. (He had come
to London to provide a temporary home for his daughter Lucy, who
appeared to be living there off the charity of friends. They were soon
joined by Aram from New York. The unsatisfactory relationship they
had with their father, which was to worsen at the time, evidently did not
preclude getting together with him as a family. In their earlier years, too,
they had spent several long vacations in his company.) By 1967 he was
able to declare, in *Days of Life and Death and Escape to the Moon* (a daily
journal kept in Paris and Fresno): "I'm free. . . . I've paid all debts, I'm
earning a living." He had acquired a second home in Fresno—though he
hated what the developers had done to his home town over the years—
and it became his habit to spend part of the year in each location.

Saroyan's next publication was a book of uncollected newspaper and
magazine articles, essays, short stories, memoirs, poems, and short plays,
each with a specially written introduction. Indulging his fondness for
long titles to the full, he called the book *I Used to Believe I Had Forever,
Now I'm Not So Sure* (actually the title of one of the plays). In his last book
of the sixties he used the autobiographical device of writing a series of
"letters" to various people, eminent and otherwise and most now dead,
who had either influenced him or remained in his memory for some
important reason. A number of these pieces were first published in the
Saturday Evening Post. He called this book *Letters from 74 Rue Taitbout, or,
Don't Go But If You Must Say Hello to Everybody.*

These autobiographical books were turning into a series. Next came
Places Where I've Done Time (1972), in which he used the theme of places
that had figured importantly in his life. But a note of rancor and
vindictiveness was creeping in as the series progressed. As a matter of
principle, he had always tried to write about people with the "largest
possible sympathy," but now he was beginning to see them in a wholly
realistic way. This trend continued (with his ex-wife as an occasional
target for his venom) in *Sons Come and Go, Mothers Hang in Forever* (1976),
though *Chance Meetings* (1978), with its delicious memories of some of
the more obscure people he had met, was something of an exception.

With the gradual intrusion of a bitter tone in these memoirs went a growing preoccupation with death, as some of the titles alone suggest. This preoccupation reached its fullest expression in the last book published in his lifetime, *Obituaries* (1979). Finding that he had known a good number of them personally, he used *Variety's* list of the show-business dead of 1976 as his basis for the book. The people he hadn't known (actually the great majority) were mentioned in passing and used to turn his writing loose in whatever direction it might go. A condition of publication was that his "facts" should not be corrected, for he believed that to write on the basis of memory only was as valid in its way as checking every last fact. (*Births,* a short sequel to *Obituaries,* written in the summer of 1979, was published posthumously). *Obituaries* was nominated for a National Book Award in autobiography (it was eased out by a more conventional effort by Lauren Bacall), providing a fitting finale to his long and distinguished career.

Beginnings

EDWARD HALSEY FOSTER

To understand William Saroyan, the place to begin is not America but ancient Armenia in eastern Turkey, from which his parents emigrated early in this century.

The landscape of Armenia is barren and dry in summer. Although once rich, fertile, and forested, the region now has few trees, and the bedouin tribes that camp here stay close to their tents, away from the burning sun.

Soviet Armenia is still occupied largely by Armenians, but few Armenians remain in the Turkish sector, the home of Saroyan's ancestors. It is a vast open land, rugged and threatening. There are a few Turkish villages with their mosques and minarets, and there are also a few Kurdish outposts and, of course, the bedouin tribes. But almost no signs exist to show that Armenians, driven out or exterminated by the massacres a few generations ago, occupied this land for nearly three thousand years.

Saroyan's ancestors came from the village of Bitlis in the Taurus mountains east of Lake Van. Now a conservative Islamic village, a hundred years ago Bitlis was an important center of Armenian culture.

Under the Ottoman Turks, Armenians became wealthy and respected merchants. (Among Turks, trade was, and to a degree still is, considered disreputable, and it was, therefore, an ideal way for Jews, Arabs, Armenians, and other minorities to succeed. It was one profession in which they would not expect persecutions.) Bitlis had been for centuries a center of trade under various Arabic, Persian, Byzantine, and Turkish rulers, and it must have seemed a very safe and respectable place for Armenians to establish their culture.

But it was not an easy place in which to live. In William Saroyan's novel *Rock Wagram*, an elderly woman remembers that "When winter came we were kept in our houses five months waiting for the snows to melt. Those five months . . . were the most terrible I have ever known. [My husband] would not be loved and said, 'Go to America, this is no place to live, this is a place to die'" (p. 74).

But for a while, Bitlis despite its climate and isolation, at least offered a sanctuary—free, for the moment, from all the unimaginable persecutions to which Armenians had been subjected for centuries.

Then came the bloody Ottoman rule of Sultan Abdul-Hamid II with its systematic extermination of Armenians. Few escaped.

Saroyan's father, Armenak, a well-educated minister, writer, and scholar, was one of those who got out. In 1905 he and other Armenians from Bitlis arrived in New York and settled near the Bowery on the Lower East Side.

Saroyan's attitudes toward his ancestors, his family, and his father could be very ambiguous, sometimes respectful and at other times distant. In *I Used to Believe I Had Forever,* he wrote that he remembered his father "as a good man" of whom "the worst that anybody was willing to say . . . was that he was too good for this world" (p.63). In fact, not only had his father, with little cash, been able to get himself and his family to America; he had also quickly established himself here as a writer for the *Christian Herald* and as a minister for a church in Paterson, New Jersey. In addition, he was soon well known as a poet, essayist, and public speaker. His writings were to have much importance for his son, who claimed in *The Bicycle Rider in Beverly Hills* that one of the main reasons he became a writer was because his father had been one, too.

On the other hand, Saroyan states in one of his last memoirs, *Sons Come and Go, Mothers Hang in Forever,* that his father was "the failed poet, the failed Presbyterian preacher, the failed American, the failed theological student" (p. 20). It is true that Armenak Saroyan, after he had established himself respectively in the East, suddenly left for California to become the minister of an Armenian church in Fresno, only to find that the congregation wanted someone who spoke Turkish, a language that he knew poorly. But the difficulties that resulted—he had to abandon his scholarly interests and, in order to support his family, take a job in the vineyards—were the accidents of fate, not personal shortcomings. Armenak Saroyan died suddenly a short time after his arrival in California, but had he lived longer, one suspects that, given his obvious ambitions and abilities, he would once again have succeeded.

Armenak's death had lasting and hated consequences for his family. His wife was unable to support their children, and they were placed in an orphanage. William Saroyan was three years old. Their mother was able to visit only on weekends. Saroyan's bitterness toward his childhood and his ambiguous attitudes toward his past may well have had more to do with the years spent in the orphanage than with his memories and impressions of his father and the Armenian community he knew in Fresno.

Saroyan's father named him for Dr. William Stonehill, a friend and Presbyterian minister who helped Armenian refugees in New York. Saroyan thought of himself, however, very much as an Armenian, and, had the choice been his, he would, he said, have taken the name Aram. His collection of stories based on his memories of the Armenian community in Fresno is titled *My Name Is Aram*, and Aram is the name he gave his son.

Clearly Saroyan's Armenian identification had considerable importance for him, and that fact is repeatedly emphasized by him. To choose a minor but revealing example, *Places Where I've Done Time* is dedicated to "Armenians, half Armenians, quarter Armenians, and one-eighth Armenians. Sixteenth and thirty-second Armenians, and other winners, are likelier to be happy with a useful book" (p. 5).

Perhaps the principal effect of Saroyan's Armenian heritage on his work is not be found in his use of his background for subject matter but rather in a deep, pervasive sense of being an outsider. In other words, what matters most is not so much his having been an Armenian as his having been an Armenian in America—and, therefore, instantly an eccentric, an outsider.

Armenians have for centuries been geographical and historical anomalies. Armenia was the first nation to adopt Christianity, but Armenian Christianity has always been distinct from other forms of Christianity in church structure, ritual, and belief. Because few Christian peoples live in Asia, the Armenians were surrounded by Arabs, Kurds, Turks, Persians, and other nations of Islam.

For centuries after their country was overrun by Arabs and Turks, Armenians were outsiders in their own land. In America, the situation was in some ways worse; although there were no longer threats of Turkish invasions, the immigrant Armenian was cut off from his land and his culture, for here he could find little of the Asian culture he had left behind. Immigrant cultures in America have generally been European, and so even among the immigrant cultures of the Lower East Side or Fresno, the Saroyans and other Armenians were alone.

American literature is a literature of outsiders; its finest books—*Moby Dick, Adventures of Huckleberry Finn,* and (to choose an excellent recent example) *Zen and the Art of Motorcycle Maintenance*—are about, and are often narrated by "outsiders." Saroyan could find within his cultural background a vision of experience that fit closely an established vision in American literature.

One of Saroyan's stories dealing explicitly with what it means to be an outsider in this world is "The Assyrian," the title piece in a collection of short fiction published in 1950. It is an exceedingly well-crafted story, equal to much of F. Scott Fitzgerald's and Ring Lardner's work, and reminiscent, in its resignation to solitude as an inevitable part of experience, to Fitzgerald's "The Rich Boy."

Saroyan's story concerns an Assyrian-American (an ethnic identity even more bizarre and culturally "invisible" than Armenian-American), a famous writer who has been a loser in everything (no friends, three divorces) except gambling and his profession. Since he is a celebrity, his opinions and activities are reported in the newspapers, but no one cares much for him as a person. He simply makes good copy. The thing which gives his life an edge is gambling, and he usually wins but gains no one's admiration; all that he has to show for his life, his writing, and his gambling, is money.

Saroyan said that he began the story to make money, but "the longer I worked at it, . . . the more hopeless the possibility of this financial coup became, for the writing would not be cheerful, would not be amusing, would not be something hundreds of thousands of friendly, normal, cheerful people might find in a magazine and know would be nice" (*The Assyrian*, p. xvii).

It is, however, precisely this inability to be amusing, this resistance to being merely entertaining, that raises "The Assyrian" above most of Saroyan's work and makes it such an effective short story.

At the center of the piece is the question of what marks a man— despite his public and private successes—as an outsider, a loner. Why is it that "in the end, as in the beginning, a man is alone" (p. 65)? The answer seems to lie in the man's heritage: "The longer he'd lived, the more he'd become acquainted with the Assyrian side [of himself], the old side, the tired side, the impatient and wise side, the side he had never suspected existed in himself until he was thirteen and had begun to be a man" (p. 17). Finally, obsessed with this solitude that he never chose, he asks himself why he has never been able to find close friends, and the answer comes back: "It was probably because the Assyrian side of him just naturally didn't believe in it" (p 21). At the end of the story, he takes a plane to the Middle East and the site of a heritage and culture that, except in the solitude of his imagination and the imaginations of people from backgrounds like his, no longer exists. But he has no other way, except death, to end his solitude.

In one of his earliest stories, "Antranik of Armenia," Saroyan explicitly rejected what has always been the easiest emotional response for an oppressed race or nation: hatred for the oppressor. The Armenian, he implied, was no better and no worse than the Turk. (See p. 257 of *Inhale and Exhale*.) The culture that survives because of its shared hatreds is not, he assumes, a culture worth preserving. Armenian identity had nothing to do with a common oppressor.

A man's ethnic identity, he suggested in another early short story, "The Armenian and the Armenians," had more to do with a personal awareness than with geography. Nationality or ethnicity is a matter of imagination, not territorial designations:

> There is a small area of land in Asia Minor that is called Armenia, but it is not so. It is not Armenia. It is a place. . . . There are only Armenians, and they inhabit the earth, not Armenia, since there is no Armenia. . . . There is no America and there is no England, and no France, and no Italy. There is only the earth. . . . (*Inhale and Exhale*, p. 437).

Saroyan's politics, which probably cost him much critical support and many readers in the 1930s, could conceivably have had foundations in this sense of national or ethnic identity. It is a sense that, in a pluralistic society, emphasizes individuality at the expense of any real opportunity for friendship and mutual understanding. The past, rather than the present, shapes people. It is an intensely conservative view, but one Saroyan apparently could not avoid. In an interview with Michael J. Arlen for Arlen's study of Armenian culture today, *Passage to Ararat* (1975), Saroyan insisted that "An Armenian can never not be an Armenian" (p. 49).

While many writers in the 1930s were dedicated to the creation of a new society, Saroyan wrote about the survival of traditional values and customs both in his Armenian community and in the country at large. *The Time of Your Life* is essentially about the survival of fundamental human values: a sense of decency, fair play, civility, and generosity of spirit. Despite a national depression and the early signs of a war abroad, the people in Saroyan's play were able to ignore the world at large and create, among themselves, the kind of decent life that, the play suggests, might be possible for everyone. It is a deeply sentimental conclusion.

Saroyan's major contribution to American literature may well be that special Saroyan "voice" which we hear echoed, however distantly, in works of such later writers as Richard Brautigan and Jack Spicer. That voice is usually whimsical, humorous, at times ironic—but also, underneath all the good fun, there is a deep sadness. One couldn't have the Saroyan voice without it. It is there in all his writings from the beginning to the end. And what is the source of that sadness, that melancholy? Saroyan's childhood? His father's early death? The years in the orphanage?

Of course, these things had their effect (as Saroyan's son, Aram, has shown in his books about his father), but perhaps the tragedies of that childhood were less important here than the history of oppression that was inextricably woven into Saroyan's Armenian heritage. In *The Time of Your Life, The Human Comedy,* "The Assyrian," and other major works, Saroyan returned again and again to his faith that basic human values survive, always survive, but while this may be cause for joy, it is seldom possible to ignore, however briefly, the fact that oppression is also a constant, unavoidable fact of history. Saroyan's Armenian heritage taught him that.

And so we have the deep sadness, the melancholy that reverberates throughout Saroyan's work, and at the least, keeps the stories, novels, plays, and essays from becoming mere diversions, entertainments. His Armenian heritage made Saroyan's voice one of the richest in American literature. To consider Saroyan without regard to his Armenian heritage is simply to miss the point.

An Orphanage Far Far Away

S. A. ROBBINS

This story begins on the porch of an orphanage, circa 1911, and ends in the attic room of that orphanage, seventy years later. It is a story of coincidence and art, a story of life and death, memory and imagination, parents and children, writers and readers, first words and last rites. It is a children's story, and like all children's stories, it contains, between the lines, a meaning that traces the author's life with images that are a part of us all.

It begins in Saroyan's *Obituaries*:

> . . . on the porch there's as small boy in Oakland in 1913 or 1912 crying in away that just won't do at all, and there I was alone . . . alone, and on my own for a moment, and nobody to tell me why the small boy, my own age, in fact, is crying that way . . . and the boy on the Oakland porch goes to sleep on the universe of ice and wakes up and remembers the death of his father and mother, and sees the sun, and forgets it all. . . .

This reference by Saroyan, late in his life, to the forgotten part of his childhood has recently been documented by several Saroyan scholars who have expanded Saroyan's own "universe of ice" metaphor in psychological terms. Catherine Burke, in her article "Impressions of William Saroyan," which appeared in the December 1981 issue of *Hye Sharzhoom,* discussed Saroyan's repressed memories of his orphan years, noting that the crystallization of those memories afforded the writer with a never-ending sense of what it was like to be a child. The consistent innocence of his fiction may be due, in part, to the subconscious recurrence of images from these forgotten years.

Aram Saroyan, in our correspondence, frequently referred to the significance of his father's orphan years in his latter art, his fascination with memory and imagination, his inconsistent manner of parenting. In his biography of his father, *William Saroyan,* Aram maintains his father's image of the "universe of ice" in the chapters about Saroyan's childhood:

> The death of Armenak and Saroyan's subsequent five years in the Fred Finch Orphanage in Oakland was comparable to the onrush of a fierce and seemingly unending winter.(P. 4)

> Perhaps Saroyan's psychic freeze at the age of three allowed him to maintain these psychic archetypes as they lived in him at the moment of freezing. (P. 4)

What remains unsaid about his "psychic freeze" and its effect upon his writing, what remains a mystery even to the most ardent Saroyan reader, is the process of forgetting and remembering. It was not until much later in his life that Saroyan could bring himself to write about the particulars of his orphanage experience. Saroyan himself, in "Growing up in Fresno," a typed reminiscence dated February 1976, admits that he did not, for many years, remember anything of his stay at the orphanage in Oakland.

To understand his process of forgetting and remembering, and to explain the eventual publication of numerous stories about the Fred Finch Orphanage in later collections, a brief examination of the natural symptoms and effects of life in "Orphan Time" is in order.

Life in Orphan Time is not easily understood by those with normal lives, normal childhoods—each day, week, and year pass by an orphan in irregular patterns, with irregular effects; it is slow, monotonous, filled with countless regrets and resentments. It contains, with every hour, images that magnify and reinforce their loneliness, their boredom. Saroyan stated in *The Bicycle Rider in Beverly Hills,*

> Boredom was the plague of my childhood. . . . While I was at the orphanage, the boredom came from being in a place I did not wish to be. . . . I was bored. I was bored the entire four years I was there.

To an orphan, every day is the same as any other, no difference between Monday and Friday, no difference between day and night but in one respect: at night, when orphans lie awake pretending to sleep, or on those nights when they run away from their cold dormitories in a futile search for a better life, at night, an orphan's fears take shape and loom large in the shadows. Unlike other children in real homes with real parents to assuage their nighttime panic, orphans can only run away, or cry themselves to sleep, knowing there will be nothing different in the morning, nothing worth anticipating except the endless and empty absence of meaning in their lives.

> The real story can never be told. It is untellable. The real (as real) is inaccessible, being gone in time. . . . There is no point in glancing at the past, in summoning it up, in re-examining it, except on behalf of art—that is, the meaningful-real. (*Bicycle Rider*)

The immense impact of Orphan Time upon an orphan's memory, as Saroyan suggests in the previous passage, cannot be adequately explained. Orphans quickly learn to forget all grief, and the sources of their grief—loneliness, anonymity, the fear of death—and in the place of this forgetting, they remember the smallest of events, the most trivial of circumstances, elevating the trivia of their lives to levels of monumental importance, attaching to each possession and brief happiness an imagined value of inestimable scope. And this is how the orphan survives life in Orphan Time, making the significant trivial, making the trivial significant, forgetting all else. They forget what it hurts to remember, forget everything they knew of the world outside the orphanage gates, until all they know of the world is what is contained within the boundaries of Orphan Time, that world, and what the orphan imagines to be true. They have no meaning but that which each creates, then pretends to be a universal truth.

"To remember something or to invent something, it comes to the same thing," Saroyan writes in *Obituaries*. This is a central proposition in his theory of fiction, that our lives include an infinite variety of persons, places, and objects for one's imagination, fueled by memory, to invest with meaning. To Saroyan, there was no need to search for metaphors; they were plentiful, found anywhere, waiting for an active imagination to inject the colors of significance into their black-and-white outlines.

Saroyan's orphan years provided a number of images that eventually surfaced in his fiction—a small, mechanical toy called "The Coon Jigger" given to him by his mother as she said goodbye on the porch of the orphanage, the miniature piano played every Sunday during lunch of duck eggs and strawberries, the Irish cook's meat pie. ". . . and it was quite simply true that the Irish cook's meat pie was one of the finest table experiences of my young life" (*Sons Come & Go, Mothers Hang In Forever*). And from those years, a large cast of characters remained with him past the forgetting, characters he seemed driven to recognize—John Wesley Hagan, the first director of the Fred Finch Orphanage; Blanche Fulton, one of the workers who accompanied young Willie to the Panama Pacific International Exposition of 1915 in San Francisco; Joaquin Miller, a bearded old man who lived in the hills above the orphanage, the first true poet whose work young Willie came to know.

But it was not the details and minor impressions of his life in Orphan Time that ignited the first of William Saroyan's genius for and obsession with writing. Thousands upon thousands of abandoned children have

Children and staff at the Fred Finch Orphanage in Oakland, ca. 1911.

The grounds of the Fred Finch Orphanage.

never survived its limbo as he did; the reasons for his particular victory
are as numerous as the biographical theories that have appeared since
his death, even theory with a kind of validity, for William Saroyan was a
complicated and multifaceted artist and man. His children have their
own perspectives, both Lucy and Aram struggling to understand the
man, Saroyan, that was their father; political scholars and sociologists
offer interpretations based upon his Armenian heritage and his place in
our historical times; students of writing identify his passion for an
absolute obedience to the daily travail of writing, his prolixity, his urge to
write down anything and everything; critics, of course, cite his irre-
verence, his inconsistency, his willingness to make a bet.

> I have been vitally aware of the Law of Opposites, and this awareness
> has kept me reasonably serene . . . the drama of life . . . the play of
> truth . . . the quarrel of fools and frauds, male and female, the classic
> and the romantic, the disciplined and the free . . . the comic and the
> tragic contrasting of the opposites in all areas of possibility and on and
> on and on. . . . *Obituaries)*

He was a man of many stories, some of them true, and each reader has
something of value to offer to our understanding. It is not my intention,
in this essay, to suggest that Saroyan's years at the Fred Finch Orphanage
were more significant, more influential than other perspectives; what I
offer is a personal point-of-view about his orphan years, his Fred Finch
stories, and their ultimate role in his overall legacy.

Jung, in his essay "Synchronicity," attempts to define the relationship
between coincidence and hidden truth, examining the "meaningful
cross-connection" of otherwise unexplainable events that serve to moti-
vate human behavior. In his hypothesis, parallel events/revelations/histo-
ries can occur in space, as well as time, and that such geographically
bound "cross-connections" are worthy of scientific consideration. Jung
was an old man when he wrote this essay, and scientists dismissed these
notions, with good reason: an absence of evidence.

They had not visited the Fred Finch Orphanage. The coincidence of
William Saroyan's history, circa 1911, with my own life on the same
grounds offers evidence of such cross-connections; more importantly,
this coincidence provides an understanding of young Willie Saroyan, his
struggle to survive his early years, his art, his relationships with family
and friends, his timeless significance to other children beginning, as he
did, on that Oakland proch, "crying in a way that just won't do at all."

That porch remains today, and Jacoby Hall, the place of so many
Saroyan stories, still stands as part of the Fred Finch Children's Home in
Oakland, California. When I was first hired as the night watchman for
the Children's Home eight years ago, I adopted as my nighttime office a

PLACE of Birth – DATE Birth
Cozette SAROYAN–Turkey "came "74" Jan 22 – 1899
Zabel   " (Home) "   ll apr 11 – 1902
Henry   " (State) "   L aug 3 – 1905
William " (State) Fresno L aug 13 – 1908

all left the Home in 1916 to live with
mother at Fresno
The records show Home received only
12.⁵⁰ per month for care of the four children
Henry and William being on state aid
at 6.²⁵ each per month as state then
(but only 70. per year per child.

The earliest admission date for the Saroyan children available at the Fred Finch Orphanage is 16 March 1912. The four children were discharged from the orphanage for the summer of 1913, then readmitted on 10 September 1913 and discharged for the final time on 15 June 1916. *(Courtesy of Stuart A. Robbins.)*

room on the third floor of that building. It was there that I first read his story "Attic Room, Fred Finch Orphanage, Oakland 1912" in his collection *Places Where I've Done Time.*

I was four years old, and had long since reasoned that it was folly to expect the big things from people. It was enough to get the little things. The biggest thing, of course, was love, the nearness of somebody you love when you need somebody to be near.

But on that night, little Willie had no one. He was ill, quarantined to the attic room on the third floor, feverish, alone. He could barely hear the other orphans, singing Christmas carols in the dining hall, listening to the words of "Oh Holy Night" as he prayed for somebody to be near, for somebody to come. Of course, no one came. Throughout the night, as his story relates, little Willie battled with his loneliness, with his sickness that seemed, in his fever, to be Death itself.

If the great one found out about my fight with Death, and came to be near me, what good things we might all expect from being in the world . . . and then around daybreak I knew I had come through, and now at last fell into real sleep—alone, and proud, and alive—now more alive than ever.

(Places Where I've Done Time)

He was only four years old on that Christmas Eve, but in Orphan Time, meaning is where you find it. Willie had already outwitted Death

HALF ORPHAN
Admitted 9-15-1913
Committed 9-15-1913

HISTORY CARD FOR CHILDREN'S INSTITUTIONS

No. 7

Name of Institution **Fred Finch Orphanage** Place of Birth **Fresno, Cal** Date of Birth **Aug 13, 1908**

Name of Person Responsible for Child **Mrs. Takoohi Saroyan** { Mother, Father, Guardian, Other } —

Address **Fresno, California 239 M Street**

NAME	Birth Date	Date of Death	Nativity	Religion	Date of Nat-uralization	Occupation	Income	Physical or Mental Defects	Marital Condition	Public Charges
F. Armenag Saroyan		7/19/11	Armenia	Presbyterian		minister		—	* MC. Div. Des. Sep. Wid. 4 Widr. UMC. UM. RM.	F. Insane County State M. Insane County State F. Jailed County State M. Jailed County
M. Takoohi Saroyan			Armenia							Property or Insurance

NAME OF CHILD	Date of Admission	Form of Admission.	**Disease	Physical or Mental Defects	Board Paid By		Amount
William Saroyan	Sept 10, 1913	Committed by Juvenile Court; (a) Needy. (b) Wayward. Transferred from other institution. Parent or guardian.			State, County, Mother, Father, Guardian, Others.		$4.25 mo.

SCHOOL GRADE		VOCATIONAL TRAINING	
At Entrance	At Dismissal	At Entrance	At Dismissal
May 9, 1916	2		

HEIGHT		WEIGHT	
At Entrance	At Dismissal	At Entrance	At Dismissal

DISPOSITION
(Indicate by check in column.)

✓ Returned to parent or guardian.
Placed in free home.
Placed for service.
Transferred to child-placing agency.
Adopted.

REASON:
Left without permission.
Transferred to Juvenile Court.
Sent to hospital.
Recovered.
Died.
Dismissed from hospital to parent.

PERSON OR INSTITUTION TO WHOM DISMISSED***

PLACEMENTS	DATE	NAME	ADDRESS
First	4/15/16	Mrs T. Saroyan	Fresno Cal
Returned			
Replaced			

(over)

*The above abbreviations mean: MC. Married Couple; Div. Divorce; Des. Deserted; Sep. Separated; Wid. Widow; Widr. Widower; UMC. Unmarried Couple; UM. Unmarried Mother; RM. Re-married.
**Record here all serious illness with date and duration.
***On back of this card or on separate card, "Alumni card", keep record of the child's history after leaving the institution.

State Board of Charities and Corrections—1914,
California
A. Carlisle & Co., S.F.

Record showing that William was admitted to the Fred Finch Orphanage in 1913, probably after his older siblings. (Courtesy of Stuart A. Robbins.)

itself, not only survived his battle but prevailed. Beginning that traumatic night, and continuing throughout the five years of life at Fred Finch, his imagination provided something to replace what life had refused him; in that attic room, Saroyan learned to transform minor qualms into conflicts of monumental significance. This victory fueled his struggle to overcome Orphan Time, propelled him into his childhood with a private weapon, a secret tool he used again and again to beat life's odds.

The Young Saroyan and the American Dream

EDWARD LOOMIS

The special issue of *Ararat* devoted to William Saroyan is interesting on many grounds, perhaps most dramatically because it presents a complex image of the veteran writer, the man of many successes and some failures as well, who continued amazingly on a track he discovered in early life, persistent, obstinate, and brilliant. This is the writer of international reputation, well known in his home country. This is the writer who visited Armenia to take part in the fiftieth anniversary of Armenia's reunion with Russia, who could make of a visit to a cemetary in Paris a memorable event for his companion and a little act of rejuvenation for himself. This is the writer whose formidable personal tone carried within it the capacity to charm the company even when the message was a little rough (and often it was distinctly harsh, somewhat after the fashion of the patriarch in *My Name Is Aram*):

> I won't have him singing all day, my grandfather roared. There is a limit to everything. When you read in a book that a father loves a foolish son more than his wise sons, that writer is a bachelor. . . . ("The Journey to Hanford")

There is of course another side to this complex image of an author going about his living—a more somber side, recalling the difficulties implicit in such a career, in such a far-ranging effort in which intellect and imagination are put on the stretch by an exuberant energy prompted by fame; this is the image we derive from the news stories about his death and about his life in California toward the end—rather definitely, there is a darksome tone to some of the details, to the rich confusion of fruit trees in the backyard of the Fresno house, allowed to go unpruned though apparently not unwanted, and to the desolation of that house in Malibu once imaginable as the proper reward for this

50

Saroyan as a postal telegraph messenger, Fresno, ca. 1920. *(Courtesy of Aram Saroyan.)*

Saroyan *(third from left)* **with his cousins Helen, Archie, and Kirk Minasian, Fresno, 1920.** *(Courtesy of Archie Minasian.)*

man's exercise of his talent. There is a complex suggestiveness in the ensemble; it seems that the success had unexpected consequences, and even may have brought about a formidable conclusion to the life-drama. It seems clear that Saroyan, the world traveler, the man who knew his way around, had his beginning in a mood so bleak as to touch on the suicidal. Consider, for instance, the famous story "The Daring Young Man on the Flying Trapeze":

> . . . Then swiftly, neatly, with the grace of the young man on the trapeze, he was gone from his body. For an eternal moment he was still all things at once: the bird, the fish, the rodent, the reptile, and man. An ocean of print undulated endlessly and darkly before him. The city burned. The herded crowd rioted. The earth circled away, and knowing that he did so, he turned his lost face to the empty sky and became dreamless, unalive, perfect. (*The Saroyan Special,* p. 39)

This mood was not the entirety of that young writer's attitude; indeed, the union of this mood with the buoyant cheerfulness of good health gives the early work something of its charm as well as its power. Certainly there can be no doubt as to the charm. *My Name Is Aram,* coming along a significant few years after "The Daring Young Man on the Flying Trapeze," shows Saroyan well on his way into a brilliant literary career, able to provide sunlit idyllic interludes for an American public already getting ready to go to war.

This little book is the center of my argument—a cheerful work of fiction if there ever was one, but coming forward at a time when a great historical catastrophe was getting ready to happen; in fact, the book is not only cheerful—it is humorous:

> . . . we could hear it [the tractor] booming in the awful emptiness of the desert. It sounded pretty awful. It *was* awful. My uncle thought it was wonderful.
>
> Progress, he said. There's the modern age for you. Ten thousand years ago, he said, it would have taken a hundred men a week to do what the tractor's done today.
>
> Ten thousand years ago? I said. You mean yesterday.
>
> Anyway, my uncle said, there's nothing like these modern conveniences.
>
> The tractor isn't a convenience, I said.
>
> What is it, then? my uncle said. Doesn't the driver sit?
>
> He couldn't very well stand, I said.
>
> Any time they let you sit, my uncle said, it's a convenience. . . . ("The Pomegranate Trees")

To be sure, this is a gentle humor. The boy scores off the man: ". . . You mean yesterday"; and the man scores off the boy: "Any time they let you sit . . . it's a convenience.: There is a mild discomfiture for the reader to consider, each time, that eternal note of the humorous, or comic, which consists in somebody else's mishap, whether of the mind (as here) or of the world of action:

> . . .There wasn't a great distance still to go, but I knew I would be able to do it.
>
> Then I knew I wouldn't.
>
> The race was over.
>
> I was last, by ten yards.
>
> Without the slightest hesitation I protested and challenged the runners to another race, same distance, back. They refused to consider the proposal, which proved, I knew, that they were afraid to race me. I told them they knew very well I could beat them.
>
> It was very much the same in all the other events.
>
> When I got home I was in high fever and very angry. I was delirious all night and sick three days. My grandmother took very good care of

me and probably was responsible for my not dying. . . . ("The Fifty
Yard Dash")

Even—as here—the discomfiture is sometimes not so mild; yet the
humorous fact prevails; the reader is allowed his laughter and the minor
purgation that comes with it. Speaking as one who read the book when it
came out (in 1940), I can recall the generally uniform response the book
elicited from the members of my family, who for a while were in a daily
competition to see who would have the privilege of reading it; and
though we laughed, we understood that we were not being misled; we
found the book to be *true,* as well as humorous, and we could believe that
it was a continuation of an American tradition of humor (*Huckleberry
Finn* was also popular in that house). It seems now a piece of amazing
good fortune that we should have had the pleasures of this book almost
literally under the shadow of a great war.

Looking back in the aftermath of the author's death, I no longer find it
inexplicable that the dire necessities of destiny so plainly marked and so
truly rendered in "The Daring Young Man on the Flying Trapeze"
should have given way to that joy in life which suffuses *My Name Is Aram;*
for Saroyan evidently had come forward to participate in that American
dream of opportunity for all, which is the pervading myth of the country, just as it is one of the important realities of the entire world. The
literary career of William Saroyan simply illustrates these possibilities.
The young writer had not actually starved to death; instead, he became
famous.

How then to account for those later episodes, that later tone suggestive
of the author's early themes? It is here suggested that the society—or the
culture, as perhaps it is best to regard it—was still not proffering the
dream to all, and still is not. The author's personal good fortune was not
matched by a good fortune universally available; quite the contrary.
Misery continues pervasively. It is with us still; the veteran writer was one
of those who could not be deceived on this matter.

Saroyan was offering something of a particular ethnic subculture to a
very racist anti-ethnic culture, and some of his near contemporaries
among the writers can make the case. I propose Booth Tarkington for
this role, though his reality as a writer is much dimmer than it was forty
years ago. Tarkington also had a genius for understanding childhood,
whether that was a matter of vivid memory or shocking intuition: *Penrod*
and *Little Orvie* retain something of their charm into the 1980s because
the charm is compounded with knowledge of real people in real places.
Tarkington, born in 1869, lived on through World War II (he died in
1946), and his books were popular through the 1930s and the war
period, rightfully so. Indeed it could seem that Saroyan and Tarkington

were almost brothers under the skin, so present were childhood things to these skillful literary artists.

One can even highlight the humor of *My Name Is Aram* by comparing it to things in Tarkington's books about the boy life in middle-class America. In *Little Orvie*, for example, there is the wonderful sequence about the dog adopted by that large-headed, gap-toothed eight-year-old; this is "good old Ralphie," to be imagined at the end of a piece of clothesline held by his lord and proprietor. And in *Penrod* there are such episodes as the barber shop sequence including Miss Marjorie Jones and her little brother; the boys' club, the IN-OR-IN; and the episode involving the Reverend Mister Kinosling's hat—and surely to mention these episodes is to invoke others equally worthy of consideration in this context.

Indeed, here was an interesting writer, if only for these two works; yet the racism of the culture is vividly present in this middle-class world, and especially in *Penrod*. It is neither avowed nor explained. It is simply not reckoned with in the author's calculus. Though Tarkington's heart may have been "in the right place," he was moving toward a different state of mind than that of the culture which produced him. A long quotation, I think, will make the case. In *Penrod*, chapter 23, "Coloured Troops in Action," two black brothers, Herman and Verman—spelled like that— who are friends to Penrod and Sam, become engaged with a local bully named Rupe Collins:

> . . . when Herman and Verman set to, the record must be no more than a few fragments left by the expurgator. It has been perhaps sufficiently suggested that the altercation in Mr. Schofield's stable opened with mayhem in respect to the aggressor's nose (Rupe Collins had been the aggressor). Expressing vocally his indignation and the extremity of his pained surprise, Mr. Collins stepped backward, holding his left hand over his nose, and striking at Herman with his right. Then Verman hit him with the rake.
>
> Verman struck from behind. He struck as hard as he could. And he struck with the tines down. For, in his simple, direct African way he wished to kill his enemy, and he wished to kill him as soon as possible. That was his single, earnest purpose.
>
> On this account, Rupe Collins was peculiarly unfortunate. He was plucky and he enjoyed conflict; but neither his ambitions nor his anticipations had ever included murder. He had not learned that an habitually aggressive person runs the danger of colliding with beings in one of those lower stages of evolution wherein theories about "hitting below the belt" have not yet made their appearance. . . .

It is a somewhat comical combat, but the implicit racism absorbs the attention of the modern reader, just as the combat against it, and against similar or analogous problems, has occupied the entire culture increasingly after the war; and what could be clearer than that the same enterprise is being carried on, with varying degrees of success, throughout nearly the entirety of civilization.

It is a startling example, but exactly *true* as to its meaning. My point is that Saroyan, beginning as a poverty-stricken ethnic himself, and in early life producing a brilliant success in spite of this, could not sufficiently shake the influence of history in his time to challenge the American Dream that had sustained him. His Armenian background would teach him that his problem was not confined to the United States—the problem of that dire copula, racism and injustice.

Surely it is not strange that such a man might suffer from the history of the country and the world since the beginning of World War II, especially as he attempted to carry the hopefulness of early life and early success into his later encounters with literary subjects. Yet it seems also clear, having in view the entire trajectory of this career, that, really, he was not wrong about the American Dream; his perception was not amiss—the dream was there, and still is, gathering range and detail however inadequately distributed to the populace. It seems that his conclusions were impetuous and his hopes grandiose; but perhaps the time will yet come when he will be perceived as a true prophet, having come along just a little early in the crescendo he proposed.

The Armenian Buffalo Bill

PETER SOURIAN

William Saroyan was a kind of Armenian Buffalo Bill, as wild and woolly as the marvelous character in *The Time of Your Life* who really and truly herds cattle on a bicycle and falls in love with a midget weighing thirty nine pounds. His feats and misadventures were no less mythic—whether it was a matter of losing tens of thousands of hard-earned dollars on the turn of a card, stubbornly marrying the same woman twice, or writing a five-act play in six days on a bet and then refusing the Pulitzer Prize for it, denying Business the right to patronize Art.

Of course, myths are myths, and that is both their strength and their weakness. They may not be true, but they are large; If you rush to apply the easier general insights of modern psychology to all this Saroyan behavior, you will manage to devastate the myth, shatter it all—truth and untruth together—into little pieces.

Saroyan, the writer, has been properly accused of being garrulous and glib, sentimental, narcissistic, and boastful. And he insisted to the end on discovering and rediscovering clichés, burnishing them, holding them up to the light for us with an insistence that can only be attractive in a sixteen-year-old virgin.

Yet, as his daughter Lucy tells us, he was "exciting, dazzling, vibrant, vital, and funny . . . and mystifying, a very mystifying man," reminding us that he was, after all, and in spite of all, an original. And so the fact is that books of his such as *My Name is Aram,* that glowing bit of radium extracted from the pitchblende of a grim Fresno childhood, will certainly be read a hundred years hence, more than one can say of the work of a slew of careful and brilliant percentage players. As for *The Time of Your Life,* it is on the boards somewhere in the world at the moment you read this, after a half-century. And in all but the worst of his dozens of books replete with silliness and repetitiousness and worldly abstractions, there is a story, a chapter, a scene, a page that really gets you.

Saroyan's exuberance first caught the fancy of the American public in 1934 when "The Daring Young Man on the Flying Trapeze" somehow managed convincingly to deny a world of depression even though the character of the title story died of starvation brought about by unemployment. He went on to perform without a net ever since. As he said of himself: "I didn't earn one dollar by any means other than writing. . . . If an editor liked a story as I had written it, he could buy it. If he wanted parts of it written over, I did not do that work. I have never been subsidized. . . . I have never accepted money connected with a literary prize or award. . . . Once I was urged by friends to file an application for a Guggenheim Fellowship. . . . My application was turned down and I began to breathe freely again."

But if he is one of that breed of California backroom boys celebrated for their limitations by Edmund Wilson decades ago, nevertheless, somewhere behind those big moustaches, flamboyant and sad, there lurked a spirit as anciently and profoundly depressed as that of the Arab who mutters at regular intervals throughout one of his plays: "No foundation. All the way down the line. . . . Whole world."

Saroyan knew it, too. When, in his later work, he is not dredging up the old peppy abstractions and hanging them out for all to see on the sagging clothesline, he is writing grave and beautiful stuff of another order:

> Something had taken possession of me, hushed me. . . . The house was dark and empty, and cold, and I didn't know what to do. In the dining room was a bench my mother had made by placing planks over two apple-boxes and putting a coarse woven covering over the planks, made in Bitlis by somebody in the family. I couldn't sit and I couldn't lie down, so I kneeled on this bench and then put my head down. . . .

And then, I feel, fleeing from it.

But he knew this. He once told his son that, if he celebrated his Fresno boyhood so lyrically, it was because it had been so god-awful, that only by making it into something beautiful had he survived it. After all, beautiful myths are made to explain things—or to explain them away, deny them.

If you think over the apparent lovely atmosphere of such tales as "The Summer of the Beautiful White Horse" or "The Journey to Hanford," you eventually find yourself thinking of how nightmarishly frightening and grubby a tyrannical grandfather can be, or how painful a time an orphan boy of immigrant parents might have in California school, or how bad it is to have no money.

An important aspect of a good story, a good work of art, involves a certain heightening of events. Sometimes this profound and strange process means leaving out a lot—not only leaving it out so it remains implied as in the case of Hemingway's famous iceberg, but leaving it out altogether. Saroyan has left things out in his best stuff, but also in his worst. When, for example, in a poor book such as *Places Where I've Done Time,* you say a marriage went bad and give no details, you're not doing anything profound and strange; in fact, you're not doing anything at all.

Another aspect involves making a world—it doesn't much matter what sort of a world—with its own dynamics, complete unto itself. Kafka's world, for example, is not *the* real world, but it is *a* very real world precisely because Kafka leaves no chinks that would let *the* real world seep in and so spoil his intact perfect nightmare of a paranoid schizophrenic. Similarly, the best of Saroyan's radically different writing keeps *the* real world out and thus maintains the fabulous integrity of the Saroyan world—with everything larger than life. The best of Saroyan's early work depicts the world of a child, vibrant and powerfully simple.

Regarding American writers, Hemingway once said, "We make them into something very strange, we destroy them," A number of victims, including himself, come to mind. Try to imagine the astonishing, utterly magical success of Saroyan (more sudden and out of nowhere than the success of Hemingway, Fitzgerald, or Thomas Wolfe); try to imagine its effect. After such an experience of dizzying fame—quick and magical and *apparently* easy—the effect, positive though it must seem, has also to be traumatic—you stop dead in your tracks, you try to do just exactly as you have been doing, and, of course, that does not work. It would be easy to preach, like a comforter of Job, to such a person that the wise and courageous course when confronted with seeping, creeping adult reality is to grow with it, rapidly and actively, to start making the best of it, to try to incorporate and thus master it. This is what mature artistic development is all about: classicism vs. *Sturm und Drang, enfants terribles,* noble savages, and so on.

Because it would be easy to preach at the dead Saroyan, one feels at least momentarily grateful to generous spirits like those of Pete Hamill and Kurt Vonnegut, both of whom have reminded us of the debt of many later American writers to Saroyan and who exhort us simply and positively to think of how marvelous his best—so often his early—work is.

Except that . . . that we are, to some extent, condemned to be what we came out of, and my background is Armenian, and—even if only intermittenly—I am obliged to be the dead, the dead who cannot speak. America is a rich country, rich in its artists and writers as in its general prosperity. Armenia is poor and devastated, and its writers were taken away and killed, systematically, many of them on one single night in April of 1915, and it has never recovered. Saroyan came out of nowhere, swift as Mercury on a bicycle, on a trapeze, on wings. People raised their eyes to him—people, not just Armenians—and cocked their ears. He was our voice, flying, and he ought to have flown higher, on the wings of the dead.

I believe that Saroyan . . . or rather, I feel that perhaps Saroyan . . . knew too late he ought not, like the overly dependent child who insists on his own magic and omnipotent divinity, to have expected God or Nature to do the job of somehow pulling everything together into a meaningful whole. Since God or Nature did indeed seem to have done this work for Saroyan a number of times, one may understand his feeling that if he sat at his battered old typewriter every morning from eight to twelve and batted away "exuberantly," it would come out divine. That he was an exception. And indeed, in May 1981, with graceful and humorous understanding, as he became "unalive, perfect," like his man on the flying trapeze, he said, "Everybody has got to die, but I have always believed an exception would be made in my case. Now what?"

Vonnegut and Hamill are right, that Saroyan is not a dragon to be slain, a balloon of a reputation to be pricked, and that we are to be grateful for what he left us, but Saroyan knew, I feel, that it was wrong, too, to praise him so readily, and he suffered grievously for it all his mature life, alone.

I suppose there may be three ways of looking at Saroyan. The view of the academics has been, don't look at him at all. The loving, lovely, nice-person view has been, don't analyze him at all. There is a third view, which is that Saroyan *has* produced literature, that is, stuff that bears rereading and transcends time and place while being rooted in it, stuff that also bears a hard, tough-minded look. It will take a fine critic like Nona Balakian, or the very sensitive, large-minded Harry Keyishian, or someone else, to describe, interpret, weigh, and strike the balance.

Ulysses in Fresno

ALFRED KAZIN

Running through Saroyan's work, and now hero of *The Human Comedy,* is the figure of a telegraph boy—a modern American Mercury, riding his bike as Mercury ran on the winds, with a blue cap for an astral helmet and a telegraph blank waving the great tidings in his hand. Like most of us, Saroyan comes from that class to which a telegram is never a message, but always an intimation of disaster or great change, the first sounding of some awful ceremony. But here, as Saroyan say it as a boy, the ceremony is seen through the eyes of the telegraph messenger, and it makes him a ubiquitous folk-character and something of a priest. As he brings news to men he symbolically brings them to each other; as he flits along the American towns, he beats his wings as if to embrace all the lonely Saroyan souls in them. Everything proximate to this boy is part of the human comedy; and he is everywhere. Homer Macauley stands for youth, for expectancy, for the keenness of an adolescence spent in the offices at night, where the sense of danger is gulped down like midnight coffee, and where each ticking brings some special knowledge. But he stands even more for the easy Saroyan knowledge of America, and the easier access to it; he stands for the struggle between his native innocence and the world's experience; and that is the point of the story.

This boy carries all the American strands in himself. In his life can be heard the pulsing of all the telegraph keys over America—the silvery piping of all those interlocked metals and wires, the grim, visored men listening to the beat of each other's hands, listening to that telegraph heart beating over America. All the locked doors open to this boy; all the reverberations of the national experience are to be heard in him. But he is not only an agent; he is a hero; and his education is the drama of the book, his learning to cry, like Blake: "O Rose, thou art sick!" He is Saroyan's white dove, singing his songs of innocence and being soiled by the world's experience. Everything about him is pure, mock-Grecian in its sunniness and youth. Part of him is Oliver Optic—a grubby American

hero supporting his widowed mother and little brother by carrying
messages after school; pure and undefeated, but with no time to play,
losing the dream girl to the rich brat across the aisle. Yet the town he lives
in is Ithaca; his California is an old earth, but the last, as it were, to be
settled by men; the last to have retained the old American innocence, the
yea-saying power; and he has a little brother named Ulysses.

Ulysses' little adventures are to Homer's as the adventures of the
classical Ulysses were to the adventures of Homer's imagination. Ulysses
is in the chrysalis, of the purely physical stage of the world's disillusion;
he has only preposterous little adventures. He goes with an idiot friend
to the public library and they stare at the covers; he gets caught in a bear
trap at a shop while people watch painfully through the window, and the
aimless frolic of Ulysses' life is defined by the Dadaist touch of deadly
simplicity that Saroyan adds when the child is freed.

But Homer has entered into the human realm; everything he sees on
his rounds leads him from the songs of innocence to the songs of
experience; and where he saw only Blake's lamb, and was the lamb, he
now sees the "tyger burning bright." But this is an exaggeration, for
there are no tygers in Saroyan's conception of the human experience;
there is only a wistful attrition of sadness. He does not even see deceit,
ugliness, violence—they are not in Saroyan's world; he merely brings the
messages of death from the War Department to the locked houses.
(Saroyan, a quick fellow, is perhaps the first American writer to have
made imaginative use of America's participation in the Second World
War.) He talks to old Grogan at the telegraph office, a sot; he hears the
sweetly delirious Saroyan lovers, lovers who can never find each other;
he is hungry and tired, and painfully conscious of his family's poverty.
And he wants to know—"*Did he who made the lamb make thee?*"; when he
weeps as a man weeps, he is still more eager to keep his capacity for tears
than to revert to his old innocence. "Otherwise I'm just as good as dead
myself." That is the height of Homer's experience, the drama in his
dismay—he wonders, he wants to know. And now the process is re-
versed—the tiger that was never a tiger has become a sweetly bleating
lamb; the resolution is Love. When he goes to his mother, the youngest,
the wisest Penelope in the world, he is comforted, as the Saroyan people
are forever comforted, when she confides:

"Everything *is* changed—for you. But it is still the same, too. The
loneliness you feel has come to you because you are no longer a child.
But the whole world has always been full of that loneliness. The loneliness does not come from the War. The War did not make it. It was the
loneliness that made the War."

There it is, and there is Saroyan. Having been baptized in the perilous
streams of Postal Telegraph, Homer the human foundling is now swim-

ming in goodness and innocence and in the easy Saroyan heartbreak. Everyone talks of Love; everyone relapses, like little Ulysses, into being a darling singing little chick. Even old Grogan hears the heavenly spheres singing together. And Homer's experience in life now becomes like the singing Saroyan describes in a cafe where some soliders gathered around the piano. "Their singing wasn't particularly good, but the feeling with which they sang was not bad at all." The feeling in Saroyan is never bad at all; at times, in fact, it is quite wonderful. I never knew, I must confess, how effective a writer he was until I read *The Human Comedy*.

The Dark Side of Saroyan

HARRY KEYISHIAN

In "Not Waving but Drowning" by the English poet Stevie Smith, a man drowns while a crowd on shore looks on in amusement. The problem was that the swimmer had a reputation for enjoying himself: "he always loved larking." And so nobody paid attention to his frantic efforts to signal for help. After he was dead, people finally understood that he hadn't been cheerfully waving, but sending a quite different message:

> I was much further out than you thought
> And not waving but drowning.

Indeed, that had been true for a long while before.

> I was too far out all my life
> And not waving but drowning.

Like the swimmer in the poem, William Saroyan also seemed all his life to "love larking," and so we were eager to see him as he presented himself: brash, confident, optimistic. The adjective "Saroyanesque" was coined to describe his particular freewheeling style of expression.

And yet if we had really looked, if we had been reading him attentively, especially in his later years, we had to see the other side of him, the dark and troubled side that existed in constant tension with his "upbeat" pose. The latter always won out, rhetorically: he insisted on the victory of creativity and optimism. But that does not absolve us, as his readers, from understanding that it is not in the conclusions he reached but in the struggle he endured that we will find truths he has to tell. The essence of Saroyan lies in that dialectic, the oscillation between hope and despair, wishes and fears, joy and tragedy.

Of course there had been a pessimistic streak in his work from the start. After all, the protagonist of his first celebrated short story, "The Daring Young Man," *does* die. But it was not until the early 1950s that this darker side began to dominate. In the collection *The Assyrian and Other Stories* (1950) and the novels *Rock Wagram* (1951) and *The Laughing Matter* Saroyan confronted human failure, loss and limitation. At the same time, his work became a search for compensations for mortality. He sought restoration in memories of his youth, his relationship with his children, certain healing actions—like bicycle riding—and, above all, writing itself.

In 1963 *Not Dying* described the period of depression, during which the author is haunted by premonitions of his own death. Saroyan tries to adopt a proper stance, "to accept the messages with grace." He is rescued from these feelings when his son and daughter visit him in Paris. They play cards, quarrel, make up, talk about writing, go to the movies; they discuss the proper way to behave and to be. His son complains about him:

> You drink and gamble and keep bad hours and all that stuff and you aren't a very good friend, you don't really have any friends at all, according to what I've heard. You speak in the loudest voice I've ever heard. You dominate every group I've ever seen you in. You almost never seem interested in anybody else, unless it's an attractive woman. You're very swift and rude with people you don't like. You're self-centered, arrogant, vain, vulgar, and really very ignorant—you know less about the details of what's going on in the world, for instance, than even I do, and you don't care anything about that, either, you don't think that is any reason why you can't explain everything to everybody, including experts. You make people nervous and uncomfortable just by being among them. You're always clearing your throat and spitting if you're in the street, or burying the stuff in a handkerchief if you're indoors. And a lot more. So how can you believe you are a good man?

Since it is unlikely that Aram, his real son, could have produced such a cogent and detailed analysis at the age he is supposed to be here, it is clear that Saroyan is really projecting, trying to imagine what he must seem like to his son. So these are really "charges" that Saroyan makes against himself. How does he answer them?

Earlier in the book. Saroyan had described what writing had meant to him, how it had changed him, as a person, for the better: "I used to believe my face was coarse, for instance, but after I had finished writing something, I noticed that my face was suddenly no longer coarse. The work had changed me so powerfully inside that you could see it in my face, which was still the same face, but no longer coarse." And here, in answer to his son's fictional accusations, he gives a similar answer: "I. . . believe that my writing, whenever it turns out to be good, is good because it is written by a good man."

These conversations and, more important, the writing of the book itself save him from his feelings of depression and mortality: "I began to write the book so that the writing of it could take the place of dying, of my own literal death." Saved by involvement with family and craft, he gets moving again, "I went to work and wrote a play for money. I didn't die."

Saroyan's swings of mood are evident in these passages. On the one hand, there is self-consciousness, self-doubt, awareness of his shortcomings; on the other hand, there is pride in what he is and what he does and the way he goes about his business of being Saroyan. First, forebodings of doom and mortality; then, the exhilaration of accomplishment.

In a later book, *Sons Come and Go, Mothers Hang in Forever* (1976), Saroyan again expressed the anguished intensity he projected as a young celebrity, an intensity that frightened people off:

> I had long known that there was something about me that was either violent or frightening for some reason. In certain three-sided clothing store images I had for some years come upon myself, with shock and disbelief, regret, and shame, disappointment and despair, for I am indeed clearly violent, mad, and ugly, all because of intensity of some kind, a tension, an obsession with getting everything that there was to be got, a passion, an insanity.

He wonders how to "cast out the demon" that was in him, "or at the very least how to . . . keep it quiet and not so terribly noticeable."

But at the same time, Saroyan sees his "incivility" as a saving force: "I have always been a Laugher," he wrote in *Sons Come and Go*, "disturbing people who are not laughers, upsetting whole audiences at theatres. . . I laugh, that's all. I love to laugh. Laughter to me is being alive. I have had rotten times, and I have laughed through them. Even in the midst of the very worst times I have laughed."

Tragically, the discrepancy Saroyan felt between what he hoped to be and what he feared he was crept into his relations with his children. We know too well the solemn accusation Aram makes in *Last Rites*—"He wanted me to die"—but we must wonder at the accuracy of that perception when we read, in *Sons Come and Go*, of Saroyan's pained awareness of his inability to make his true feelings known to those closest to him, to his children. Saroyan describes his despair as he listens to a tape record-ing he made of a conversation with Aram and Lucy when they were seven and four:

I was abashed by the monster I had clearly been—loud, swift, impatient, unable to slow down, unable to be disciplined enough to make serene my nearness to each child, alone with me in an office. I *sounded* insensitive to them, and yet, this is the terrible and puzzling thing, I had been full of nothing but profound love, easy intelligence, abundant comedy, enormous health—and yet unmistakably a monster.

Perhaps this passage makes it easier for us to credit Aram's account of his father's apparent hostility towards him; but we must also see the anguish of the father, torn between the wish to love, simply, directly, and spontaneously, and his inability to express that love.

Keeping that failure of communication in mind, we can well understand Saroyan's deep admiration for George Jean Nathan, the noted drama critic who was Saroyan's booster, friend, and teacher. In *Sons Come and Go,* Saroyan remarks that Nathan:

never had anything *instructive* to say about the *writing* of plays, but knew more about the theatre than anybody else I have ever talked with. He passed along what he knew in a way that was easy for me to take or leave. And his talk both invited and compelled participation on my part, and the part of anybody else who happened to be at the table.

So what Saroyan could not do for his son, Nathan had been able to do for him; and that created, in Saroyan, a sense of gratitude and awe.

There was also his admiration for Nathan's style, for in that too Saroyan saw exemplified qualities he wished he had:

He dressed neatly and he went out among the thieves and assassins. . . .And everything he wrote had a laughter in it. He was one of the most serious men in the living world . . . but he refused to burden his writing, or his readers, with the agony of his unconverted and apparently indestructible soul.

Saroyan concludes, "There can't ever be anybody like him again."

Was Nathan really such a paragon, or is this only Saroyan's hero-worship? We cannot say. What does emerge from these lines, however, is a sense of what Saroyan held precious, and seemed to see in his admired friend: the ability to combine in one personality the capacity for laughter and seriousness; the ability to have and convey knowledge; the style that permitted a person to walk untouched among "thieves and assassins."

The conflict between the energies of life and the undeniable fact of mortality is the focus of *Obituaries* (1979), the book in which he used the 1976 necrology list in *Variety* for an extended commentary, memoir, and

meditation. Although he was never a man of traditional pieties or orthodox religious beliefs, it nevertheless startles us to read his head-on
confrontation with the finality of death—all death, his own included:

> A stiff is found in bed, bereft of sleep and dream, and God knows
> where the person has gone, some say to heaven, some say to hell, some
> say only to graveyard, some say back to nature. . . . I don't believe in
> such silly stuff as going to heaven to sit on the right hand of somebody
> fictitious and damned foolish, or going to hell to be roasted by some-
> one else even more fantastic and silly—just dump my beloved ashes
> . . . into the raging ocean, which as you know, as you surely re-
> member, was the character of my soul, and the style of my eight
> minutes of dances, songs, and witty sayings.

But we will be startled only if we have failed to hear what Saroyan has
been telling us right along. "Don't tell me I'm sentimental, you sons of
bitches," he roared elsewhere in *Obituaries*. Indeed, there was sentiment
in him. But sentiment was only one part of his personality, and he wills
and compels us to understand his wholeness—his spiritual and his physical hungers, his idealistic and his pragmatic sides; he demands that we
understand his lifelong dissatisfaction with himself, the people he knew,
the life he lived, and the terms of existence itself.

If we would honor Saroyan, we must strive to understand him, to
confront what he strove to tell us. We must not codify him, but treat his
writing for what it was, a dynamic product of the interplay between the
opposing forces within him. In this is revealed not only the meaning, but
the courage of his confrontation with life.

The Time of His Life: A Shavian Influence

DANIEL LEARY

I recently came upon a passage by William Saroyan in which he claims:

Shaw . . . is the tonic of the Christian peoples of the world. He is health, wisdom, and comedy, and that's what I am, too. . . If you must know which writer has influenced my writing when influences are real and for all I know enduring, then that writer has been George Bernard Shaw.*

This is from the preface to the one-acter *Hello Out There* (1941), a preface that energetically, uncontrollably and most Shavianly spills over the material ancillary to or independent of the play. Saroyan seen through the eyes of Shaw: *The Time of Your Life* shifts into the dialectical mode.

My original delight in the play's anarchism and overblown romance is still there, but now I find it coming alive with irony and pertinence. The play remains a social fable set in 1939, but the Shaw parallel sets it in a wider context, one where the characters are neither waiting for Lefty's aggressive socialist promise, nor for Godot's existential nonexistence. "Nick's Pacific Street Restaurant, Saloon, and Entertainment Palace" has just become a microcosm for a world that is still evaluating its possibilities just as Shaw's disordered ship set in *Heartbreak House* conveys the shipwreck of European values at the time of World War I and thereafter.

What had seemed like a peripheral passage in *The Time of Your Life* (Joe's comment on the Arab) becomes central: "That man, in his own way, is a prophet. He is one who, with the help of beer, is able to reach

---

*Saroyan visited Shaw at Ayot St. Lawrence in 1944, when he was in the Army. He writes in "The Bicycle Rider in Beverly Hills, ". . . he was a gentle, delicate, kind, little man who had established a pose, and then lived it so steadily and effectively that the pose had become real. Like myself, his nature has been obviously a deeply troubled one in the beginning. He had been a man who had seen the futility, meaninglessness and sorrow of life but had permitted himself to thrust aside these feelings and to perform another George Bernard Shaw, which is art and proper."

The cop, the longshoreman, and the comic in a scene from Saroyan's most famous play, *The Time of Your Life,* **directed by Jose Quintero, at the "Tribute to William Saroyan" (Circle in the Square, 1982).** *(Courtesy of Martha Swope.)*

that state of deep understanding in which what and what-not, the reasonable and unreasonable are one." We recall Shotover in *Heartbreak House,* who seeks, with the help of rum, "the seventh degree of concentration" from which vantage he may see even the destructiveness of war as healthy. The comment on the Arab gives the basis for an all-pervading dialectic in the play: for Joe's unresolved conflict between the need to have money and the desire to hurt no one, for Kitty's needing the loneliness of being separated from Tom to better love him, for the threat of world war intensifying both the challenge of a pinball machine and the wonder of life, in short, for Nick rhyming with Blick.

"Health, wisdom, and comedy." The health and wisdom are coupled concerns for both Saw and Saroyan. Shaw's defrocked priest Peter Keegan in *John Bull's Other Island* dreams of a wise and therefore healthy society.

in which the state is the Church and the Church the people: three in one and one in three. It is a commonwealth in which work is play and play is life: three in one and one in three. . . . It is a godhead in which all life is human and all humanity divine: three in one and one in three.

It is a dream whose pursuit structures such plays as *Man and Superman, Major Barbara, Heartbreak House,* and *Saint Joan.* As Saroyan puts it in the preface to *Hello Out There,* "No man's guilt is not yours, nor is any man's innocence a thing apart." When Joe explains that if you have *"not time of living"* in the time of your life, there's "nothing but minutes and idiocy," he is using one of Shaw's favorite etymological tags. The root meaning of "idiot" is an individual, someone separated from the rest. Health begins with a dream that includes more than your own wants. As the central figure, Joe seeks to find and confirm the vitalizing dreams of others. Kitty Duval dreams about a home and family, Tom dreams about a home and family with Kitty. Wisdom has nothing to do with prescribed education in either Shaw or Saroyan. In a two-page Shavian-like stage direction, Dudley Bostwick, one of the characters in *The Time of Your Life,* is described as a "swindled young man. Educated, but without the least understanding. . . . Ordinary and yet extraordinary. . . . He is a great personality because, against all these handicaps, what he *wants* is simple and basic, a woman." Shaw's Jack Tanner in *Man and Superman* has multiple plans for changing the world, but he finds that what he wants—in spite of himself—is Ann Whitefield. As with Shaw, romance in Saroyan's play leads to thoughts of eugenics and the evolving human race. The forthright longshoreman McCarthy explains: "I'm a man with too much brawn to be an intellectual, exclusively. I married a small, sensitive cultured woman so that my kids would be sissies instead of suckers." He is aware of what is actually driving Kitty and Tom into each others arms. From the early *Cashel Byron's Profession,* novel and play, to the late *The Millionairess,* Shaw has marriageable characters seeking their opposites, hoping for the vital synthesis of progeny with sane minds in healthy bodies.

The dramatist's dream becomes flesh in words and rhythms. Shaw has Jack and Ann in *Man and Superman* embody their wants, project their dreams, against a mythic backdrop,—explicitly, the fourth act, "Don Juan in Hell," which combines the terrestrial wants of man and woman with the mythic exploits and neurotic drives of Don Juan. Caesar steps out of Egyptian darkness to answer, like Oedipus, the riddle of the Sphinx, Liza Doolittle is as much a self-liberating Cinderella as she is Galatea to Higgins's Pygmalion. In *Back to Methuselah,* Shaw first takes us back to the Old-Testament Eden and then projects us through five plays to a time as "Far as Thought Can Reach" and a place in which new Adams and Eves watch a fabricated "old Adam," filled with idiotic self-importance, kill its maker. Saroyan also gives us characters whose individual dreams have allegorical resonances. It my be Nick's saloon, but "The Missouri Waltz" floating "dreamily and softly" from the juke box evokes the tender dream of an America that exists only in the imagination. Joe is the dreamer whose imaginative control over the doings in this world makes him a surrogate for the creator-dramatist himself. He initiates the actions of others whether it is making an errand-boy of Tom or opening conversation with Kitty by asking her "What's the dream?" a question he puts to everyone in one way or another throughout the play. Under Joe's direction, Nick's saloon becomes mythic: Tom and Kitty, the new Adam and Eve, face the age-old, idiotically self-important serpent, (this time called Blick) in an American garden as innocent, eccentric, and wild as that which Kit Carson recalls and helps re-create, while Willie pits his skill and daring against Frankenstein's monster, technology, and wins to the accompaniment of flags, lights, and the song "America."

Like Shaw's heroes on the evolutionary way to being Supermen, Saroyan's Joe is a permanent resident of "Heartbreak House"; that is, he lives without illusions about the way of the world, without hopes for personal happiness. Joe may sing songs with the Salvation Army (the derelict's calculated confession conjures up *Major Barbara*), but he knows you must pay the piper with money that comes from munitions makers, slums, and brothels. Joe's last-act revelation to Tom could be Barbara— no longer a major—explaining her tortured state to Cusins:

> If anybody's got any money—to hoard or to throw away—you can be sure he stole it from other people. Not from rich people who can spare it but from poor people who can't. From their lives and from their dreams. I'm no exception. . . . I stole it like everybody else does. I hurt people to get it. Loafing around this way, I *still* earn money. The money itself earns *more*. I *still* hurt people.

For a moment the promise of personal happiness glows as Joe talks to the mysterious and beautiful Mary L who rekindles his earlier dreams. But like Higgins, Caesar, and Dick Dudgeon, Joe won't dance. He tells her he is occupied in trying to find out "if it's possible to live what I think is a civilized life. I mean a life that can't hurt any other life."

In the first stage direction of *The Time of Your Life*, a sailor enters "moving thoughtfully, as though he were trying very hard to discover how to live." That description contains the Stanislavskian infinitive, the concept that motivates the play—"to discover how to live." All of Shaw's major plays share in that search for a working synthesis, a viable morality. We are back to health and wisdom again. Dream and imagination, yes, but only as the cue for passion, the vision that will move the will to action. Joe looks back on the dream of woman nostalgically and now finds "I don't do anything. I don't *want* to do anything any more." He suffers from the same sickness as does the capitalist invalid Mopsey in Shaw's *Too True To Be Good.* The disease, as Saroyan sees it, is expressed by the Arab who mutters throughout the play, "No foundation. All the way down the line" and for Shaw by Aubrey in *Too True* who preaches that "we have outgrown our religion, outgrown our political system, outgrown our own strength of mind and character." The answer for both dramatists is the same: become involved with others whether it is finally leaving Nick's bar to help a young couple or founding a sisterhood of working women. But to take meaningful action demands a unified person, a person with faith in himself. In *Back to Methuselah,* Shaw has his serpent in the Garden of Eden succinctly answer that problem by dissecting the creative process: "You imagine what you desire; you will what you imagine; and at last you create what you will." Saroyan tells us much the same when Joe bets a large sum on a horse named Precious Time and wins. Like Shaw's heroine in *The Millionairess,* money comes to him because he has will. He warns Nick about gambling only fifty cents: "You've got no more faith than a flea." It is desire, imagination, will, in a word, faith, that makes things happen. It is the conviction of *The Time of Your Life* that we must bet everything on Precious Time so that in the words of the play's epithet "in the wondrous time you shall not add to the misery and sorrow of the world, but shall smile to the infinite delight and mystery of it."

Shaw for Saroyan is not only health and wisdom, not only temperament and content, but also a model of "comedy." Saroyan's *The Time of Your Life* utilizes some of the calculated formlessness of Shaw's late comedic structure. In part the formal resemblances come from the Shaw-Saroyan healthy tendency toward self mockery. Saroyan has one of the characters suggests that all the world's war-causing maniacs are frustrated writers: "Print everything they write, so they'll believe they're immortal. That way keep them from going haywire." They both permit the authorial presence to be felt, the voice to be heard. Shaw often has characters hold up fun-house mirrors that distort the Shaw that is holding them up. Jack Tanner in *Man and Superman,* for example, obviously a Shaw surrogate, is breathtakingly articulate and delightfully wrong on every evaluation about human motives he makes. Even in his early, Isben-influenced plays, Shaw's ebullient self broke through the dramatic unities, but in the plays after *Saint Joan,* there is an extravagant willfullness, a breaking of conventions, a shorthand of the stage, that demands attention because—so the message rings out—the time for redeeming the time is short. Saroyan conveys the same personal and frantic urgency. Man has to repair himself—on an individual level learn to function with all four faculties, on a community level learn to live as one with other individuals. The voices of both authors become their forms, and they are saying—shouting, cajoling, demanding—that man must "try . . . very hard to discover how to live."

Shaw and Saroyan knew that voices as forms must be entertaining if they are to be heard. Joe's explanation of what a toy is for nicely reflects the author's thoughts on the drama he is constructing: "This is a toy. A contraption devised by the cunning of man to drive boredom, or grief, or anger out of children." And as everybody gathers around to look at the toy—just as the audience has gathered around to look at the play—he adds, "Delightful. Tragic, but delightful." The tragic part is that we are grown-up children not coming to terms with our boredom, our griefs, our anger but letting them individually and collectively, metaphorically and literally, kill us. As the children watch, Blick comes in—a frustrated author if ever there was one—and immediately disrupts the bar's harmony. As head of the Vice Squad he had come to make vice. He is an embodiment of man's destructive urges and, in the context of 1939, of Adolf Hitler's rise to power, though the children of Nick's bar can barely bring themselves to glance at the headlines. In spite of the Blicks, the human race continues producing Nicks. Dudley's dream girl Elsie agrees to go with him "to a room in a cheap hotel, and dream that the world is beautiful," but cautions, "Let's hurry, before they dress you, stand you in line, hand you a gun, and have you kill and be killed."

In act 2 Joe returns to his musings about toys and observes that they help you to stop crying because they get you "curious about the way they work and you forget whatever it is you're remembering that's making you cry." Dramatic toys are somewhat more complex. Saroyan's play is full of attention-catching distractions but, as in Shaw's extravaganzas of the thirties, they are often calculated to make you think about what you are seeing as well as feeling about them. In Shaw's *The Simpleton of the Unexpected Isles* (1935), the Angel of Last Judgment comes to earth to do his job. It's an outrageous tour de force, with the Angel being winged by artillery as he decends and having takeoff trouble on his departure. We are distracted into laughter, but when we consider how it works the message comes clear: most people do not know how to live and any sane judge would have them removed. In the middle of *The Time of Your Life* a Greek-American newsboy claims to have a great lyric tenor, sings "When Irish Eyes Are Smiling," and is promised a job someday. It is a vaudeville turn that seems outrageously irrelevant to the play until we start thinking about the way it works. The Italian-American Nick listens in delight to a Greek-American singing an Irish-American ballad. The moments of harmony in the bar, carefully choreographed in the stage directions, are living demonstrations of how all men can live together.

That newsboy is happy and brings pleasure to others because in Nick's bar he can do his thing. His imaginative want is given approving space for willed action. Nick touches on the secret when he soliloquizes about his bar and the people it attracts: "Maybe they can't feel at home any-where else." The black man Wesley plays the piano, the Arab plays the harmonica, the Assyrian Willie plays the pinball machine, the American Harry delivers comic sketches that fail because they are sad and dances to express them in another way. (Gene Kelly, the original Harry, must have delighted in these interpretive dances.) They all have what the newsboy has. Saroyan describes the ensemble health and wisdom just before Blick's arrival:

> Every man innocent and good; each doing what he believe he should do, or what he must do. . . . Although everyone is dead serious, there is unmistakable smiling and humor in the scene; a sense of the human body and spirit emerging from the world-imposed state of stress and fretfulness: . . . Each person belongs to the environment, in his own person as himself.

Anyone acquainted with Shaw would catch in this passage something of his delight in the body and spirit of man functioning in an environ-ment based on vital economy rather than cash nexus. It is found in Joan whose will is one with the wind, the laying of eggs, the playful discovery of a king, in Caesar who revels in his plunge into the ocean and freedom, in the dithyrambic cadences of Undershaft, Cusins, Barbara when the Life Force moves them, in the ensemble vitality, verbal and physical, in all the plays. For Saroyan and for Shaw the real tragedy in life was the loss of this exuberant sense of life. I think of Mrs. Warren's daughter Vivie who withdraws from the life of the heart for the Victorian equiv-alent of a yuppy M.B.A. Saroyan's policeman, Krupp (first played by William Benedix), would have known what to say:

> All the corruption everywhere. The poor kids selling themselves. . . . Nobody going quitely for a little walk to the ocean. . . . Everybody trying to get a lot of money in a hurry.

When the sad comic and interpretive dancer Harry complains to McCarthy that nobody laughs at his routines, the wise and healthy longshoreman assures him "that I *am* laughing, although not *out loud*" and suggests that maybe "you've stumbled headlong into a new kind of comedy." I again detect the authorial presence. Like Shaw, Saroyan senses the absurdity of human behavior but finds that a direct mirroring of it bores, angers, grieves his audience. Harry's first sketch reminds them that a world war is imminent. However, after that unsuccessful monologue he does "a goofy dance . . . with great sorrow, but much energy." His second sketch, which focuses on the have–have not situation in America, falls equally flat, but the accompanying dance prompts McCarthy's observation that it is "a most satisfying demonstration of the present state of the American body and soul." Harry's monologues reveal the sickness and the lack of wisdom in America, but his "goofy" dance in which sadness and energy collide enacts the spirit of Saroyan's plays and those of his major influence, Bernard Shaw.

Saroyan's typically candid and expansive acknowledgment of Shaw's influence on his work opens that work to an expansive deconstructionist interpretation. Viewing *The Time of Your Life* from a Shavian dialectical perspective, we discover the play is healthier and saner than it has seemed in decades: it escapes its time and place and becomes part of the evolving body of world drama. The shift from individual talent to creative continuity is a critical application of the health and sanity embodied in the plays of Saroyan and Shaw. Beyond "the anxiety of influence" we begin to experience the camaraderie of kinship. Time dissolves. Shaw's shipwrecked house, yes, but also Harry Hope's backroom in O'Neill's *The Iceman Cometh*, Dr. Relling's manipulating of dreams in Ibsen's *The Wild Duck*. Joe's involved distancing, his pivotal position inside and outside the action, his foreknowledge, his direction of others, makes him something of a stage manager recalling that godlike entity in Thornton Wilder's *Our Town*.

The new comedy Saroyan stumbled on was a mode of contemplating and of dealing with a world that seemed to be unhomelike, inhuman, unpredictable, mad. Saroyan was not alone in seeking new approaches. The 1930s and '40s were tragic or threatened tragedy, but Shaw insisted throughout his career—even taking on Shakespeare—that we cannot afford the luxury of tragedy in our theaters. The playwright must contemplate the sickness of his time and seek for a healthy solution, must attempt to balance conflicting forces in plays open in both form and attitudes. While contemplating and balancing, the dramatist must distance himself through comic perspective to avoid his own paralysis and to prevent his audience from leaving. When we permit Saroyan's work to echo in the company of his fellow experimenters of all times, his new comedy gains in richness and significance. When we accept Shaw as Saroyan's major influence we are less inclined to dismiss his solution of togetherness as naive sentiment, more willing to envisage a world in which the children are at home, with the space and time to grow up.

Saroyan Shoots a Film

DICKRAN KOUYMJIAN

William Saroyan wrote, produced, and directed just one film, *The Good Job*, for Metro-Goldwyn-Mayer in 1942. The title remained an obscure reference in film guides—Katz in his *Film Encyclopedia* of 1979 called it a documentary—until it was ressurrected in 1980 for an Armenian film festival at Columbia University. It has since been shown at festivals in Fresno, California (1981), Los Angeles (1982), Lyon (1983), at the Cinémathèque française in Paris (1984). There exist both 35- and 16-mm copies. An example of the latter is preserved in the Armenian Film Archive at California State University, Fresno.

The genesis of this "M-G-M Miniature," as the studio called it, is inextricably enmeshed with the production of the Academy Award–winning *The Human Comedy*, based on a scenario Saroyan prepared especially for Louis B. Mayer in January 1942. At the end of the same year Saroyan turned it into his most successful novel; it was published in early 1943 by Harcourt Brace. Through a series of chance meetings, described in Larry Lee and Barry Gifford, *Saroyan* (Harper & Row, 1984), William Saroyan, a nationally admired writer of Broadway plays, some of which he directed himself, met the powerful head of M-G-M in December 1941. He entered into a gentleman's agreement to prepare a film treatment.

This was not Saroyan's first try at Hollywood; he had gone there in 1936, newly famous as a short-story writer at a weekly salary of $300 with B. P. Schulberg at Pathé (Paramount) and later went to Columbia Pictures.* Nothing tangible seems to have materialized from this first en-

---

*Budd Schulberg describes Saroyan's arrival in Hollywood in his *Writers in America* (Stein and Day, 1983):

So Saroyan came down [from San Francisco], bringing to our sunkist, overly routined dream-factory town his unruly, creative vitality, his tongue-in-cheek but effective defiance of artistic and commercial conventions, his outrageous, inimitable individuality. His sense

counter with the big studios, except that Saroyan saw lots of films made and understood how the industry worked. He especially liked to be on the sets when his fellow Armenian Rouben Mamoulian was turning. Five years later, just at the moment America got involved in the Second World War, it was a different matter for Saroyan. In one month he wrote a three-to-four-hundred-page scenario, *The Human Comedy,* and delivered it by hand to M-G-M. On 11 February 1942 he signed a contract to direct his own film.

Mayer was moved by *The Human Comedy.* At the meeting he said, according to Al Hirschfeld as reported by Lee and Gifford, "Anything you want, Bill. The thing to do is try it out first, see how you like it. Write a short. Work it out. I'll leave it up to you. You can take the studio . . . do whatever the hell you want. . . . Write the script. You direct it, you hire the people, you produce it, you're the whole works on this short" (p. 69).

On 23 October 1980, I asked Saroyan about the film because I had been invited to introduce its first contemporary showing in New York at the end of that same month. Saroyan said his expectation of directing *The Human Comedy* was met by skepticism from Mayer and especially the pragmatic sycophants surrounding him. According to Saroyan, Mayer said, "But Bill, how can you direct *The Human Comedy* since you've never made a film?" It was an affront to a Saroyan who had successfully directed stage works. He replied, "Mr. Mayer, give me three days and I'll prove that I can direct and bring in a professional film on schedule." Mayer said, "Fine, write a script first." "I've already got it," retorted Saroyan, who recalls borrowing equipment and making the film in "about three days." With an office on the M-G-M lot and all necessary facilities, he began filming what would become a two reeler (twenty minutes) on 19 March 1942.

Saroyan chose the story "A Number of Poor" from his 1939 collection *Peace, Its Wonderful,* calling it according to Lee and Gifford, successively *Jazz,* then *Corner Store,* and finally *The Good Job.* In April he edited it for in-house screening.

Testimony on the merits of the film are contradictory. Saroyan said that those who saw it liked it, even Louis Mayer. Victor Flemming, the

---

of motion-picture construction was nil, and he hardly made a secret of his disdain for the kind of vehicles my father had chosen. But in spite of shortcomings and misgivings, he was able to run through those routine scripts and give them a little something of his own offbeat ebullience. There was something called *A Doctor's Diary* in which the obstretician's delivery of a baby was accompanied by a page of hackneyed sentimentality. Bill's attack on this scene was to have the doctor slap the baby and say, "Okay, baby, this is the world . . . inhale, exhale . . ." launching into one of those high-spirited Saroyanesque monologues. Coming from a doctor it was pretty strange and wild talk, but it did shake the scene out of its pedestrian mold. Some of it was even heard in the final version, and all of it was tenderly preserved for a subsequent Saroyan short story entitled naturally, "Okay, Baby, This Is the World." (p. 76) director of *Gone with the Wind,* said, "Bill, that's wonderful, but there are no close ups." He pleaded that in three days he had no time for such luxuries. As it exists today, *The Good Job* is a single reel film, just under eleven minutes long. This reduction was done by M-G-M, who, again according to Saroyan, commercially distributed it. "The film won several awards," he even boasted.

"Those who saw it (it never was released to theatres) recall work-manlike performances by the contract players and an unforgettable moment when a woman drops a watermelon down her decollatage for safe keeping," report Lee and Gifford (p. 84). But did Larry Lee see the film? He visited Fresno State at least twice and once addressed my Saroyan class. A videotape can be viewed there with permission; if he saw the film he forgot its details.

The Good Job opens with all the formal trappings of a commercially released film, including the M-G-M lion twisting its head and roaring. For this reason Saroyan's version is more credible. But its release, must have been after the summer of that year, for in the introduction to a segment of the scenario of *The Human Comedy* published in *Theatre Arts,* September 1942 (p. 584), the editor says, "Meanwhile, Saroyan has written and produced *The Good Job,* a short picture which should be soon released." A search in M-G-M's archives will someday settle the matter. As for the dignified, middle-aged woman (she is fifty in the original story) suffering hard times, she discreetly puts a small cantaloupe (in the story too) in her very comfortably fitting blouse with the shopkeeper-narrator's secret acquiescence.

M-G-M's vice-president for publicity at the time, Howard Dietz, during the feud that developed with the writer, said that *The Good Job* was the most expensive short subject Metro had filmed in two years, but that no one could determine whether the finished product represented simply exposed film or, as *Variety* paraphrased him, " 'just what the public subconsciously wants' " (Lee and Gifford, p. 86).

Recent audiences have voted, by their admiration, for the latter view. The seven episodes of the film are sensitive and warm and succeed in doing much the same that M-G-M's interpretation of Saroyan in *The Human Comedy* did for an America caught up in an all consuming world war. Saroyan's own work certainly depended less on sentimentality than M-G-M's manipulation of *The Human Comedy.* Lee and Gifford feel that the film "leaned heavily on talk, including the crutch of narrative, and it lacked visual texture. This latter problem may have been a result of the short shooting schedule, but the absence of satisfying close-ups or dialogue reverse shots made the movie look stiff and stagy" (p. 84).

It is true that narration holds the film together just as it does in the original story narrated in the first person. That's why Saroyan chose "A

Number of Poor," and, despite Saroyan's own disclaimer, there are a few close shots. Though there is dialogue (as in all films), its use is not excessive, the camera doing most of the work in four of the seven vignettes.

"One summer I worked two months in a grocery store," the narrator begins in the story "A Number of Poor," "a little store on Grove Street, near the slums." There are four others in the story, all customers: the lady of the cantaloupe, Casal the Spaniard, twelve-year-old Maggie who thinks she looks like Ginger Rogers, and four-year-old Callaghan. The film includes them all, in the same sequence as the original, starting with the lady and ending with Callaghan, an expert on candy. But Saroyan added at least three more episodes—"at least," because as the characters file by the camera during the credits at the beginning and end of the film, there are actors not to be found in it, presumably edited out by M-G-M. The new sequences are Mike the discontented popcorn man and a boy who does not like popcorn but rather vitamins; it is placed between the lady and Casal stories. Then, after Maggie the redhead, is a sketch of kids on the street sharing cracker jack. It treats the budding power of materialism on young children, but also makes a strong antiracist statement. That is followed by the speaker of strange languages who in strongly accented English asks for Smyrna figs. He occasionally speaks and counts in his language, which is Armenian. After buying, then caressing, a whole box of California black figs, he says, *Iskapes kaghtzer en, erkar jamanak koutem* ('They are really sweet, they'll last me a long time')."

The Casal episode, the longest in the film as well as the most touching, is the only one about whose inspiration we know something. In his last memoir, *Births,* written in 1979 and posthumously published (1983), Saroyan explains the origin of the story. "My cousin Kirk Minasian told me thirty or more years ago about his customers at a small grocery store patronised mainly by winoes on Grove Street near Laguna. I remember vividly the small man who told Kirk that as soon as he got home from work his large son would kneel down and demand that his father get on his back, whereupon the young man would solemnly carry his father in and out of all the rooms of their apartment. It was a ritual of love, and the small father worshipped his son no less than his son honored him. I loved that story but it never did it justice, although I mentioned it, somewhat in passing, in a story entitled "The Good Job," which I also made into a two-reel movie, in order to demonstrate to Louis B. Mayer that I should be the director of the story 'The Human Comedy'" (p. 18).

Never one to research while in the process of writing, Saroyan forgot the original title of his story—worse, he was uncertain about the importance of the Casal section. In the short story Saroyan did fail to do it justice, but in the film the lines are written better and enhanced by the camera to recreate a remarkable and unusual father-son relationship.

The film opens with the shopkeeper saying, "Every person I met . . . was like some one I had known all my life but had forgotten," and ends, "That was the best job I ever had . . . because of the wonderful, funny little people . . . remembering them, I remember you."

Of course Saroyan did not get to make *The Human Comedy*. It was directed by Clarence Brown from a screenplay by Howard Estherbook, starring Mickey Rooney, Frank Morgan, Donna Reed, and Van Johnson. (Saroyan never liked the film, saying Brown's directing was not very good and Estherbrook was famous but stupid.) For Saroyan it was not just a disappointment—he was furious because he had been tricked, deceived. Al Hirschfeld proffered this version to Lee and Gifford: "Well, the short having been made, there comes along *The Human Comedy*, which was the big property. And Bill said he wanted to direct it. And Louis Mayer said, 'No, that's not for you, Bill. We have directors here.'"

"But I have a contract with you that I am to direct my own film."
He says, "Well, you've directed your own film."
"What are you talking about?"
"The film that you've just directed."

Artie Shaw, one of the heroes of Lee and Gifford's book, remembers it this way: "That's when the mania began, that obsessive thing when they screwed him. . . . He assumed that if he did this short, *The Good Job*. . . . He was thinking merit. He didn't understand that they were thinking the bottom line. . . . So they gave him the short in order to get rights to *The Human Comedy*. And he signed over that assuming they would give him the directorship. . . . I can't say it was ethical. Anyone who gets in the film business looking for ethics is like a guy who goes into court looking for justice. Dumb. I was astounded by his reaction. He was so bitter."

Saroyan instantly left M-G-M and his $1,000 a week job. He wrote a scathing letter against L. B. Mayer, which was published in *Variety*, the one magazine that everyone in show business reads. For Budd Schulberg, "It was unheard of. . . . In terms of begining in the industry, it was like writing your own exit, your pass out of there" (p. 85). Saroyan's bitterness never lessened. Back in San Francisco, he quickly wrote the play *Get Away Old Man*, a devasting portrayal of Mayer and an exposé of filmmaking Hollywood style. It was produced on Broadway in November 1943. A decade later he took up the Hollywood theme again in the novel *Rock Wagram*. The solid values of the young Armenian movie star from Fresno are contrasted with the cunning of the big studio moguls.

Saroyan's offer to buy back *The Human Comedy* for the $60,000 he had received was refused. As late as 1946 in a letter to Eddie Mannix at M-G-M he again offered to buy back the rights. This letter is now in the collection of Saroyan scholar David Batten of Fresno, who also has another letter addressed to Mannix from London in 1944 in which Saroyan says he recently had the opportunity to see "my one reel two-reeler," *The Good Job,* commenting "it stinks." If he did see it, further support is added to the notion that the M-G-M miniature was released and even offered for G.I. viewing. In the letter Saroyan finds his work too ponderous, wishing he had lightened it up, but he also complains about an employee of the studio who kept coming around telling him he couldn't do this or that because it would be too expensive.

In 1980 Saroyan had not yet gotten over it. "I made that film free of charge. I got nothing, not for my work as director, not for the literary property as author." He claimed not to have seen the film after he left M-G-M and complained that he never even received a personal copy, an unusual circumstance in Saroyan's case since he had a fetish about saving examples of all his works. The episode so marked him that in nearly everyone of his ten or so published memoirs he mentions his struggle with Mayer.

The Good Job is uncontestably a fine first film for a writer turned director. The fallout from the explosion between two strong person-alities hardly affected one of them, but ended the film career of the other before it fairly began. It deprived cinema of Saroyan's magic, for there is no arguing his genius with story, dialogue, drama. In the Oc-tober 1980 conversation he confided, "Film would have been perfect for me. But I couldn't do what I wanted, if you understand me, I couldn't do what was needed, but had to do what was necessary to get ahead, and I was not able to do that. The industry was and is full of bankers, crooks, hustlers, liars, and worse." I asked if he had ever thought of directing again after *The Good Job,* away from Hollywood, in Armenia for instance, where he was king. "Twenty years ago I suggested it (there), but no one really could follow through. There too there is administrative red tape, their system too can be overbearing. When in Yugoslavia I saw their problems and understood that it cannot easily be done anywhere."

That Saroyan would have been a natural in the world of cinema was clearly perceived by *Theatre Arts* in the same introduction of 1942 cited above: "There is a peculiar affinity between this poet's vision, which can wander freely from one image to another with no need for literal transitions, and the film, whose greatest talent lies in the same ability to fade smoothly from one vista to another with only the most tenuous and nonliterary relation. It is right that a poet such as William Saroyan should bring his powers to the release of films too long hamstrung by stage and literary convention."

With an imagination both fertile and furtive, Saroyan would have served cinema well. His timing was impeccable, his speech authentic, natural, and graceful. Such plays as the *Beautiful People, Love's Old Sweet Song,* and *The Cave Dwellers* seem perfect properties to translate into film. Only one other Saroyan work, *The Time of Your Life,* was made into a feature film and that by the independent production company of William Cagney in 1948, though released by United Artists. It starred James Cagney, William Bendix, Wayne Morris, Jeanne Cagney, Broderick Crawford, Ward Bond, and James Barton. But it has never been re-released and remains a rarity in the film archives.

Saroyan's vision of filmmaking was clearly articulated to Nathalie Sarraute during an interview published in *Cahiers du Cinéma* in December 1966. "In my opinion, cinema can do everything or be everything, it all depends on who gets involved." Saroyan never really had the chance to find out if he was one of the select. In 1942 the successful scenario of *The Human Comedy* and the direction of *The Good Job* suggested he might have been. That short film was not just a modest testament to a creative talent whose major interest was centered around people and the qualities that gave them their humanity; it was also the unappreciated, aborted creation of a would-be filmmaker.

Saroyan in the Ranks

R. C. McINTYRE

To most of us in Comany A, 3rd Batallion, SCRTC (Signal Corp Replacement Training Center) Camp Kohler, Sacramento, California, in November 1942, he was just another unlucky draftee.

To the mere sophisticated, he was known as a modern American writer, who had made the American Lit. text book. I had read his first novel *My Name Is Aram* before being drafted.

William Saroyan was stuck with the rest of us in a Signal Corps four-weeks basic training course. [Apparently in November of 1942, Saroyan was trying to arrange a transfer from the Signal Corps to the Air Force base at Mitchell Field in Mineola, Long Island, where a film-making unit was being formed. The plans to form the unit fell through and the Saroyan transfer never materialized, though several high officers in the Air Force seemed keen on enlisting his advice in the making of "information" films. (From a letter of Robert Breen to William Saroyan, dated November 16, 1942, in the editor's possession.)]

The rumor was that he had a $50-a-week room in a Sacramento hotel to which he retired each evening after training.

To us, including Saroyan, $50 was the pay Uncle Sam gave all privates each thirty days to show how appreciated you were that month.

The hotel rumor must have been true because at 5:30 each morning, when the rest of us were rudely awakened, Saroyan wasn't in his bed. But about the same time, he would could in the back door of the long tar paper covered barracks, fully dressed in his class A uniform. That was the tailored one with all the gold buttons. The one you wore in public. The rest of us were hurryig into our rumpled green fatigues and lacing up our leggings.

We were all racing for the front door and the parade ground to stand reveille. Saroyan was the only enlisted man who stood it dressed like one of the officers. It was so dark at that hour, in November, that no one could tell how you were dressed or if you were.

Saroyan and his cousin Ross Bagdasarian *(second from right),* **with whom he later collaborated on "Come On-a-My House," Paris, 1945.** *(Courtesy of Aram Saroyan.)*

After reveille, making up the beds, and breakfast chow, came time to fall out for the day's training. But first came "Anyone for sick call?" Saroyan daily accepted the sergeant's offer. He always announced loudly, "My feet are killing me!" While the rest of us were learning the rudiments necessary for soldiering—first aid, military courtesy, camouflage, the firing range—Saroyan went off to see the medics. The result was that he got to spend the rest of the day assigned to his barracks. The opinion was that he rarely attended a training class.

Saroyan practiced the art and science most of us only dreamed about—"gold bricking." A simple definition of that is: faking, usually through pretended illness, to keep from doing what you were required to do. Among the troops, this practice made him a hero figure.

If you passed him in the company street after training hours and he noticed you were looking his way, he always gave you a gracious nod. Your reward for recognition, no doubt.

The only GI he seemed to associate with was a thin, pasty-faced trainee from somewhere in the camp to whom he eagerly talked and walked to the barracks for further conversation.

Mail call was twice a day. Mail calls were usually conducted by the mail clerk—a PFC or corporal, at the most. Ours was presided over by our regular army first sergeant. I have the feeling he purposely took over in order to taunt and embarrass Saroyan.

Standing on a loading platform, the sergeant, short in stature but long in military know-how, methodically called out the names of the draftees receiving mail as they clustered below him. Last name called first. All mail carefully alphabetized by the mail clerk. As your name was called, you responded with a loud "YEO" and raised your hand from somewhere in the crowd. If you were not down front, your mail was carefully passed from hand to hand to finally your hand.

That is, it went that way until the letter S was reached. Saroyan's mail was first in the S category. He received a terrific amount of mail—letters and packages, mostly books—at each mail call. Slowly the sergeant picked out each item for Saroyan and just as slowly placed them at the back of the bundle well behind the X, Y, Z's as he continued calling names.

After all the mail was delivered, except Saroyan's stack, sarge would announce, "That's it." A long pause. "Oh, wait a minute—THE GREAT SAROYAN!" At which point, he threw all of Saroyan's mail high in the air. As it fluttered to the ground Saroyan would remark, "Thanks, sarge. I really appreciate that." Many hands went to work picking up Saroyan's mail and handing it to him.

Today people have forgotten, or are unaware, that early in his career, Saroyan gave himself the title "The Great Saroyan" and acted as his own press agent by presenting libraries and reviewers with his published efforts at his own expense. Who has the better right to blow his own horn than the guy who owns the horn?

One Saturday evening while waiting for our weekend passes, we got a look into the world of writing as seen through the eyes of William Saroyan.

Saturday afternoon was reserved for inspections by a company officer. Everything was inspected—barracks, latrine, foot lockers, draftees. If all went well the reward was a weekend pass good from the time you got it Saturday until 11 P.M. Sunday.

For the few weeks at Camp Kohler inspection was favorable. Except one. For no reason, that we could find, passes were held up. First for half an hour, then an hour, and then another half hour without any explanation. For many the best part of Saturday night was slipping away. Except during that period of waiting Saroyan kept our minds off ourselves by talking about himself.

His cot was next to the stove. It gets cold in Sacramento—or at least it did during World War II. The stove warmed our exteriors while Saroyan's writings exploits warmed our inner man. The troops knew he was somebody. The sergeant during mail call had made that clear. They knew they were in the presence of greatness and Saroyan honored their attention.

Everyone listened. If he thought they weren't he talked louder. More citizen-soldiers came to sit at his feet.

The first item on his agenda was an attack on Hollywood for buying and then distorting his work *The Human Comedy.* He claimed that when he saw the finished product he didn't recognize it. He was amazed they hadn't tampered with the title. "Hollywood will never get their hands on anymore of my efforts," he stated.

He then launched into a discussion of a contract he had with an editor to provide a manuscript by a certain date. The date approached and he had not hope of delivering as promised. In desperation he put a piece of paper in the typewriter and started a letter to the editor. He tried to explain his failure, the daily circumstances that had kept him from writing the story. "As I typed page after page of explanation the story took place on the paper and when I finished my letter I had the manuscript I needed." Saroyan summed it up: "I'll never again write to meet a deadline." He failed to mention, and no one asked, the title of the story or the name of the publication—or that of the editor.

About 9 P.M., a second lieutenant burst into the barracks to announce that passes could be picked up at the orderly room.

Saroyan interrupted himself and headed for Sacramento, stopping first at the orderly room to pick up the much-needed pass to freedom.

On to civilian life and his hotel room. Personal reminiscence time had abruptly ended.

A few days later, Christmas of 1942, was a most happy occasion. Partly because of the holiday, but mostly because the next day we would depart for our various specialized training centers. For me Portland, Oregon, and a future as another face in the crowd. For Saroyan, Fort Monmouth, New Jersey and an ascending personage on the American literary scene.

In the 1970s Saroyan's book *Places Where I've Done Time* was published. Every year from 1912 to 1969 is verbally illustrated with a personal ancedote from somewhere in the world. He mentions the army and his experiences in and around Governor's Island, New York Harbor, 1943, but gives no recognition to his Signal Corp basic training, 1942.

Such an abrupt change from the easy street of civilian life to the rugged dirt roads of Camp Kohler with its black tar paper on the outside of the barracks and its unpainted 2x4 supports inside would make an unfavorable impression on anyone—especially on a writer. I can't think of a better site than Camp Kohler to be described as a "place where I've done time."

This acquaintance between Thanksgiving and Christmas, 1942, in Company A, 3rd Battalion, of the Signal Corp Replacement Training Center, twelve miles outside Sacramento, California, at Camp Kohler may not have been an important aspect of an American writer's life but it was an interesting moment in my life as draftee.

My Saroyan

JACK WARNER

The moustache-heavy face of a bloated Balkan "brigand" scowled up at me from the obituary page of my morning *Times*. William Saroyan was dead! Something was all wrong—this was the picture of an absolute stranger, another man from another time.

My Saroyan was a smooth-faced, black-haired and healthy young man in an Army uniform one size too large with perhaps a single chevron stitched on the sleeve. Was it Private First Class or just plain Private Bill Saroyan who came to my office in the Signal Corps Photographic Center so long ago in 1942? Rank meant very little in that strange outpost of democracy. All that mattered there was talent and the ability to turn out millions of miles of training films to help transform raw recruits and dismal draftees into future victors over the battle-hardened Germans and Imperial Japanese.

Saroyan introduced himself and we both read the orders sending us next day to Camp Lee, Va. The Quartermaster Corps School desperately needed a very special training film and impatiently awaited a project officer and a writer to turn their ideas and requirements into something with the provocative working title of "Abandon Ship!"

Whatever the exciting title and its implied theme had to do with the stodgy, stolid Quartermaster Corps, purveyor of food, clothing and heaven only knew what else, was not made clear. The title excited us though and we sat in my office until past closing time recalling great disasters of the sea—the *Titanic,* the *Lusitania,* and, of course, the *Hesperus.*

Private Saroyan had never written about the sea as most of his plays and novels were set in and around Fresno, California, a long walk from the Pacific Ocean, even for a very active Armenian. He was a genuine celebrity, even among the many Hollywood names populating the Army Pictorial Center. Nobody could recall a Pulitzer Prize winner who had actually rejected the coveted award. It was almost as though a movie star had spurned an Academy Award, something that George C. Scott would do many years later, but without the grace and elan shown by Fresno's favorite son when he turned his back on a Pulitzer. A very talented young man, and as many jealous writers at Army Pictoral suspected, perhaps more than a little nuts.

The post transportation officer issued us rail vouchers and we shared a drawing room from New York City to Camp Lee, located in a part of the south neither of us had ever seen. In any normal military situation a captain would have first choice over a private for the upper or lower berth, but nothing connected with the Army Pictoral Center was quite normal.

Filled with creative people from every part of the film industry, added to miscellaneous movie-struck "connivers" who had somehow wangled themselves into this off-beat Army post, privates, sergeants, and corporals mingled casteless among colonels, majors, captains, lieutenants, and, now and then, a very puzzled general up from the Pentagon.

Many of the enlisted men lived in the finest Manhattan hotels, driving to the war each day in Cadillacs, one even in a chauffeured Rolls Royce. Most of the officers scrambled on the BMT subway under the river to Queens Plaza, where they transferred to the G.G. Local and finally ran four long blocks from the Steinway Boulevard exit to the old Paramount Astoria Studios, which had been taken over by the U.S. Army Photographic Center.

Movie history had been made at Astoria long before the war and ghosts of the departed still stalked the stages, no doubt wondering at this bunch of olive drab clowns who had taken over.

Saroyan tossed me for the lower berth and I lost. No matter, I enjoyed heights and by the time we finished talking and watched the lights fly past, we had only a few hours left to sleep before the train disgorged us in front of a waiting Army sedan driven by a staff sergeant.

Our quartermaster technical advisor, a Colonel Henry, sat in the car with his wife, a full-blossomed blonde who clutched several of Private Saroyan's books under her arms. She popped out and rushed over to surround the author, opening books to their flyleaves for him to sign then and there, all the time gushing that the ladies of the post had arranged a luncheon in his honor later that same day. Of course he would autograph *My Name Is Aram, The Human Comedy,* and *The Time of Your Life* for the ladies, wouldn't he? The private looked at the colonel, then at me, and finally back at the colonel's lady. He would be very happy to have lunch with the ladies and to autograph all their books. The colonel fussed a little. After all, Captain Warner and Mr. Saroyan had come here on serious Army business ... frivolous things shouldn't interfere with duty. The lady speared him with a sharp look and the colonel surrendered. It appeared he too had some books written by the eminent Mr. Saroyan that he had picked up and would the author sign them too? I marveled at how quickly Private Saroyan had been transformed to Mr. Saroyan. There was a war going on and all that, but how many privates in any army had been awarded a Pulitzer Prize—and how many had turned it down?

We were put up at the post guest house where we unloaded our meager baggage and went immediately to join Colonel Henry and an assortment of Quartermaster and Transportation Corps officers, each with his own idea how the training film should be made.

First of all, we were told that the basic message and purpose of this film was to tell every American soldier boarding a troopship that in the unlikely event of disaster, say a lucky submarine meeting an unlucky troopship, he was to remember that all of the equipment issued to him had been paid for with the hard-earned dollars of the American taxpayer. Under no condition should this equipment casually be tossed into the ocean to more easily escape a stricken ship. There were plenty of ways, the colonel insisted, to get off a sinking ship and into a lifeboat and still remain custodian of the taxpayer's property. This film would show "even a middle-grade moron" how it could be done.

"We have the perfect title for it!" piped up a thin-faced lieutenant whose sunburn and nautical manner revealed him to be a yachtsman, wise in the ways of small-boat river seamanship. "It's to be called, 'You *Must* Take It With You!' The title *is* the message! Every soldier in the Army who sees it will remember that message when he boards a troopship. Think of the millions it will save!"

"Dollars or lives?" asked Pulitzer's despair.

"Uh, both, of course, Private Saroyan," said the colonel, and I noticed how suddenly mister had been busted to private. For several hours we were told how web-belts, canteens, first aid kits, entrenching tools, gas masks, bayonets, cartridge clips, and all the other body-hung paraphernalia had to go wherever the wearer went. "Abandon Ship!" did not mean "Abandon Equipment!"

"If the soldier keeps his head, remembers what we will be showing him in the fine motion picture you people are going to make for us, he will save not only the cost of replacement, but he will immediately be ready for battle when called upon. This afternoon we are taking you through a troopship which is being refitted here so you will see. . . ." The telephone on the colonel's desk rank sharply and he broke off to answer.

"Yes . . .yes. Of course, dear. We'll be right over. I had no idea it was so late. Tell the general and Mrs. Smith we're on our way and apologize to him for the delay. All right. Yes, of course he's here with me and . . . goodbye dear." He hung up, rose to his feet and started for the door.

"Come along, Mr. Saroyan—you too, captain. We're late for a luncheon and the general is waiting. My God, where did the morning go!"

I was happy that the private had made it back to mister so quickly and followed the colonel to the waiting sedan which carried us to the Officers' Club. The dining room was filled to its walls with ladies, each holding one or more books written by William Saroyan. Several male officers, included the general, were scattered throughout the room and all the eager faces glowed with delight at having a real live Pulitzer-rejecting author among them here at Camp Lee.

We had lunch and the author graciously signed stacks of books for all the ladies. The general, Colonel Henry, and assorted majors, captains, and lieutenants came forward to present books for autographing. Several of the offerings were paperbacks, but Private Saroyan treated them as regally as the hard covers, even though his royalties on them would be smaller. Sales were sales and no doubt it warmed his creative, commercial heart to see all his works laid out for the personal touch. I wondered how many of those books had actually been bought to be read, or if they were meant only for show and tell.

The ladies hoped their guest might speak to them and he stumbled through a brief thanks, seeming relieved when the colonel whispered that we had an appointment with a troopship in the harbor. A few final autographs and we were off.

When you've seen one troopship you've seen them all. Of course if you were looking at the *Queen Mary* back when it was in the super-troopship business, that was something very special. The one we visited was no queen—not even a duchess. It was being scraped, "un-rusted," de-gaussed, repainted, and rewelded. It looked like a big, floating dormitory-junkyard. Bunks were tightly crammed into all available space and I wondered if there would be room enough to be reasonably seasick in a heavy storm. Was it even possible to climb through the maze of pipes, bunks, junk and debris to where the ship could decently be abandoned when that unlikely torpedo struck its mortal blow?

After a cluttered walk through the ship we were invited to go over the side and down a rope cargo net to a clumsy whaleboat floating alongside, far down in the calm and filthy water. What would it be like in a violent sea among waves of fleeing panic-stricken men bent on personal survival without abandoning all that Army-issue junk fastened to their bodies? At least we did pick up some vital information which I shall always remember and hope never to use.

Always hold tightly to the up and down ropes of a cargo net when you go over the side of a ship. Grabbing the crossropes, which seems the most natural thing to do with a ladder, is an invitation to having your hands flattened by the feet of the fully loaded soldier following you down the net. We were lucky that our Quartermaster hosts trod lightly on our misplaced fingers so that we made it down with a minimum of damage.

The nautical lieutenant from the meeting room was waiting for us down in the whaleboat and again piped up.

"See what temptation there is to toss all your equipment over the side in an emergency! Our training film has to get the message across to every soldier boarding a troopship that 'You *Must* Take It with You!'"

Saroyan craned his neck to look up at the high side of the ship looming over us. He turned and gave me a sick smile, then leaned close and whispered.

"The first damn thing I'd throw over the side would be that lieutenant. Frank Capra should sue them for stealing his title, 'You Can't Take It With You.'" ·

"Ah—that's where I heard it!" I replied, "Say, Capra is a Signal Corps colonel shooting morale pictures for us at Army Pictoral! Somebody should tell him what the Quartermaster School is doing."

For several more days we sat in endless meetings with the experts and soaked up data, drams, and doctrine. Now and then the colonel's driver would bring more books for Saroyan to autograph, and one evening the colonel and his wife took us to the city for dinner, where they could show off their visiting celebrity to a larger audience. A general asked us to lunch in a private dining room where none of his regular Army colleagues would see this unmilitary mingling of the ranks at mealtime. Saroyan was completely gracious through it all. He smiled a great deal and I could sense a future book coming together in his creative mind. His script notes and my production memos grew until we had a briefcase full. After he signed a last carton of books, we made our farewells and took the train back to New York.

Now came the real work of putting it all together into a stirring and vital training film which would keep the boys awake and attentive in the hot and cramped training camps across America. It inspired us that our film would be seen by every soldier, sailor, marine, and civilian involved in the war before boarding a troopship and sailing off to rescue democracy and the free world. It was mind-warping to realize that we would influence so many millions and ensure victory for our side by convincing them that they "Must Take It With Them" as they intelligently abandoned ship.

Three exhausting weeks later we presented our first draft screenplay to the Quartermaster Technical Advisor who told us it was exactly what they had wanted, only they didn't want it anymore. Somebody in the Pentagon with a constellation of stars on his shoulders had called a meeting and with rare good sense decreed that when a soldier went over the side of a sinking troopship he could strip himself naked if it meant saving his life. The project had been canceled.

"Thank God! Now I am convinced we are going to win the war. We've got brains as well as guts on our side!" said Private Saroyan as he turned to me and sighed with relief.

We shook hands and parted. Saroyan went on to his new assignment, a first draft script on the disposal of human waste in the field ("Part I— The Basic Slit Trench") while I was reassigned to barrage balloon projects. Within a few months I went overseas via torpedoproof air transport to become photo officer on Gen. Omar N. Bradley's 12th Army Group Staff.

Just before D-Day shook up the world, I was standing in the middle of Grosvenor Square in London watching an all-women crew raising one of their lovable barrage balloons high in the sky on a cable tether. Those British "girls" knew their jobs better than any of the all-male crews in the training films I had worked on. Suddenly I sensed a khaki presence at my elbow and turned to find Private William Saroyan also admiring the hard working gas-bag ladies.

There were a few minutes of joyful reunion and we recalled the aborted film we had nearly made and wondered how much valuable equipment paid for by the suffering Americans taxpayers had ended up in the ocean. A last look high in the sky at the balloon, and we said goodbye to each other.

The next time I heard of Bill Saroyan was in newly liberated Paris where a rumor reached me that he had slipped off a bar stool at the Scribe Hotel, a spot favored by war correspondents and other "word mongers." He had managed to injure sufficient discs in his back to be shipped back to the United States for treatment. His war was over, and soon Private Saroyan was once again legitimately mister. I was tempted to visit the Scribe's bar and try my luck on Saroyan's stool, but was told there was a long line already ahead of me, with Ernest Hemingway in first position.

The years had rushed by and now the heavy face of a scowling stranger looked out at me from the newspaper. It was somebody I had never known. It was not William Saroyan at all.

My Saroyan was back there in the corridors of my mind, forever young, eternally thin-faced and clean-shaven in his ill-fitting uniform, full of boyish wonder watching a fat barrage balloon rise in the sky high over London as the two of us laughed about all the lives we had saved by not making a training film.

Which Saroyan Visited Filene's?

JAMES TASHJIAN

Late in August of 1968, or thereabouts, my office phone tinkled. It was William Saroyan, and I was sort of surprised because I had not heard from him since 1964 when he published his minor masterpiece, *One Day in the Afternoon of the World.* Then he had again faded back into the woodwork—travels, Paris, present Armenia, San Francisco, Fresno—but here he was back on my phone, his voice its usual sonic boom.

No "Hello, James? How are you? Well?" No amenities. Nothing.

"Say, James Tashjian? Is that you, James? This is William Saroyan. Say, I'm over here at your one-horse, no surrey, of an airport, and I just got lifted of all my folding stuff and since I am in the People's Republic of Massachusetts and can't understand what your mercenary Irish cops are trying to say to me, and since they don't understand my Armenian—and although my Armenian is certainly no more abominable than yours and neither is a candidate to replace Esperanto as the official international language, and of course English is out of the question in Boston, I'm now in my usual state of being broke, had to tear up my credit cards since the banks demanded that I do so after I ran up a real whopper in Belgium, in Enghein, and no longer had any credit, so to speak, and I need help."

We Armenians are practical people, more or less, although anyone would dispute that after a few hours with Saroyan; and so I asked him— no amenities, nothing—if he had a place to stay that night. He never stayed overnight at anyone's house. So, my house was out of the question, and we both knew that.

"I called up the Ritz (Carlton)," came back the artillery, "and they won't accept my credit, so I thought it best to ask you to take over. I'm in Boston overnight. Just came in from Shannon. Can understand their Irish over there but it's like a Bitlistsi trying to follow a Vanetsi. Find me a room near Filene's Basement, the department store—you know where it

95

is? I'm not interested in meeting your Cabots or your Lowells. They speak only to God, I understand, and good luck to all of them."

I asked him where exactly he was in our one-horse, no surrey, of an airport. I would get there as soon as I could. "I appreciate that," he screamed over the background bustle and roar of the airport.

The first thing, then, that had to be done was to find him a place to stay. I tried the Ritz. There was a convention of bankers on Boston. Sorry, full up. Then it occurred to me that a nice Armenian girl from Stoneham worked in the front office of the Statler (now the Park Plaza). Why try everywhere? If Ida can't help me, who can? I dialed.

This time, amenities. How's Ida? How were her landmark of a father, her brother, her second cousin Archie in the Marines, her third cousin, still not working? Then, "Say, Ida, I'm in a bind. . . Now, you know William Saroyan? Well, he just got into town and needs a room for tonight." The Statler, Ida said, was booked solid, but hold on. . . I did. Ida got back to me. A house suite was being put at Mr. Saroyan's disposal.

I found Saroyan at Logan having an earnest academic discussion with a red cap. "This man," Bill said to me, "says he's read the works of Thurgood Marshall but he's never read my stuff, although he is sure I'm a great writer. He went and got me a ham sandwich and wouldn't take a cent for believing in me, adding to my knowledge and faith, and feeding me. Say, give him a fin, will you—on my account? As you know, I'm broke."

Honest, that nice red cap refused to take anything at all. Moreover, he insisted on helping us to the cab—and let me tell you that the man's luggage cart and his broad back was a boon, because I honestly had never seen such a huge collection of immigrant gypsy junk as Saroyan's "luggage."

In the first place, Bill had stuffed his belongings into shopping bags bearing the brands of boutiques, booteries, and shoppes all over Europe—large, small, medium bags, each with old socks and various items of clothing and otherwise overflowing its brims—and there wasn't a single piece of luggage, as one knows that term—just bags and bags full of, well, whatever they were full of.

As for Saroyan himself: at the height of a murderous summer, Bill was wearing an enormous greatcoat that sheathed him from shoulders to shoes, which were unlaced beneath the cuffs of grease-stained double-woven slacks and he had on some sort of jacket. And there was his cherished enormous brown snap-brim on his head, he obviously needed a haircut and a shave and, as I moved closer to him to clasp him

Kharpertsi style, I regretted that he was a candidate for a good American shower.

Anyway, we finally threw all that bagged refuse into a cab—by the way, as our good friend the cultured porter was placing one of the shopping bags into the trunk of the amazed cabbie's vehicle, a fully restrung skeleton of what must have been at one time a little simian fell out of the bag and rattled to the ground. William was literally appalled. He howled in pain, ran over and reverently picked the thing up and dangled it before his eyes, and then carefully laid it back in the bag. The stately red cap fled, casuals who had witnessed the scene shook their hips out of joint—and the astonished cabbie shook his head all the way to the Statler.

We finally got up to his room, and Bill immediately started unpacking some of his stuff—you will never believe what he had with him, and I will not try to describe the once plush suite a half hour after he got there. He shaved, he showered, he sang Antranik's song, he found some fresh longjohns somewhere in his stuff, he threw everything on, shouldered into his greatcoat—William Saroyan had a circulation problem and was always complaining he was cold—and we went down to the Hungry Pilgrim and ordered late lunch.

Bill called over the middle-aged waitress, attired nattily in her pilgrim black-and white, bonnet pinned to her hair.

"Say," he said to the woman, "what kind of getup is that? I can't place it, although I have been around the world and have seen getups I would rather forget."

"Why, sir, I'm a Pilgrim lassie, don't you see?" she said as she tripped around our table, coquettishly. "Now, what'll you have?"

"O, so that's it! Why, I thought you were a puritan dame. Now back in Bitlis, in Armenia, I knew several Puritans and let me tell you, they *believed*. Now, do *you* believe?"

The woman fled. Seconds later, she was back with the manager.

"Sir," he said, "what will you have?"

"Bring me a huge salad; if you haven't got a huge salad, bring me three smaller ones, and a large bowl, and never mind that ham and anchovie stuff. Just greens—onions, radish, lettuce, celery, black olives. . ."

Bill had his enormous salad, three shots of tequila, laced with horseradish. I covered the whole mess with my Mastercharge, and so Bill arose. He said, "And now, James, Filene's Basement! Can we walk there?"

So we walked from the Statler down Boylston Street, crossed Tremont past the old Touraine on Essex, down into the heart of the Combat Zone, past the seedy peep shops and all that gaudy fascination. There was much to see and marvel at, but I wager that the principal attraction on lower Washington Street that day was William Saroyan.

As we sauntered past the old Gayety Theater, Boston bums and simply people stopped to observe, with open amusement, this August apparition with his winter coat, his great handlebar moustaches crossing his face like the mounted headpiece of a Texas longhorn, his battered fedora screwed down over one eye, and his great booming voice remarking on the sights seen, some of which we common gentry simply could not see, for this man had the sharpest, most incisive eyes I have ever encountered. He actually spied and picked up a copper penny in the gutter of Washington Street. You have to admit it takes keen vision to find *anything* of value along that strip of despair.

We reached the intersection of Washington and Summer where some say civilization resumes in Boston, and there William spied one of Boston's finest astride a splendid broth of a mare. At that time, through traffic was still permitted along Washington Street, but Bill couldn't have cared less. Ignoring the howling traffic and the cop altogether, he made his way to the animal, and started saying something into its cocked ear. The horse sort of balked, and the officer clearly ordered Bill to "be off, y'a bum." When I finally got to the scene, Bill was chiding the horse. "Look, you nag," he was saying, "I used to ride better leather than you back on my uncle Mihran's ranch in Fresno. Good day to you!" And I dragged away William Saroyan to the safety of the sidewalk, where stood the entrance to both the Boston El and Filene's Basement Store. We proceeded down the stairs and finally into Filene's Basement.

Bill stood there for a good five minutes, his mouth agape at the battle scene before him. Obviously, he forgot me, and he forgot himself. He turned to his right and pushed through the crowds at ladies' intimate underthings, the mountains of other stuff with their great presses of determined women trying like Sisyphus, to reach the top of the mountains of merchandise; he stood at ladies' shoes and offered to try one of them on so that a lady could see what it looked like on someone else; a uniformed guard thought he was a pervert and told him to move on. We did. We continued pushing our way through the delicate ladies of Boston, being jostled around, and William Saroyan gleefully doing his share of jostling.

Bill was like a kid. You could see that he had fallen into the spirit of the place, and it was clear why he had wanted to see the Basement Store for himself. Here he was enjoying every moment of the good-natured manhandle, the giddying confusion, the utter disorder of the display tables. We went into the men's section. He saw pairs of sox, piled up, with people pulling out choice specimens, like anglers' worms; he roared in glee at the slacks intertwined like the serpents of Laocoon. He ran over to the racks of men's clothing, tore down a jacket, tried it on, and although I thought it fit pretty well, discarded it, tried on another. It was obviously too big, and the smiling salesperson tried to tell him this, but Bill said he would take it.

Amen, I said to myself, here's a fellow who's just been robbed, who has holes in his pockets anyway, who's starting to buy everything in the place, and me with a couple of dollars on me, a brace of credit cards that Filene's will not accept, and how pray were we to get out of this one?

I said, Bill, I'll be right back, and I went and found the floor manager and I said to him, "Sir, do you know William Saroyan?" The fellow said airly, "Nope, never heard of him." I knew I was up against an ignorant clod, so I got down to cases. "If I identify *myself*, will you accept *my* credit?" The manager looked down on me. "Got your license?" I pulled that out and also my Mastercharge. He called somebody; two minutes later he came back, gave me back my stuff and said, "When you get everything together that, uh, Surewen? guy wants, bring it all to me and we'll check it out . . . a personal favor, you understand."

I went back to Bill standing among a whole rash of men's goods. Thank God, there was even a new hat among the stuff, a suit of clothes, a pair of shoes, neckties, shirts, Fruit-of-the-Loom underknits, and more, and I explained to him that we were going to check out the stuff and we found the floor manager and he took us to the check-out counter and the clerk totaled up the cost against my Mastercharge, and we walked out of the bedlam with some $315.06 worth of goods.

Finally, out of the unconditioned precincts of sweltering Filene's, out now in the cauldron of that sweltering Boston day, we hailed down a cruising cab, got in, bearing our loot; and for the third time that day I met another William Saroyan.

The elation of the last hour had left him. He was withdrawn—how shall I say it?,—contemplative, submissive, thoughtful, and almost child-like, and quite obviously he had lost interest in his bagged acquisitions, which lay all around us. As we swung around to Charles Street and started making our approach to the Statler, Bill started to speak in a low voice not to me, not to anyone, but to a specter, as if he were soliloquizing at his father's grave in San Jose, by the railroad tracks. I have tried to remember what he said in that remarkable confessional:

"People are part animals, part people, wherever they are. Open up a bargain center in London, Warsaw, Moscow, Canton, or Lagos and you'll have the pride on you in a moment, snarling and searching for your jugular, just as I instinctively reverted to the beast on the hunt. . . We're all carnivores. Scratch our surfaces and you will find more of Cain than

Abel, not Solomon but Hamid, not Christ but Caiaphas, not Luis the Pious and Henry the Fourth but Richard the Deformed, or Stalin and Hitler the Mad. We're beasts of the jungle, clothed and refined, until there is prey before us; we then gleefully shed our elegant robes and become the lion-sheathed ogre, the Goliath. Dogs becomes wolves, and sparrows ospreys. We tear ourselves asunder for a choice morsel of flesh, and we'll seize from our friends the fruits of their inheritance, and we will steal and cheat, and we will embezzle. Within us rest the seeds of violence, ready to burst their pods and devour us all. We are really frames of greed and violence, and our vanity is uncontrolled."

He then turned to me.

"James, was it the great Pope Hilarius who preached that mankind must at long last depart the kingdom of the wild beasts before he might fulfill the glorious destiny bequeathed Man by Our Lord? James, we must grow out of our cupidity, we must practice love and we must be humble. . . ."

I looked at him in utter atonishment. The first thing that occurred to me was that I had just heard and witnessed William's lamented father, the Presbyterian preacher without a pulpit, and Armenian poet without an audience, exhorting his small flock gathered together in a shabby little church in Paterson, New Jersey, on a Sunday long ago. I just looked at this man of many contrasts. He sat there, a man sorely tormented, a puzzled man, a savior who was too human to become a savior, a messianic man who bore within himself uncontrollable animalisms, a man much too *human* to transcend the feral appetites of the flesh; who had just allowed himself again to become one of the howling mob. This was only a mood, a passing moment with him, but to this William Saroyan, I suspected, the matter was one of eternity . . . and he was fully of worry . . . ashamed, penitent . . . *afraid.* . .

The very next morning I went to the Statler and was told that William Saroyan had checked out, but that I should see the bell captain, for he had a note for me. I was directed to the baggage room and given an envelope pasted to all the Filene's stuff wrapped together in heavy twine.

I read the note. It said, "Thanks, may Khaldis and Lutipris watch over you, and may you sing Armenian songs all your life. I think that of all the peoples of the world, the Armenians are the purest. We love each other, fight one another, bravely die together, although we can't live together, but we all go up there purified of the evils we have done for usually we have died martyrs to the future of a better world. There *has* to be a better world for all of us. Now, I can't use this stuff. Why not take them out on the street and give them away, or to some charity? *Bill Saroyan.*"

A couple of days later, I got another note from Bill, written and mailed in San Francisco, and a bank draft meant I supposed to cover what had been spent at the hotel and Filene's. I returned the check and took the clothing to the Morgan Memorial up on Columbus Avenue, and handed it all to the proper functionary, in the name of William Saroyan.

Looking suspiciously at the new, unused items, and wondering of course if the stuff, still bearing the retail tabs, had been shoplifted, she asked, "What he do? Die?"

"In a way," I said, "I suppose in a way."

The woman looked at me and shrugged.

"Well, I don't understand."

"To tell you the truth," I said, "neither do I. . . ."

And I continued not to understand what happened that day in Filene's Basement. I found myself puzzling over the incident and, finally, the whole thing became a sort of obsession with me. It troubled me. It had been so unlike his deportment on other occasions, and I didn't think I liked it, liked seeing Bill Saroyan with his hair down.

Bill had shown a hidden side of himself. He had gone half crazy in a well-known madhouse. I put aside everything I had thought I had learned about the clock-works of the remarkable man, and I started my apprenticeship all over again.

Slowly, it dawned on me as I read along in the stuff I had thought I had already read and appraised, that Saroyan in Filene's was as thought-provokingly "insane," as profoundly a tissue of contrasts in personality, or personalities, as those he had written into in his *Sam Ego's House* or his earlier *Sweeney in the Trees,* or into some of his better known characters in *The Human Comedy* or *Love's Old Sweet Song,* and in other stories and plays. Whatever William Saroyan wrote, he wrote *about* himself. His writings were all autoiographical, and one endless autobiography, more autobiographical than his critics had supposed.

And in thinking over the scene at Filene's, I concluded that although I had the perfect right to judge at least one of Saroyan's alter ego's as eccentric, or at least terribly unusual in terms of the William Saroyan I had thought I knew, that shocking side was generally definable and acceptable as normal behavior, for I had found it being demonstrated by hundreds of other folks in Filene's basement that day.

Now, what all of them, Bill included, were doing was something they would not ordinarily do, and yet, no one looking on thought these antics as particularily odd, except me, not because I am a Rogers Peet snob and have never battled to a purchase in The Basement, but because I expected the great William Saroyan to be above all that and above the rest of us, the intellectual he was, the great writer he certainly was, the demigod we Armenians thought him to be.

Although I ought to have taken warning from his writings, it never occured to me that basically William Saroyan was like most everyone else; he was as complex as any other, and as simple as any other.

It was only after my visit to Filene's with William Saroyan that I really began to know and understand William Saroyan. There has probably been no other American author quite like William Saroyan. He was a self-taught peasant genius, a populist, a man of the fields, plains, and mountains of Bitlis, Armenia; through some marvelous chemistry, some selective process of which we know nothing, the creative, homespun genius of his parental stock the Armenians, centered in him.

Was William Saroyan an Armenian writer? Try it yourself. Pick up any Saroyan product, read his words and sentences and translate them (if your can) into Armenian to understand how astonishingly similar are his English-language expressions, his grammar, his syntax, the construction of his phrases and sentences, his idioms and his thoughts, to what is found in the Armenian (this may not be good advice to *odars*).

Then, mull over his career both as a writer and as a human being. How many parallels we see between William Saroyan and our Armenian psyche. We are, generally speaking, more a good people than we are not good. William Saroyan fits that mold. Absent from the Armenians are many of the glaring, characterizing vices attributed to other peoples. And yet, the Armenians are *not* saints, and William Saroyan certainly was not saint; but he was a man of conscience, and that is the best thing that can be expected of a human.

William Saroyan once said to me, "James, this will come as a surprise to you, but the best thing that every happened to me, in terms of my ambition to become a writer by remaining myself, and there is no other way for anyone who wants to write, was that I never went to college, less finished high school, where I specialized in absences and the only subject that interested me was typing because I knew that I would have to type out my stories, which everyone proceeded to throw into ashcans anyway, even though they were carefully typed, until your Reuben Darbinian (editor of the *Hairenik* of Boston) liked my neat typing and accepted my first story. I remained exactly myself. I have to laugh when some New York critic likens me to Jack London. Hell, I thought London was all right, he was an amusing afternoon on a park bench in Fresno, but I knew I couldn't ever write like him, just as he couldn't have written like me. The point is, college, and Jack London, were not for me, and I remained exactly myself. I wrote exactly what I wanted to write, without the ornamental ribbons of any acquired learning. Now, I have nothing against an educated writer, but somehow I rebelled against a kid from Bitlis going to Yale and writing loftily about things only Yale men think they understand, but that Bitlistsis understand *better* in their *own* way. I remained what I was born. Otherwise I would be working today in my uncle Aram's elegant law offices in Fresno, playing golf when I wasn't sorting out deeds, and that sort of thing."

After the 1981 passing of this remarkable man, I wrote in my notes to *My Name Is Saroyan* while trying to plumb the many sides of the fascinating nature of William Saroyan: "(William said to me): 'Now I am different, and that is the way it must be. Each person must be different from all others. What a helluva gray world this would be if we were to all *look* alike that we are asked to *think* alike. But my difference has never been understood, and I'm not sure I understand it myself. I've done many mad things in my life, but something in me drives me to do such things. I regret my *having* to do them. It isn't easy for me to be me. I have always been in full rebellion against the world, *and* myself. But—and this is something crucial about me—there are *convictions* and *beliefs* within me which, were I to allow myself to express them, would type me as more of a conservative, a religious man, than anything else.' Saroyan opposed war and violence, although when his own toes were stepped on, he would drop Gandhi's 'passive resistance,' which he so admired, and would raise Cain. He deplored poverty and want, which he himself had experienced, and scorned the affluent; and yet he readily sought and accepted enormous fees for his works, banked very little of his earnings and sank a good deal into the pleasures of the rich. He buffooned the so-called 'qualities of greatness,' and he was cynical of society in general, although he firmly believed that, individually, people were essentially good. He would bridle, however, when anyone tried to characterize him as 'humanist.' He said to me, 'In the first place, I'm not sure what the word means. Are you? I looked it up in the *Collegiate* and found the word absurd. Sure, I deal with humans, but so did Stalin, Hitler, Mussolini, Tamerlane, and Cromwell. Were they 'humanists' because they swore that the evil they were doing was after all for the good of the human race? Didn't (the Turk) Talaat argue that in exterminating the Armenians he was benefiting both the Turks and other humans? Now, this man said he was a 'humanist,' so why place me in such company? I ask no one to define what I am. The fact is I am simply William Saroyan, I represent only what *I* am, there may be no other like me, and if I am a 'humanist,' it is only in terms of *my* understanding of myself—and the term. Classifications are usually meaningless, any way, and nobody is an expert on anybody else, just as nobody is an expert on himself. I've never understood myself, so how can anyone else understand me? If I have a philosophy, it has to be sought for in my writings; but such a search will usually get the seeker nowhere. But no harm done; let people classify me any way they wish. Let them have their fun. The only thing I won't stand for is their forgetting that Bill Saroyan is Armenian. I guess I'm not a typical Armenian in the way I live, but you've got to admit, I always come out an Armenian.'"

It was that Saroyan who visited Filene's.

Drive, He Said

BRENDA NAJIMIAN-MAGARITY

The first time I ever saw Saroyan was in the late sixties, when Fresno State College hosted a "Saroyan Week." I watched my English professors trail behind him as he marched across campus and I listened to his talks, but I never dared get close to him.

The same thing happened a few years later when I worked as a page at the Fresno County Library. Each time he came to the library a whirlwind of traffic revolved around him. If he entered alone, he left with an entourage. Even when I was promoted to the information desk, I still dared not breach his path.

My dream of meeting Saroyan was beginning to fade when in 1970 he brought his hat into our dry cleaning shop for repair. My mother and father studied the tear carefully and, after much discussion, decided the mend would be most succesful with a simple piece of scotch tape. After this, Saroyan brought in his dry cleaning regularly. Because my father would not charge him for the work, Saroyan began bringing copies of his books. This is how I came to own a copy of *Letters from 74 rue Taitbout or Don't Go, But If You Must Say Hello to Everybody.* My father had told him I was an English teacher at Madera High School, and an admirer of his writing. His inscription read: "Hello Brenda (Najimian) I hope to visit you in class at Madera High School soon meantime all best William Saroyan Fresno October 27 1972."[sic]

After reading *Letters from 74 rue Taitbout,* I wrote a letter of thanks to the address of the title, knowing he spent half the year in Paris. I wasn't sure that he would return, but I now had an opportunity to think about what I would say if he did.

A few months later I was walking across campus to the faculty room when a student stopped me and asked if my father had found me. At first I was confused, but then I knew who it was.

When I arrived at the faculty room, Saroyan was waiting for me with his friend, Buck, who had driven him. During the next few minutes Saroyan did most of the talking, in a booming voice that filled the room. None of the questions I had planned seemed appropriate. Finally I asked if he would talk to my classes. He said no, he had done that a lot and preferred not to do it just now.

In August of 1975 we gave my parents a surprise fortieth anniversary party. Saroyan was invited. He called the night of the party to ask for a ride. Saroyan had not driven a car for many years, so he always rode his bicycle or relied on others for transportation. This night he was carrying a cane. "I fell off my bike and banged up my leg," he said, making it very clear the cane was not an affectation. For those of us who had seen him riding his bicycle this was easy to believe. Heedless of traffic laws, he usually rode wildly, leaving irate drivers honking and yelling.

But Saroyan came to the party to see if my parents were really surprised. He stood at the front window of my sister's home waiting for them to arrive. "Do you really think you fooled them?" he asked skeptically.

"Yes," I said, "their anniversary is two months away. Why should they suspect anything?"

"I'll know when I see how your father is dressed. He doesn't know about it," he said, when he saw my dad get out of the car.

It was a magical night indeed. My sister's garden made a lovely backdrop for this happy celebration. Saroyan enhanced every conversation, every mood, every thought. Yet he was careful not to upstage my parents to whom the night most belonged. He became a part of my family that night.

It came as no surprise to anyone in my family when I began to chauffeur Saroyan about on his errands. Even though he told me I drove like a Parisian taxi driver, I think he actually enjoyed the ride. What does it take to be a good chauffeur? Nothing more than a decent car and a passenger who knows where he wants to go. For Saroyan that was usually the Westland Shopping Center where he would leave his wash at the coin-up laundry while we went through Longs Drugstore and Mayfair Market.

Breezing through the candy section of Mayfair, Saroyan snatched two caramels out of a bin and handed me one as he popped his into his mouth. I followed his lead with great trepidation. I chewed and swallowed the candy quickly, positive we were about to be arrested. I was still trying to free the candy lodged between my teeth as we walked through the check-out. Fortunately I jogged the candy loose just as Saroyan, who was five feet ahead of me as usual, stopped and looked over his shoulder to see what the trouble was.

Another time as we stood in the same store, Saroyan gave me a talk on the delicious simplicity of stewed chicken. Once again I asked him if he would visit my classes. The boldness of my question stunned me much as his reply. "Yes," he said. Then he continued about stewing chicken. "Add some mint leaves to the water for flavor."

On 26 January 1977, I pulled my Toyota into his driveway and knocked on his front door. I watched in disbelief as a well-dressed Armenian, his great mustache meticulously groomed, stepped out. That day with him was to be dazzling: it was like having the entire Armenian population with me at work.

My oversized classroom was filled to capacity four times that day. The one hundred plus students who listened to him each session were respectful and acutely aware that this might be the only genuine writer they would ever meet. Each student who asked a question or answered a Saroyan query was invited to shout out his or her name while Saroyan wrote it down. "Please forgive my eccentricity in wanting to know your name," he said. Little did we know that he was to use the names in the book he was writing at the time, *Obituaries,* his last published work.

Saroyan told them "I was very lucky in believing that I was a writer at an early age and that this was the real work of my life." As a youth he believed books came into being like trees, from God or nature. He thought this was logical because the first book his grandmother gave him to study, The Bible, came from God. After he realized that books, people wrote, he decided he would like to do that too.

One day Saroyan's third-grade teacher, a Miss Chambers, kept him after class. "What did I do wrong how?" he asked. She was leaving the school the next week and wanted to leave Saroyan with some advice. She insisted that he go to college. Saroyan took this to mean he was a writer, and her suggestion had a significant influence on him.

Saroyan in a serious moment as he gave Ms. Najimian's students "the time of their lives." (*Courtesy of the* **Maderan.**)

When asked why he became a writer Saroyan said, "I became a writer to change the world." He wanted to change the human race in the way that is most difficult: for people to change within themselves—within their own hearts. And because he loved language, especially the words of Mark Twain, Charles Dickens, Guy de Maupaussant, and Anton Chekov.

When a student asked how much money was made from *The Human Comedy* Saroyan answered without hesitating, "About a million dollars, but that was over a period of forty years." He was fortunate, he said, to make his living as a writer. He had published forty-four books in forty-three years. "The only real reward of writing is that you want to do it," he said, "and whatever you get besides is extra." He added that most of his writer friends around the world had to supplement their income by teaching.

Saroyan said he would not accept the Pulitzer Prize for literature because he didn't like wealth patronizing art. Yet he encouraged his audiences to take full advantage of the National Endowment of the Arts. "My son won $750 for a poem that had only one word. That's my idea of the proper usage of the government's money," he said.

In answer to the question of whether he patterned the character Aram after his own life, Saroyan said, "A writer saves enormous time and provides reality by writing what he or she knows. Most of the character of Aram is myself. And all the episodes in the book were my own or those of my uncle."

In mid-August of 1981, two days before my birthday, I stood in a Fresno Bookstore thumbing through Saroyan's last book, *Obituaries*. A friend told me there might be something in it I would like to see. She was right. In chapter seventeen I found:

"And so why did I get up at half past five yesterday morning in order to go to a high school and talk four times instead of only once at a college, for which I might have been paid anywhere from $1,000 to $3,000—instead talking for free, as the saying is? . . . I was asked if I might pay such a visit to that school by a girl who teaches English and Drama there, and during the past three or four years this Armenian girl has been a good kid at filling me in about life in a high school in a small town. . . ."

Although he is gone, Saroyan's published words continue to speak for him; that is as it should be. I still feel that one day I'm going to run into him in a coffee house or a Laundromat in Fresno some hot summer day.

The *Obituaries* Lunch

PENNFIELD JENSEN

"Boredom!" exclaimed William Saroyan. "Boredom is the worst thing!"

He was talking about Ernest Hemingway, about his suicide, and now had passed judgement: that it was a sin, a cardinal sin, to find life—the great miracle of life!—boring. The subject had arisen as a surprise ending to a classic four-hour publisher's lunch in the Garden Court of the Sheraton Palace Hotel honoring Saroyan and his most recent book, *Obituaries.*

The lunch was a small one, as such things go, consisting of Saroyan, novelist Herb Gold, publishers Don Ellis and Barry Gifford of Creative Arts Book Company in Berkeley, and myself. Saroyan had made a special trip up from Fresno for the day dressed in a bright high-Sierra, sky-blue suit to meet his new publishers for the first time. We, in turn, were there to pay discreet homage to this man and his work, collectively acknowledged as one of America's treasures. Herb Gold, who has known Saroyan for twenty years, was greeted as an old friend. The rest of us, however, were subjected to the legendary Saroyan scrutiny beginning with our names. "Pennfield! What kind of Danish is Pennfield? Ellis! What was it originally?" (Elyisch changed to Gluckstein then back to Ellis), and Gifford, we learn, being a contraction of Giddingsford, an ancient crossing of the Little Gidding river in England. The history of our names revealed, each was an identity poker chip anted up as the menus were dealt out around the table.

The Garden Court, with its great glass dome, colonnaded arches, and starburst crystal chandelier, was Saroyan's choice and a perfect one for this encounter. Literary lunches are not like other kinds of lunches. They are more like stages upon which, in no regular order, reasonably good minds aspire to cabaret, to a kind of exalted inconsequence, self advertisement, and general celebration that is uniquely satisfying. The star, of course, was Saroyan, and from the cornerstone information of our names, the conversation careened and follicked through a thousand twists and turns as we devoured our sole meuniere, poached salmon hollandaise, and other gastronomic delights of the Garden Court. Inevitably, we spoke of children, of writers' children, and of writers' children who write. Of these latter, we could think of very few, a fact that stood in sharp contrast, Saroyan noted, to the many generations of Armenians working the fertile San Joaquin Valley content to follow in their ancestors' footsteps. One exception, and a noteworthy one, was Saroyan's one son, Aram, who had recently published a book about the Beat poet Lew Welch entitled *Genesis Angels*. Welch had committed suicide, a puzzling and disturbing act that led Herb Gold to ask more or less rhetorically—who, after all, could possibly know?—"Why?"

It was this question that had led Saroyan to make his pronouncement about the Great Suicide of Hemingway. The oblique, looping route of the conversation was very like a chapter from Saroyan's *Obituaries*: to start with a name and conclude with an epitaph, or more rightly, an epigram, a parting word meant to guide rather than warn, and all meant to celebrate one thing—Life.

"*Obituaries* is an astonishing book" wrote *Publishers Weekly* in its April review, "a profound and even original meditation about death and our only possible answer to it: the way we live. . . . *Obituaries* is solemn, beautiful, hilarious, raunchy, a heartbreakingly sad and funny testament and one of Saroyan's finest books." It is also a very wise book based on a clever notion: the Necrology of 1976 from the big annual *Variety* magazine of that year. A necrology is a list of the dead, and Saroyan writes about the names he reads there in a steady, conversational stream of consciousness that starts with the letter A, jumps immediately to Z (for Adolph Zukor, the Hollywood legend) and then rafts straight through the alphabet all the while railing at us, the readers, cajoling us, joking and laughing with us (mostly at himself), and generally conspiring with us in all manner of gossipy and sprightly treason against the dead. Saroyan's genius is in this book, and it pours out big-hearted and all-embracing, even though it proceeds from a chilling premise: that his own name, William Saroyan, is not on that list. Not yet, at least, and he makes the most of it.

Saroyan at seventy-one looked sixty, and carried on as if he were thirty-five. He was deaf in his right ear and spoke with the volume turned up.

Herbert Gold, Barry Gifford, William Saroyan, and Don Ellis in San Francisco. *(Courtesy of Pennfield Jensen.)*

He lived half the year in Fresno and the other half in Paris. Thirty or so years ago he was very nearly the most famous man in America. Seemingly, he knew everyone and everyone knew him. His were the marvelous memories of a marvelous age, one that is noted as much as by anything else as the great flowering of Hollywood. With *Variety's* Necrology before him, he invoked much of that magical time and let his mind range freely through the images each name inspires.

On Billy Rose and Mike Todd: "But the fact is that with all their fraudulence, I miss them both, for they used up some of my time, and that time is gone forever. Poor little old, and poor large young clever millionaires: the mothers of thousands of sad souls didn't know enough about them to hate them."

On an unknown: "Joe Bigelow. He died, too. And I never knew him. I am sorry to say, for I like the name. It is a rollicking name, O, O, Joe Bigelow. I hope he had a good life and a very good death, for of course it would be absurd not to know that there are as many kinds of death as there are kinds of life, pieces of action and experience, or marbles."

On lawyers: "The bastards that do me, that seek to do me in, that plague my soul, that rob my purse as they say, that belittle my name, that very nearly drive me mad, I am proud to say I loathe, despise, hate and patently dismiss from my mind forever and ever, and am only reminded for a flash of profound gloating when I hear that death has done them in, the dirty little mothers. I hate the breed. . . ."

On the dead: "Do we mock the dead by staying alive, by reading their names in lists, by remembering them in the world, by speculating about those we never knew? Do we perhaps take pleasure from our own survival and even from their sad or joyous failure to do so? Bet your life we do."

On writing: "Is it worth it? Bet your life it is . . . and this is why: there is no movement after something has died, and it is action alone that permits anything—and out of anything it is always possible to make something, or even something else, and in anything it is possible to find whatever is needed for the continuing of everything, for the dance of life, for the deep waltz of the soul in all things."

That Saroyan has produced a late-inning masterpiece is not really as surprising as the fact that he chose to publish it with a relatively obscure press in Berkeley called Creative Arts. The obvious question, of course, is "Why?" Saroyan himself dismisses the question with a laugh and a rather ambiguous "it's all part of my system." He does not employ an agent, despises them as a matter of fact, and would appear to take an altogether dim view of publishing in general. He even writes about it. "But let's you and me, reader, forget it, and let me just suspect that no publisher is going to publish this book, and that I am not going to publish it, and that my standing and working every day early in the fine and fantastic year of 1977 has been solely for itself: I have stood faithfully and produced a whole book because I have wanted to."

It is a rebellious statement, defiant and possibly even a little spoiled, and vintage Saroyan. "Saroyan has always been a maverick," Barry Gifford explains. "He published with small presses back in the Forties when he was probably the most famous man in America and had won the Pulitzer." Don Ellis, the bearded, 41-year old owner of Creative Arts, has a more practical point of view. "We got the book," he states, "simply because we asked."

Ironically, the query to Saroyan came as a virtual afterthought to another request—to review *Tilt!*, a C/A title on pinball machines that uses a publicity still from the motion picture version of Saroyan's *The Time Of Your Life*. "At the time," Ellis confesses with a chuckle, "we didn't even know whether or not Saroyan was alive! It was only later when Barry and I were sitting around that it occured to us to ask him if he might have a manuscript lying around that we could publish. In practically return mail," Ellis recalls, "we received a jiffy-bag with *Obituaries* in it."

But how could it be that a major American writer could have a potentially top-selling book "lying around?" Apparently, Saroyan had written a letter to his previous editor at W. W. Norton in New York asking him if Norton might be interested in this new work. The editor, however, had jumped to another publishing house and the letter went unanswered. Feeling slighted perhaps, the query from Creative Arts was all Saroyan needed. But what of Saroyan's reputation as a hard writer to work with? "Sure, Saroyan has a reputation for being an irascible, demanding writer," Gifford states. "But I am considered an uncompromising and contentious *editor*. Somehow," he notes, "the contrast of our two iconoclastic styles was ideal. Saroyan," he concluded, "was a lamb."

During the entire edition process, Saroyan was in Paris, and he approved all of the editorial changes from his home there including the book design by George Mattingly that makes artful use of a tombstone-plaque motif for the running chapter heads. The high praise from *Publishers Weekly* launched a barrage of requests for personal appearances ("Today Show," "Johnny Carson," etc.) but Saroyan, perhaps wearied of the vicissitudes of fame and fortune, took an encouraging but detached view toward the publisher's eternal struggle to sell his books, leaving some doubt as to whether or not he would actually go on the shows.

"They're so dull!" he exclaimed "and the people are all exactly stupid the same way. But I do like the animals," he admitted. "I love when they bring animals on the programs; they are so perfectly honest and alert. They don't try to sell anything, or put on an act, they are just totally *there*, totally *real!*" Besides, he had a schedule to keep: a few more weeks in Fresno then back to Paris for six months. He had a book he wanted to write.

"I write according to how much time I have," he explained. "I never set out to write a 'novel,' or a 'short story,' or a 'play.' If I know I will have six days of solitude someplace, or even six weeks, I'll write what I know I can get done in that period of time. I let the amount of time set my goal, and that determines what the piece will be."

In person, the most striking thing about Saroyan was his eyes. There were Einsteinian eyes, and contain that same compelling blend of sadness, humor, and dreamy tenderness that seems to see all things equally and in equal measure, to register them and absorb them directly into the shape and substance of his own world. He regarded the tray of desert *gateaux* wheeled by with the same droll curiosity as he regards the nationality of the waiter (Spanish, said Saroyan; Italian, said Gifford and Gold, who were right) and the unspeakable conclusion to his own marvelous parade of days.

"Why do I write?" he asked in an *Obituaries* chapter. "Why am I writing this book? To keep from dying, of course. That is why we get up in the morning." But it was not an effort of will that kept Saroyan going, it was the process of celebration. "I'll tell you something, reader, I'll tell you something good: you are the star of your life, knock on wood. You are the living one, old soul, inside your own skin: even when you lose, you win . . ."

Not unsurprisingly, there was a bittersweetness to this uncorked spirit, an unmistakeable flavor of life persevering in the face of death. As the conclusion of *The Human Comedy* Saroyan describes a woman who welcomes into her home the battlefield friend of a favorite son she had only just learned was dead. "The mother stood and looked at her two sons, one on each side of the stranger, the soldier who had known her son who was now dead. Sick to death, she nevertheless smiled at the soldier, and said, 'Won't you please come in and let us show you around the house?' "

Some thirty-seven years after those lines were written, *Obituaries* reveals just what that tour was like: witty, ribald, occasionally angry, self-contradictory, and always joyous. To the sorrowful anguish of an irrevocable and all too real fact of death, he turned a conveniently deaf ear. Sick to death, he may be, but in the end, we are given our own room, invited down for breakfast in the morning, and left with a typically insouciant word of advice: "Reader," he states, "take my advice, don't die, just don't die, that's all, it doesn't pay. . . . Don't do it."

It's impossible advice, of course, outragous, ridiculous, absurd advice, but nevertheless the very finest, if you can take it. Saroyan certainly did, stubbornly, defiantly, and uproariously. He was, of course, toying with us, stringing us along, proving that after thirty years he was still the daring not-quite-so-young man on the flying trapeze and we still capable of being children, mouths agape, looking up enthralled.

As I lingered to pack the camera gear, the waiter came over to me. "Who *was* that?" he asked. I told him and he looked at me with surprise. "Saroyan? Why, I thought he had died years ago!"

Not hardly. Not hardly at all.

Hello Out There, Bill Saroyan

EDWARD HAGOPIAN

For years I had tried to persuade Bill to visit the famous cemetery of Père Lachaise in Paris where hundreds of the world's best known writers, painters, poets, and composers are buried. He always had an excuse, even though he knew that General Antranik, the legendary warrior and patriot, whom he had met in Fresno, was also buried there. Graveyards are not Fun Cities and Bill avoided them like the plague, along with funerals, mortuaries, wakes, slumber rooms, and places that deal with death—including hospitals.

Then one Sunday in November 1974, while I was finishing lunch, the phone rang. A booming voice said, "Ed, ole boy, what are you up to? I've done a good morning's work and I'm through for the day. Got any plans?"

"Nothing special," I said. "Might go out to Issy-les-Moulineaux and visit Armenak Mikaelian. [Armenak passed away in the spring of 1983.] Want to come along? He's nearing ninety and who knows how long the old fadayee would be with us?"

"Sounds like a great idea, but first let's go and pay our respects to his commander, General Antranik. It's a good day for it and if you bring your camera we can take some pictures."

"See you in a half an hour at the Eglise La Trinité," I said. Then checking the camera for film, it was loaded, I took along an extra roll of 35mm color film for this historic event and drove down to Place Estienne-d'Orves where Bill was waiting. Driving across Paris we talked up a storm. He wanted to know who else was buried at the cemetery besides General Antranik. He scribbled down the names as I called the roll: Balzac, Proust, Oscar Wilde, Colette, and Gertrude Stein among the writers. Chopin, Bizet, and Rossini, composers; Sarah Bernhardt, Isadora Duncan, and Edith Piaf from the stage.

As we walked past the massive portals and entered the silent stone metropolis, Bill's lighthearted mood became somber and more reflective.

**Shot of Saroyan by Paul Kalinian for David Calonne's full-length study _William_
Saroyan: My Real Work Is Being.**

Even on a bright summer's day with birds singing everywhere, and this was a grey autumn afternoon, cemeteries have a depressing, forbidding air. Driving across the city we laughed and bantered about the trite and the trivial, and now as we walked with the gravel crunching under our feet and a gentle wind whispering through the pine trees, our conversation turned toward our own mortality.

We made our way around the Avenue Circulaire toward section 89 where General Antranik was buried with Bill picking up odd pieces of stone for his rock collection while I caught him in the act on film. For Bill stones were precious nuggets of everlasting time, enduring, eternal.

Is there a grand design of which we know nothing, which is beyond our comprehension? A grand illusion? A phantom reality as in a dream? Or was it created by chance, an accident of atoms, of different elements that sparked the source of all living matter? And this planet is it not a droplet of water under a celestial microscope being studied and experimented upon with all its creatures and life forms as in a spatial laboratory by the unseen eye of Ominscient Nature?

As we made our way around the perimeter of the cemetery, we came to the Mur des Fédérés or the bloody wall, where the last of the 150 Communards were executed by firing squad during the French Commune in 1871. Their bodies lie in a trench along the eastern wall with a plaque and visible bullet holes to mark the spot.

Moving along we came to the Jewish section with its chilling memorials of those who perished in the Holocaust of Nazi concentration camps. Bill was visibly moved by the emaciated men in chains clawing at the sky and by the poignant inscriptions chiseled in stone for the victims of Belsen, Dachau, Buchenwald, Auschwitz, and Mauthausen to name only a few of the death camps. The calamity that befell 6 million European Jews, along with the genocide of nearly 2 million Armenians in the Turkish-occupied provinces of ancient Armenia, added another sad chapter to the Doomsday book under the heading: Man's Inhumanity to Man.

From the holocaust memorials we continued on towards General Antranik's tomb. In his youth Bill had met the great hero who had come to live in Fresno and where he would die in 1927. Now 47 years on, Bill had come to pay homage to the old warrior. He stood bareheaded before the life-sized statue that covered the grave of the old soldier astride his horse that seemed to be climbing over the craggy mountain slopes of Mother Hayastan. He gazed in silent reverence for what seemed an eternity, while I discreetly photographed him before the weatherstained rider that time and the elements were slowly eroding.

What would remain of the sandstone horse and rider exposed to rain, wind, sun, and snow forty-seven years hence? Would future generations remember the legendary guerrilla leader or would he become a forgotten hero whose remains would lie forever in alien earth?

Bill selected several bits of stone from around the tomb, regarded them with affection, then carefully put them into his shirt pocket next to his heart. These fragments were sacred for he believed that in some mystical way they embodied the soul and spirit of the Armenian warrior, who slept in that hallowed piece of French earth, which had now become forever Armenian.

After taking more photographs, I suggested that we walk to the nearby plot and visit the graves of Edith Piaf and of Oscar Wilde. Bill brushed aside the idea saying that it would be an affront to the general's memory to include others, however celebrated, during our pilgrimage. To behave like ordinary tourists and wander about the tombstones searching for the graves of Chopin, Balzac, or Bizet would border on blasphemy. Our sole purpose was to pay our respects to Antranik and leave it at that. Someday we could do the tourist bit, but we never did. Now he wanted to immortalize that afternoon with a single act of remembrance, witnessed and recorded in diary of his mind. I took one final photograph of him standing before the monument, then we left without looking back.

The visit seemed to exhaust him physically as well as emotionally, and in the short space of an afternoon Bill had suddenly aged, the spring from his step had gone and now he trudged like a man older than his years. We walked in silence, each lost in his own thoughts, with only the sound of our footsteps to disturb the quiet of the dead.

Bill hated the burial business and had contempt for the interminable rites along with the long-winded orations that only distressed the living. "Can you imagine me," he said, laughing heartily, "lying with my arms folded, listening to some bearded windbag praising me to the heavens? I'd bust my guts laughing, jump out of the coffin and tell him to cut out the bullshit and get on with the business. He was boring everybody, including me." Nope, he wanted none of it. Death was embarrassing enough without all that malarkey.

When his time came to turn in his hat and his trapeze tights, Bill would do it his way. He didn't want to ride in the back of a hearse leading a long line of cars to the crematorium. If he had his choice, he'd rather drive than ride. Since that was out of the question, he'd rather go alone, without the cavalcade of a commercial production for the death industry. Nope, on that day, all his friends and relatives should go out and celebrate—everybody—for it was truly the time of their lives, and they should be out celebrating.

As we distanced ourselves from Antranik's tomb, Bill's spirits swiftly rose and soon he was posing for more pictures standing besides the more baroque monuments of common, uncelebrated French citizens whose families had spared no expense to honor their loved ones and to enrich the stone cutters.

I never got to see any of the dozens of photographs I took that afternoon, save one, which appeared on the dust jacket of *Sons Come And Go, Mothers Hang In Forever.* Bill insisted on having the films developed himself to preserve that afternoon for posterity. The last time I inquired about the negatives was in 1977. He claimed they were around somewhere among his papers, drawers, or in his files at his house in Fresno or in Paris.

When we finally stood on the sidewalk on Boulevard de Menilmontant with our backs to the high-walled cemetery, Bill was completely rejuvenated and bursting with joy.

We were glad to be alive.

The Last of the Armenian Plays

DICKRAN KOUYMJIAN

William Saroyan's last major statement on the meaning of being Arme-
nian is expressed in an unpublished play, *Haratch,* written two years
before his death.* Curiously the purely Armenian side of this Pulitzer
Prize–winning American author's writing remains obscure and to many
totally unknown. Yet there was never doubt about his Armenian identity;
Saroyan asserted it openly and directly. The early stories, such as those in
My Name Is Aram (1940), are filled with Armenian characters set against
Armenian backgrounds. In the largely autobiographical novel *Rock
Wagram* (1951), the solid, genuine Armenian life of the lead character,
Arak Vagramian, an actor from Fresno, is pitted against the sham values
and hyprocrisy of the outside world exemplified by Hollywood, a way of
life Rock/Arak refuses to succumb to. Immediately after, Saroyan began
writing a series of memoirs. *A Bicycle Rider in Beverly Hills* (1952) was the
first, followed by various collections of autobiographical sketches
culminating in *Obituaries* (1979), his last published work. Each of these
directly or indirectly discusses things Armenian.

Saroyan's voluminous diaries and massive correspondence, all carefully preserved, will some day also contribute to an analysis of his
Armenian side. However, much of this material only indirectly treats his
Armenian roots. It was in two other genres that Saroyan directly confronted his ethnicity. The first of these comprises a series of introduc-
tions and prefaces to the works of various Armenian writers—novelists,
historians, translators, essayists. When solicited to contribute such opening pieces to help promote a new writer by adding the prestige associated
with his name, Saroyan rarely refused. The very first was the introduc-

---

*Haratch and two other plays discussed in this essay, *Bitlis* and *The Armenians,* were
published in the fall of 1986 by The Press at California State University, Fresno, under the
title *An Armenian Trilogy: Three Plays about Armenian Life,* edited with an introduction and
notes by Dickran Kouymjian.

tion to an anthology: *Three Worlds (Hairenik 1934–1939)*. One of the most extensive and incisive statements on the Armenian reality is the introduction to the 1970 publication on the Armenian village of Chunkush by Karnik Kevorkian. To the best of my knowledge the last of these prefaces was for a volume of English translations under the title *An Account of the Glorious Struggle of Van-Vaspouragan* (1980).

The second and more important medium through which Saroyan explored his Armenian identity and expressed his personal reaction to current Armenian problems, was the theater. It may seem strange to those unfamiliar with Saroyan's writing that the theater rather than the essay or memoir should be the vehicle for Armenian expression. Saroyan liked play writing perhaps more than any other literary form, including the short story. His early success was based in part on such plays as *My Heart's in the Highlands* and *The Time of Your Life* (1939). Those who knew his working habits were well aware of his instinctive, almost uncanny ability to transform all experience directly into dialogue and drama. Some of his numerous unpublished plays are really diaries written in dialogue form. In the last decades of his life, during the Paris years, he used to boast of writing at least one major play and several minor ones every year, putting them aside for future publication and performance because he felt the present state of theater arts, especially in the United States, was poor and unconducive to proper presentation of his works.

Saroyan's bedroom with pianola at 74 Rue Taitbout, Paris. *(Courtesy of Dikran Kouymjian.)*

In the fall of 1980 Saroyan brought to my attention three new plays only one of which, *The Armenians,* had ever been performed and none of which had been published. During a discussion of some of his early stories and plays, which were being studied by my class in Armenian-American literature, at California State University, Fresno, Saroyan said he wanted to give me a typescript of a play called *Haratch,* because, he said, I knew most of the characters in it through my Paris connection. He allowed a few photocopies to be made for the class, adding that this was the first time he had ever permitted anyone, let alone an entire university class in literature, to read an unpublished work. In a loud and emphatic voice he said the play was "the greatest ever written on the Armenians." The next day, October 2, he telephoned and apologized for his bravado about *Haratch,* yet commented, "It is still a good play, and perhaps even great."

At this point, a digression on Saroyan's method of composing is appropriate. Whether by conscious imitation or by the instinctive, almost Jungian carrying out of a millennia-old ritual among Armenians, William Saroyan was a great practitioner of the art of the colophon. Like Armenian scribes, stone masons, and artisans of old, he ritualistically recorded on every piece of paper he typed, wrote, or painted on, a precise formula inscription containing his name, the place of execution, the date, the day of the week, often the hour of beginning and ending of writing, and at times terse commentary. Thus, the typescript of *Haratch* reveals very clearly that its thirty pages were written in exactly thirty consecutive days from June 23 to July 22, 1979, at 74 rue Taitbout, Paris. Each page, bearing some 800 to 900 words, was typed, single spaced to the very bottom with virtually no margins. An average of 15 to 20 minutes was spent of each day's work, usually in the early afternoon. He had always prided himself on being a skillled typist, something he learned in his early teens at the Fresno vocational school after deciding he would become a writer. His speed was remarkable, for working without the aid of preliminary notes or a draft he produced 30–40 words a minute including the time for the formulation of his thoughts. The typescript is relatively free of syntactical, grammatical, or mechanical errors.

It might be assumed that such a technique would lead to an episodic work, but Saroyan's innate mastery of words and ideas keeps the play together, a unified whole. No doubt when the play is published in normal fashion it will no longer reveal this underlying peculiarity of composition. It was widely known—he was fond of bragging about it— that from his earliest writings Saroyan would set up very rigorous chal-lenge-schedules for himself, somewhat like Handel writing *The Messiah* in 17 days. His first collection of stories, *The Daring Young Man of the*

Flying Trapeze, consisted of 33 stories (actually only 26 were printed in the volume) written in 33 days; *The Time of Your Life* was completed in a New York hotel room in six days; and *Haratch,* the Armenian play, in exactly 30 days. "During that summer," he said "*Haratch* was one of seven works that I was creating. When I write I prefer not to be obsessed night and day by any one work. By laboring at one time, at the same time, I don't know which one to think about at the end of my day's writing, and therefore, I think of none of them consciously, but allow them to just be there as I take my walk or eat or visit or just sleep." During our very last conversation in Fresno on Christmas Eve of 1980 before I left for Paris, he brought up the subject once again: "A play must be an accumulated story."

That is exactly what he did with *Haratch:* accumulated its parts, its ideas, not just during those 30 days, but really all his life. The one-act, one-scene play takes place entirely in the editorial offices of the Armenian daily *Haratch* on rue d'Hauteville not far from Saroyan's Paris flat on rue Taitbout. Dramatic action has been almost totally suppressed; there is only the pouring of drinks (whiskey) from time to time. In this, his final statement on the Armenian condition (unless the last work he was so intensely writing prior to his death has an Armenian theme), Saroyan eliminated all distractions, all extraneous activity. In his own mind *Haratch* was the last of several plays that circumscribed his own Armenian experience while affording him a way of presenting commentaries on its significance. Let us examine the earlier plays first.

In the fall of 1974, on the eve of the sixtieth anniversary of the Genocide, *The Armenians* was enacted at St. Vartan's Cathedral in New York. Allegedly written at the request of Archbishop Torkom Manoogian, the original typescript dates back to 1971. In the next year, Saroyan went to the Middle East, where among other activities he gave the commencement address at the Armenian-American Haigazian College in Beirut. He was deeply immersed in his Armenian past during this period. He seemed to derive a bouyancy and strength of spirit from the adulation, honor, and unconditional support the Armenians gave him in Beirut and Soviet Armenia, in marked contrast to the diminished attention he was experiencing in America. It was as though he replenished himself at the very source of his creative power, the Armenian experience, his own specific cultural antecedents. He was more optimistic than ever before, more extravagant than usual. During the trip to Beirut he also endeavored, as an act of homage, to get his father's Armenian poems and other writings edited and published (he carried the aging manuscript with him as though it were a hallowed relic of his own past). It is in this context that *The Armenians,* a one-act play in twenty-one scenes, was created. The action takes place in Fresno in 1921 after the fall of the Armenian Republic, moving from Armenian church hall to Armenian coffee house; the main characters are three Armenian clergymen, Apostolic, Presbyterian, Congregational. During a series of discussions various aspects of Armenia's fate are passionately argued. For Saroyan the Armenian spirit in this play is synonymous to the human spirit; the exercise of studying it, disputing its meaning, is of itself a form of redemption for Armenia and the Armenian.

An even earlier unpublished play was considered by Saroyan himself as part of his statement on being Armenian. One day he called to say he wanted me to read another work of his. It was *Is There Going to Be a Wedding?* a one-act play of forty-eight scenes written in 1970–71. It takes place in various locations in Fresno between 1919 and 1923 when Saroyan was entering his early teens. The main characters are himself and his older brother Henry, his mother, and two opposing uncles, Mihran, the idealistic and intellectual tailor, and Aram, the materialistic and pragmatic lawyer. The play creates the Armenian environment the young writer grew up in while at the same time exposing the opposing forces after his soul. It is the least philosophical of the "Armenian" plays.

These three works of the 1970s show a steady artistic movement toward a progressively less complex dramatic environment where external considerations such as stage directions and scene changes are reduced until they vanish completely in *Haratch*. In this final play, Saroyan settled for a newspaper office—not a church, not a coffee house—in the dispersion, not in Armenia proper, as the most appropriate place for an analysis of the Armenian condition. This setting was not absolutely new, for already in *Rock Wagram* the protagonist and his cousin pay a nostalgic visit to the office of *Asbarez* in Fresno, described in most poignant, nearly desperate language, yet suggesting that this newspaper, and by inference all Armenian newspapers, though feebly surviving with an ever diminishing readership, was nevertheless, the embodiment of the Armenian spirit in the dispersion.

The time and setting of *Haratch* are real, late morning or afternoon on a summer day in 1979 when the next day's edition has already gone to press and the staff and whatever visitors might have congregated there are free to just talk about things. Saroyan himself often "checked-in" at *Haratch* to announce his arrival in Paris and at times would "check-out" before leaving on a trip through Europe or for the winter in Fresno. In the opening pages of the play he informs the audience that the writer as a young man had already in 1935 on a trip to Soviet Armenia made acquaintance with the founder of the daily, Shavarsh Missakian. The suggestion then follows that a continuous relationship has been established since that time between him, the paper, and its current director, Arpik Missakian, who has spent the past quarter of a century continuing her father's work. Saroyan also draws an analogy between *Haratch*, which means "forward" in Armenian, and the *Daily Forward*, the famous Jewish newspaper of New York, bemused that the names of these papers of two diasporic nations with similar histories should be the same.

As the play unfolds Saroyan assembles his characters one by one in the office and printshop in Paris' tenth arrondisement. All are Armenians and once they enter this environment, which is symbolically transformed into a piece of Armenian soil, they do not leave it during the entire play. The *dramatis personae* are: Arpik, the editor and director; two Paris associates, the poet Zoulal Kazandjian and Zorab Mouradian; two Americans, Khachig Tololyan, a professor of comparative literature, and his girl friend Sylvia; Hrachia, also poet and most certainly Hrachia Hovannisian, editor of the Soviet Armenian paper *Sovetakan Grakanoutiun*, who is passing through Paris; Bishop Stepan, modeled on the late Archbishop Serovpe Manougian, Primate of Europe; an old man from Bitlis who is a writer of simple memoirs; Anoushavan Kapigian, and Saroyan the writer. No such meeting or assembly as the one described ever took place in exactly the manner given, nor were these individuals ever together at one time; however, it is certain that Saroyan had met and talked with each of them in the office of *Haratch* or in Paris, and the language and ideas expressed are conceivably those of each of the characters he has speaking them, though in the final analysis they are all Saroyan's.

The play develops as a series of questions and answers with comments by various participants. Like *The Armenians* and *Is There Going to Be a Wedding?*, *Haratch* contains absolutely no stage directions. Saroyan attached great importance to the role of the director; he often commented that his plays needed the right person to successfully interpret them and bring them to life. He expressed his disappointment with the only production of any of these plays, that of *The Armenians*. Though he was not present for its performance he had a tape recording about which he commented, "The director, Ed Setrakian, was off-base; he had the characters get too shrill, a bogus trick. Armenians are not shrill. Elia Kazan uses that trick too, everybody jumping up and down and all of it very shrill." He added whimsically, "These plays have to be produced and directed either by me or some Armenian who is well acquainted with me." I suggested the obvious Armenian directors in America and abroad who might undertake the work and told him I would try to arrange a reading of it in Paris or back in the U.S. in the following autumn.

As it appears on paper, the play is more of an intellectual exercise than a dramatic action. Saroyan was quite aware of that just as he was of the earlier *The Armenians;* in his mind this never detracted from its theatricality; like all of his plays it had to be "prepared" for the stage. As a self-contained work, history and background are provided as it moves deeper and deeper into the enquiry of being Armenian. In the process there are the humorous stories, a part of most of his writing, and the commentaries on life and death. There is the constant Saroyanesque insistence that every life has a tangibly important meaning, best illustrated in this work by the octagenarian "man from Bitlis" who regularly brings in a new installment of memoirs on his native city (also that of Saroyan's family), which Arpik at first refuses but, only later accepts, having learned through Saroyan in the play the value of this work, a value which contributes to the continuity of the nation, its culture, its ethos. Each of the characters is based to one degree or another on the real-life traits of the individuals they represent: Zoulal, the somewhat cynical poet; Arpik, the energetic, no-nonsense editor, out of whom a latent sentimentalism must be forced; Bishop Stephan, the pagan idealist working within a church which is more national than Christian; Khachig, the dry-witted American professor; Hrachia, the bon vivant Soviet poet and publicist; the man from Bitlis, the self-effacing romantic, enchanted by everything; and the writer, Saroyan, the perpetual investigator and observer.

The play is full of profound and provocative statements on questions that continue to obsess the thinking Armenian. Saroyan himself had long reflected on the dilemma of being an Armenian, especially a diasporic Armenian. Among the topics discussed and debated are: the role of the Armenian press, the role of the church, death and its meaning, individual identity, Armenian-Turkish relations, the return of lost Armenian lands, and questions such as, What do Armenians want? Who is an Armenian? What is an Armenian? Why is an Armenian? Do you like being an Armenian?

It is impossible to go into detail on even a limited number of the subjects dramatized in *Haratch;* that must wait for a more detailed study, perhaps after publication or performance of the play. Any one of the subjects mentioned above would lead the reader back into other works of Saroyan; their proper understanding would require a familiarity with certain basic ethical principles that he carefully maintained, and an explanation of some of his attitudes on the importance of national identity, national culture, inherited tradition, and the relation of all these to the common feature shared by all beings, namely their humanity. Because Saroyan was from start to end a humanist whose concern was in the definition of the species as a living, ethical, interracting being, worthy of study, the center of all systems of thought, he wrote endlessly, usually in tersely pitted contradictions, of the nobility of all men and women, of every nation, of every social and economic class.

Yet in this enormous universe each person has his or her own individuality and Saroyan's was being Armenian, an accident for him to be sure, as all birth was accidental, but still an important, undeniable reality, one which deserved attention and study (his posthumously published *Births* elaborated on this concept). His method of study was Socratic; that is, through conversations with his fellow humans. It is this constant search to clarify, define, understand his Armenian identity, and of course through it his humanity, that Saroyan was always asking, looking, reading, experiencing. He was obsessively curious about everything and everybody. The expression of his curiosity and research was often manifested by a kind of continual theme and variation on favorite subjects. Of these death—dying and not dying—was certainly the most prominent. However, second to death as a theme was probably "being Armenian." *Haratch* was the final attempt to synthesize his feelings about this, to provide an existential handbook or roadmap of the problem. To underline the importance of the ideas about being Armenian contained in the play, I believe he consciously chose a very elevated formal structure, that of the Socratic dialogue as we know it through Plato, especially in "The Symposium on Love." The choice must have seemed "just right" for Saroyan, since Plato's works are eminently theatrical with dialogue raised to a level certainly as high as that of the tragedies contemporary to the period.

In Saroyan's play-dialogue the subject is not love, but one he considers to be no less important, one he wishes to raise by this deliberate literary creation to the same level, namely, being Armenian. For him, in his later as in his very earlist years, being Armenian, living as an Armenian in the twentieth century, either in Armenia or in diaspora, was, after the confronting of death, the most vital question. The most appropriate place for a debate on being Armenian was that environment where the native language and all it contained was being produced daily: a newspaper office. Near the end of the play Saroyan even asks if such a spontaneous exchange of ideas could take place anywhere else and after answering "no," he has Zulal say, "Armenians are never so at home as when they are in an editorial office and near printing presses." On the other hand, though the settings are dissimilar, the number of characters in both the *Symposium* and *Haratch* are exactly ten, Saroyan probably adding Kapigian late in the play with his one or two insignificant lines to achieve that precise parallel.

There are many remarkable messages in *Haratch,* but in ending the dialogue that has no ending, the writer convinces all present that the meeting itself, the discussion, the exchange of ideas between humans, in this special case Armenians, quite separate from the content of the ideas (though this too is significant), is the continuity of the experience that allows the human race, and the Armenian portion of it, to endure, survive, flourish. It also affords Armenians, especially in the diaspora, a way to perpetuate the heritage passed on to them through centuries of cultural inertia. On the penultimate page Saroyan the author has Saroyan the character say it all loudly and clearly, "Who shall remember us if we don't? Who shall remember the Armenians if they don't remember themselves?"

Saroyan always talked about Bitlis as "the hometown" and strongly identified himself with it. On the first page of *Haratch,* he introduces a major character, the old man from Bitlis. During the probing of the "identity" question, it is this old man who is most secure and clearly joyful in his Armenian and Bitlis origin. His whole life, after sixty-five years of exile, now centers around the writing of his recollections of Bitlis. When Saroyan as Saroyan discusses his own visit to Bitlis near the end of the play, the reader senses the writer's discomfort and confusion. In 1964, Saroyan journeyed to his ancestral home with Bedros Zobian, editor of *Marmara,* an Armenain daily of Istanbul, and another friend. In the play Saroyan has the old man from Bitlis ask, "Why did you not write about your return to Bitlis?"

At this point, Saroyan responds in his own voice, "Well, there was only one Armenian in Bitlis, and the rest were Kurds, and I told them that they seemed to be not only Armenians but that they were Saroyans or Garoghlanians, and on top of the Fort a Kurdish *ahshkhukh* (*sic* for Armenian *ashough,* minstrel) sang improvised songs about my visit to beautiful Bitlis—well, when I got back to Fresno I didn't know where to start, and in the end the only thing I wrote was a kind of poem called Bitlis, but it does not really tell what is in my heart to tell, which I don't really know how to tell—for the old Armenian only asked us to please get him to Beirut so that he could die among Armenians. He had been born in Bitlis, he was nearly ninety years old, he was mocked as an old man by the young wild Kurdish kids. . . . The old Armenian became to me all of us driven out of Bitlis, and yet I was not at all unfond, I hope you understand, of the lively ill-mannered Kurds living in our fine stone houses. It is a difficult thing to make sense of loss, and absence, and displacement, and destruction—but whoever is alive in a place, he is the owner of the place, that is the law of history, and Bitlis is gone, and I wish I knew how it might be brought back to us."

KHACHIK: Only by fighting.

HRACHIA:. . . . No, there are other ways.

In this passage Saroyan is not being completely candid, probably because of the lingering irresolution is his own mind about *Bitlis.* I have not read Saroyan's poem on Bitlis, but four years before he wrote *Haratch,* in the spring of 1975, he wrote in Paris a short play called *Bitlis* which describes in detail his visit to the city. On the last page of that work as he and his friends are leaving the mountain town, Saroyan says:

> I find myself deeply saddened to be leaving the place, but also glad to have it behind me. I had to come, I had to see it, I came, I saw it, I am saddened by it, I am glad to be leaving it, but—there is more, there is something nagging me and I don't know what it is. What is it?
>
> **BEDROS:** It's quite simple. It is simply that the place was ours for so long, it was yours for so long, it was the home of the Armenians and the Saroyans for so long, and even though you were born far away from it you were really still here, as if you had been born and had lived here, and you came back and everything was in ruins, and even in doubt.

The play *Bitlis* ends with a speech by Ara, the other traveling companion, speaking for Saroyan, full of hopelessness and despair before this unresolvable dilemma. If there is any resolution, it is given in part by the play itself, which took Saroyan eleven years of preparation to write in seven days.

Candid Conversation

GARIG BASMADJIAN

(25 May 1975 in Paris)

GB: In February 1934 *Story* published *The Daring Young Man on the Flying Trapeze*. In October Random House brought out your first book. In less than one year you became one of the most read, discussed writers of the time. You were 26. Looking back forty years, how would you explain your sudden and spectacular appearance in American letters and what was the key of your success?

WS: I am obliged to reply that there is an element of the unaccountable in such things. It will be a little bit mistaken for me not to acknowledge the unaccountable. I certainly wanted only to have my writing published, so that I could make a beginning and a living. I was hoping for the kind of reception which would permit me to continue (I had much writing to do) and at the same time not to need any financial assistance from anybody.

GB: Was that the best reception you've gotten as a writer?

WS: I would have to say that I received from the outset perhaps the best that any writer has ever received for a first work. Later, with both *My Heart's in the Highlands* and *The Time of Your Life*, there was another order or reception, which had to same mingling of astonishment and gratitude on the part of both the critics and the public in general, that was very pleasing to me. The first book made me famous and made me rich.

GB: Wasn't it too sudden?

WS: Not to me!

GB: Could you resist it?

WS: I didn't want to resist it. I made a fool of myself. I was young. I enjoyed it. I have never been reluctant to make a fool of myself. But we are losing sight of the writing that was involved. My writing also was a kind that somebody might say "Well, you're only making a fool of yourself." There were experimental things, there were unusual things that I was trying for, and so it was not uncommon for me to risk a great deal. Remember that I accepted being a kind of character in the literary world: loud, outspoken, enthusiastic, confident, cocky.

GB: Innocent, Naive.

WS: Well, very naive, but at the same time very sophisticated. A mixture of both, and with the kind of arrogance I think a writer should have. I did not believe for instance, that anybody in America or anywhere else, was writing better than I was writing, or was potentially a better writer than myself. I have no reason to correct that now. If that constitutes my being naive and arrogant and so forth, let it be so. But the writing must not be overlooked as being part of the reason for what happened. There has got to be something. It isn't just nothing that they are writing about. So the real answer to how do you account for its happening and so forth, I would say that basically, the proper answer is the writing. It was the writing, it was a new writing, it was a dynamic writing, it was a lively writing.

GB: Horace Gregory relating your phenomenal success to the psychological needs of the Depression Era has said: "At a moment when people did not trust themselves to speak aloud, it was good to have someone else, someone like Thomas Wolfe and William Saroyan, assert a vigorous inflated personality."

WS: I never read it. Where was that?

GB: *New York Herald Tribune,* February 23, 1936, page 7.

WS: All right. In other words he says that apparently I was speaking for a kind of body of inarticulate sentiment or intelligence or feeling or involvement. Could be. But just remember this, [pause] we are able to say many things about many things. An element of truth will be in anything that we choose to say. I have come upon very fine writers the first year that I was published and every year since then, and I swear that I can't understand why they do not have the recognition which I think that their writing entitles them to. And so again we come up against something which (without putting ourselves into the dimensions of mysticism) has to do with forcefulness. I have always been just a little bit more than people are, I have always been just a bit, an edge more than one person [pause]. I am trying to be respectful as possible to your questions . . . [long pause].

GB: Let's pass to another question.

WS: No! We will not pass to another question. Let us not be afraid of getting bogged down and coming to an impasse or dead end. Because we do it all the time in experience and in writing in any case. We can get out of it. I would like to answer [pause] and it takes a moment for such things, because this is brand new to my own head at this point . . . The answer is as follows: I am none who is, I am not stoppable and apparently that was felt from the beginning.

I have to be a writer, I have to be Saroyan, that's all, that's the end of it. There is nothing indecisive about my being. It is very decisive, and it is loud and it is forceful and it is larger than life. It is art. None of this is Gospel, but then no question is Gospel. I am a writer and my first book announces that I'm a writer, and they've got to listen to me. Now if you say, suppose you didn't deliver your second book and the forty-four other books? Well, that's the whole point, you do deliver it.

GB: I'd like to suppose something else: suppose *Story* and then Random House refused to publish *The Daring Young Man* and you remained an unpublished solitary writer?

WB: I would be stronger than ever.

GB: Did your success disturb you then?

WS: It didn't disturb me, but it did have the effect which concerns all of us. How much are we willing to give over to courtesy, to acknowledgment, of nice people's response to our work, to routine civility and neglect of the large mixture of anger and of love, which is essentially the blend in art. I'm still the angriest writer I know.

GB: But your writing is full of love.

WS: Aaaaaa! Don't be deceived; it's not as full of love as people imagine. Besides, a lot of my writing just hasn't been published. Remember that I'm at the mercy of magazine editors. Do you know of the stories of mine that they have received and sent back? No, *I* know, and they have sent back many, because it wasn't good writing? Not necessarily; it's just something they don't want. So it's hard to say. I know all about the whole theory of Saroyan, the warm-hearted Armenian embracing everything and so forth . . . I have more true, powerful annoyance, anger toward man and his vulnerability and corruptibility than almost anybody I know. Now, if you say "Then how can you have all this love?" That love is discipline on my part. I insist upon that. I know everything that's going on. Nobody would ever suspect that I'm not with him. As a matter of fact there was almost nobody else at that luncheon or the wedding that I could be in agreement with. I couldn't be in agreement with any of them, but I am not going to become estranged from the human race. This is my family, these lunatics, and I love them. I love that crazy Bitlistzi, you remember him, don't you? What a wonderful man! Eighty- seven years old, tears coming down his eyes . . .

GB: And so that nobody would ever suspect that you're not with him-you start acting?

WS: I act myself everywhere, all my life: we have no choice. We choose who it is out of ourselves that we must be. We choose differently depending upon the arena and the circumstances. The first impulse that you

Saroyan as seen by Paul Kalinian.

have, that might be called creative or aesthetic, is the infinite variety that is in the human being for performance. I think essentially that all writers are actors. Not in the crude, exterior sense, but in the sense of being equal to knowing everybody; knowing about everybody, approximately everybody, in essence being everybody. Yet, I act.

GB: And how often do you change masks?

WS: According to the moment! I meet your son, I'm another actor. I couldn't be the same with you as with him. I have to say to myself, now wait a minute, this is a little child, you could quiet down, remember, he might be full of fear, you look very strange, you smell strange, your eyes are wild, so be careful, don't frighten this child, see if this child can see you as somebody that he doesn't fear. And he didn't fear me, when I squeezed his hand he liked that, he smiled. You change even to birds and to buildings, you change to streets, you change your act where you are. Don't you see that we are fluid? We are flowing. An identity is not static, it's a continuous flux.

GB: Let's talk about your family. *Inhale & Exhale* had this dedication: "To the English Tongue, the American Earth and the Armenian Spirit". How much did your "Armenianism" help you in shaping your being and your writing?

WS: I am unable to conceive my identity apart from being Armenian. It is as central as the spark of life from the beginning. It is part of me. I could never live not being Armenian, because of the fact that's what I am. If somebody came today to me and said "Mr. Saroyan, there has been a terrible mistake, your father and your mother both were Turks, and you also are a Turk," I would repudiate that. It could not enter into my being, because if it had been let's say genetically possible, the life that supplemented that genetic falsehood would turn out to be a falsehood. I owe everything, everything to the unaccountable, which is in each of us arriving in the center of himself and a part of a family and a part of a region and a part of a culture.

I am not a very good student. I do not know cultures historically and in terms of scholarship. I know them by living only. And so the answer to that question is: my debt to Armenia and therefore all Armenians is incalculable. It is enormous, that's what it is.

GB: Is your Armenian background the best element of your literary output?

WS: Yes, yes, in the sense of my being anything. That is: what usage do you make of your identity? What usage do you make of the accident of what you are? That's the important thing. Am I satisfied that I'm making usage of my talent? Yes, I am satisfied. I'm making excellent usage, I'm making better usage than perhaps I might have made.

GB: Were you even an American?

WS: Always

GB: You are always an American, and you were always an Armenian. Let's talk a little about this duality.

WS: Definitely. I have heard the word, and it is a laughable word, but it is very much the style among the intellectuals of New York and also of Hollywood: dichotomy. We are a product of two things well-known and established by everybody. The inherited and the environmental. I am an American by environment. I am an Armenian, that's who I am. I was born an Armenian. But you put me in California, that's my home. So somebody told me "What does California mean to you?" I said, to be perfectly honest, it's my native land. I have a very deep attachment to it. He says "As much as to Hayastan?" Yes, as much as to Hayastan, as much as to Bitlis. In an allegorical rather than sentimental sense, Bitlis is supreme. But this is another dimension of experience. This is almost a dream. This is almost beyond anything that we need. Try to measure in terms of the reasonable, because, remember, Bitlis has become a kind of monument of our loss. And I have a feeling about regaining, which is almost psychopathic. I wrote a book called *Tracy's Tiger* in which the theme of regaining the lost is mad, insane, obsessive. This son-of-a-bitch cries to bring back the past, and that is madness. But in regard to Bitlis I know it's beyond any further expectation. I was there ten years ago. I didn't want to leave. But it's not ours. It *is* ours but other people occupy it. I did long for the day when that would be ours and I'd go there. I would go there. Go there and live there. I would settle down there and die there, and put the bones with the other Saroyans that have died there for may be who knows. Forever. Our bones are there. We are there, as far as memory of our old timers goes, *saroyannere hos en, ouskitz ekan? (The Saroyans are here. Where are they from?)*

GB: How much did criticism affect your instinctive methods of writing? Were you really indifferent, as you say, on many occasions?

WS: I must make a terrible confession. I have never learned one thing of any use to me from any writing favorable or unfavorable by anybody. I have received some nice letters from readers that enlightened me, and said more about something that I had written and I had suspected, but nobody in writing about anything of mine was of any use to me. As a kid, because it was fun, I used to answer every critic and I'd be deliberately critical of the critic. I would be sarcastic. I did it recently about the guy who reviewed a book of mine, *Places Where I Have Done Time* in the *New Republic*. He says Saroyan is forever young. I replied to him and pointed out a couple of things which I thought he had missed. I said, "Do you think I'm writing about myself? I'm writing about you. I'm writing about everybody and most people feel that. Most people read me when they want to feel reassured about their own reality."

GB: Do you read books?

WS: I wouldn't give up reading for anything in the world. I like the solitude, the quiet. I like the whole connection with the multitude of people who have written. I like even bad writers and trash books. I like to read what they are doing. I buy a lot of books like that for 20 centimes and I love them. I read them every day. One book ten minutes another book two hours.

GB: Of the classics whom do you generally read or reread?

WS: I like to read Russian writers translated into English at least once a year. I like to read Tolstoy especially when he repudiated his novels and wrote his cranky philosophies.

GB: Only the "cranky" philosophies of Tolstoy?

WS: Oh yes. Because I don't believe in it at all, but I love his preoccupation trying to improve the whole human race. This is a fantasy which only a man like Tolstoy could have. You are not going to improve anybody, maybe yourself. He failed improving himself. . . . I have an old 1901 edition of translated Russian stories. I love to read those. Gogol, "The Overcoat." I like to read Pushkin. I love to read all "The Ace of Clubs" [sic]. There is a quality that satisfies a sense of being in a large spirit which has .a fusion of these things, which Russian writing has; honesty, tremendous vulnerability to wrong, to failure, to mistake, to embarassment, to folly, a zest for the comic in character, and essentially a profound love which is not sloppy, but is a general reality. Go ahead.

GB: Are you unliterary?

WS: It would be pretentious if I say I'm unliterary. I'll tell you how it is now. I am a craftsman whose apprenticeship has been more than forty years long. I have done my best revising over these years, so that now when I write the revision is already taking place. By instinct I write good writing, whether I wish to call it literary in the sense of the stylists who use English, no! I'm not that kind of a stylist and don't want to be, because the words I use are not to stand as much as possible in the way of what I'm doing. The stylist lives in the words he uses. I don't. Anything that you write, which is not totally private, must win the reader. You'd say how do I win the reader? You must give him something, right smack from the beginning. And he says "This guy is talking to me, I better read this." I am simultaneously literary and a writer of very simple straight usage of English, which is the only language I work with.

GB: You also make mistakes.

WS: Oh yes, many, and I allow them to stand.

GB: Which means that they are deliberate?

WS: Yes, I want them to stand, if something is to be learned from them. You'd say something about who? About me, about a writer, about people, about mistakes. I do not accept anybody's telling me that this is the way. Do I have the way? Well, for myself I have it to the extent that I'm sixty-seven years of age and continue to work, in that sense I may have it.

GB: Have you always expressed contempt for rules and stylistic traditions?

WS: Not contempt, oh, contempt is the wrong word. For instance, I couldn't have contempt for things that so many people believe. But I cannot for myself see it as something that needs to be unduly prolonged; as as matter of fact I think it is on its way out, I think so many things are on their way out, you'd say but when? Maybe five hundred years, that's nothing for nature, but for us it is, we don't have very much time. We are Armenians, we take pride in being the first officially recognizers of Christianity as our state religion. Well, I think if we were pagans, we may have been much more interesting, but that's irrelevant, we became Christians, and we saw the costumes today at our church, we saw the ritual, we saw the theater, it's beautiful. You'd say, would you want your children to be baptized. I say certainly, it's fun, it's no harm, sure it's nice.

GB: Is suffering beneficial? Is it good? How much is it Armenian?

WS: If it is unavoidable, what it can do to our soul and character, is usable. It's useful. Too much suffering is not good, and it is not Armenian, it is human in spite of our long history of being geographically, in the equivalent of constant vulnerability to change, which is disastrous in its potentials. We have suffered possibly a little more than some peoples, but not more than all peoples.

GB: Misery in your writings is sometimes treated so poetically, that it seems the reader is invited to live in it . . .

WS: Then it ain't misery. If there is such a thing, then it can't be misery. I am an old man, sixty-seven years of age, I have failed. My children have grown up and gone away and don't love me. I have no wealth. I have no fame. I have no real reason to be glad. And yet I go on. I've got a room and in the room there is a table, and in the room there is some paper and there is a pencil and I take the paper and I write down over here [writes down] *the world is a great big fat falsehood* (yeah, that's interesting), so I'm writing now, I got nothing. The room is cold. Now, how can I be miserable? I cross out *the world is a great big fat lie,* and I say it may hurt somebody's feeling, so I put over there *the world is really not real,* then I look at that, and I am working. And I say the world is really not real. It is certainly not real, the way Howard Hughes and Paul Getty and Calouste Gulbenkian thought it was real. They were wrong. And so I'm off to the races. There's something going on, there's the beginning of art. Or I take the pencil and I make a drawing. I think about the drawing, or I start to write a poem. Now I do write poems and I keep them, and I almost never look at them again.

GB: What do you think of your poetry?

WS: My mother gave cake to Najar Levon and Najar Levon said "Mommy, your *gata* is good bread." My poetry is good prose. The hero of my poems is and always has been for the past forty years one body and that's the sun, and in one connection to the body, and that's the eye. My son once asked me "Pop, if you could take one part of the human body as the one that would mean most nearly yourself, what would it be?" I said, the eye. Because I can't conceive of any of us having anything like reality apart from it. We have to have it. "Suppose you are blind?" I answered, then I'll have an interior eye and I would see. In the sun I would probably see great abstract paintings.

GB: You have always been the substance of your books.

WS: Absolutely.

GB: Seldom have you created an imagined character.

WS: Well, I am an imagined character. I have a whole play called *An Imaginary Character Named Saroyan,* it's a good play.

GB: Haven't read it. Was it published, produced?

WS: Oh no! Not published, not produced. Henry Fonda read it for instance (they are such children, the people of the theater). He would rather do a bad job in *The Time of Your Life* (and he did a bad job of it), than get out there in a brand-new play and really work hard and create that character. He read it and was afraid of it. It's a hell of a play. It's a good play.

Have I created characters in the sense that some writers have? No sir, I am everybody. That's all I can say. It may be a terrible limitation, may be a terrible oversimplification, but true. I will write *Lear* or rewrite *Lear* in due course. As a matter of fact I've partly written it already. I have not written *Hamlet,* because perhaps I don't like him very much. And I am trying to think of the parallels of the so-called created characters. Aaaaaaaa! These are all variations of the man who wrote them. We know that. They are not invented. Best, I think, are some of my own characters because of this reason: My characters in my plays do not get so falsely involved as to need to commit murder or suicide, and at the same time do not lack passion. Now the thing that we want in drama is passion so that there can be that intensity of a context, otherwise you wouldn't have a drama. I honored the play that I wrote in my 59th year in Paris, day before yesterday. Because while I'm here doing other work, I sort of catch up on stuff that is in my files. It's a play called *Going Great,* going to the graveyard, going well. It doesn't have violence, no nothing, but it is dramatic as any play. It's a hell of a play. Someday it will be done. Who has seen it? Nobody! [laughs] I don't care, it's none of my business. Somebody said: "Well what do you write them for?" What do you want me to do? That's my work, I write, I like to write, I am a writer.

GB: You have already published more than 40 books. Do you have as much unpublished?

WS: More unpublished.

GB: Novels, stories, plays?

WS: Everything. You see, that's none of my business. That's the business of whoever is a scholar or whoever wants to. My business is to live. Writing is living and there comes a time when writing and living, art and reality, come very close and I want them to come close in my life. You'd say are you desperately (I hate to use the word) unhappy? And I would have to reply, unhappiness is impossible for me. Don't you see? Then are you a terribly happy person? I'd say, that also is impossible for me. I am an involved person. And that involvement is writing. That involvement is moving, that involvement is the participation in simple daily things: drinking tea, meeting people, listening to them, trying to understand them, watching them, having them watch me, they watch me.

I will not cry. I will not moan and groan about the hideous predicament of man, the impossible hell of man's soul, the imprisonment of man's destiny. For Christ's sake! We drink tea, we look at children, we look at old men, we hear them, we walk the streets and we see madness and we see beauty and we see folly, and we see wisdom and we see charity and we see love. What the hell! I'm going suddenly to make myself into the biggest fool of all time and pretend that I know anything more than to accept it? Ah! You say that's Saroyan's sentiments again, that it's his big yes-yeah saying and so forth. Yes, I'd day yes, that's by deliberate choice. If anybody might be said to have had a feeling for the other side of the choice, it should be me. My whole life, from the very earliest time was not easy, but I never quit.

GB: Do you think that you will stop writing altogether one day?

WS: I don't think so, I shall write up to my death, if possible. If not write, then I'll speak into the [pointing at the tape-recorder]. I'll say: *vazek perek an pane, es kani me khosk ounim eselik. Tzdesutioun eselen aratch, sireli hairenakitzner, yes aysdegh barkel em vor biti satkim hima, tzezi parevner ge ghrkem.* (Run, bring me that thing. I want to speak a few words to it. First, to say, "Goodbye until we met again, dearest compatriots. I am going to sleep in this place where I am going to depart for good. I will send you my goodbyes.") [laughs]

GB: Let's talk about death. You have written: "There come a day in the afternoon of the world when a man simply wants to lie down and close his eyes." How often do you have this feeling?

WS: At the writing of "One Day in the Afternoon of the World" I really meant to lie down on the bed and close my eyes. I only have thirty years to go before I'll be ninety-seven. At that time I'll close my eyes and so forth. But I am drawing near the time when death is an increasing reality. But don't forget that youth knows proximity and nearness to death more than maturity does. Because youth is swift, risk-taking, and aware of the fact that other youth die all the time. I have always felt death since my father died at thirty-six. I have had some very good friends who have had heart attacks, and they know that they are not going to recuperate, and they cry like babies. Now I ask myself, it if happens to me, will I do it too? It could be. We don't know. But it's such a humiliation to cry before death. You cry about other things. A man should cry. But because you are going to die, it's such a terrible thing. One of the toughest kids I knew used to cry all the time; he said "Bill, I'm going," and he cried, and he went forty-eight hours later. You see? Something tells them. The doctor doesn't have to tell them. I think the message comes unmistakably. I said you are going to be all right. He said "Bill, not this time." So we wonder about that. I have noticed that dying people have an irritability which is rather large, and one can use that as a measure, a probable closenesss to death. I'll give you an illustration: I had a Cadillac, I was taking my mother and my sister from Fresno to San Francisco and I turned the Cadillac up to get to the Skyline Boulevard. My mother said something when I turned. It was so irritable, unlike her, that I figured she had a slight stroke then, and this was retaliation to that stroke, and she died of a stroke. Apparently this was a hint, and I said that kind of unreasonable irritability isn't towards the event of turning, it's toward the event of death. And I"ve seen that happen to other people, and of course to be perfectly honest I've seen it happen to me, and it makes me realize, watch it!' [laughs]

Somebody said, "we die when we want to, we don't die until we want to." There was a girl in the Bagdassarian family (Dickran Bagdassarian married my mother's little sister Verkin) and Dickran was dispatched to help this little girl die of TB. She had been in the hospital and her family had become bankrupt. And he told me one of the saddest stories in the world. He said, "Penny, *me vakhenar, keghetzgoutioun bidi ella, anoushoutioun bidi ella, arev bidi ella,*" and little Penny said: "Uncle Dickran, *chem ouzer mernil.*" ("Penny, don't be afraid. There will be beauty, there will be sweetness, there will be sunlight" and little Penny said: "Uncle Dickran, I don't want to die.") Isn't that beautiful? Just don't ask me to die. I'll give you another little story: A friend of mine had many daughters and the daughter who was most like a butterfly was famous for playing a little piece called "The Butterfly." She got leukemia and I visited her two days before she died. Her little brother and father visited her the day she died. Her eyes closed and this what she said: (her little brother's name was Vahan) "Vahan, I've got to go now, I've got to go," and she died. Also my grandmother Lucy died at the age of eighty-eight and this is what she said at the end: *Ul chem grnar:* Isn't that beautiful?

"Can't hang on." How near are we to death in our experience? Any of us? How near are we to be willing to regard death as freedom? Sometimes that happens and I think it's lack of suicide that the people do feel that they will finally be delivered from all of that agony they're experiencing, it will be a relief.

GB: Have you ever thought of committing suicide?

WS: Never. But I will tell you something: When I was a kid I used to black out the universe before going to sleep, and I must confess that I used to be able to will in my mind the effacement of all things, not including myself. Now that was helpless. I'm interested in the fact that it was helpless. Is there a physiological longing in early life? Is there a longing for the void? The nearest suicide would have been (if we could interpret it that way) the effacement of matter, all matter, the universe, the sun.

I flipped my wig when I was in the army in London, I was going to kill some of the officers or myself. Suicide is also murder, you understand. I could have gone to the army psychiatrists, and I might have killed them. But even then, my impulse was to wait. I have some writings from those days which someday, if I look into it, must be incredible. I have a grim play called *Don't Go Away Mad*. The setting is a cancer ward in a San Francisco free hospital, overlooking the Golden Gate. The sun is down over there, all they can do is take away your pain with shots. They've got cancer. And this man called Brick, because he's got red hair, says to the other guys "no more tricks, we will break out of here, I've got 120 bucks, we'll drink in every bar on Pacific Street, we'll cruise and die." And he arouses a little bit of interest and they all collapse.

Death is death only when unwelcome, premature, wrong, humiliating, belittling, and a deprivation of one's own true character and fullness. Otherwise death is a benediction, and important expectation lying ahead. I don't mean that we yearn for it. For in closing the eyes in that allegorical sense, the only thing that would be is totality. Having reached the totality, if you can ever decide that there was such a time that the reaching is concluded, then why not?

You might ask me, do then you believe in the deciding party to the totality? I know of one great suicide. Morley Kennerley, the publisher, gathered his kids together, he said "I'm eighty-four years old, I see many things coming upon me, we are going to have this big celebration right here tonight, eat and drink, pretty soon I'm going to stop my life." Nobody objected to it, and he did.

GB: Hemingway?

WS: I would be embarrasssed though by such a violent suicide as poor Mr. Hemingway's. And remember, I speak with tremendous sympathy and understanding of the predicament of a man who can no longer endure himself. I sympathize profoundly, but I wish medical science, psychiatry, his luck, might have been different. I wish he hadn't done it, because such a humiliation was so painful to him. His wife, Mary Welch (I knew her too during the war), at first said that it was an accident, and so *Time* asked me (they phoned me in Paris) "Was it an accident?" I said certainly it was an accident. The man kills himself, that's always an accident, it's an accident that he has to kill himself. This is an accident of a failure of his identity. Failure of his being able to sustain himself to continue with himself. He used to try to walk into airplane propellers, those little airplanes. They just would grab him the poor guy. I saw him in the army, when he was a foreign correspondent and I was a private, we had some times in London [pause], it was getting sad, he equated reality with a continuation of his posey writing, and by posey I mean that hero character he invented, which the whole world would love and be influenced by it, couldn't be continued. I don't want to call Hem a dishonest writer, but essentially this is a fantasy writer.

GB: Did he influence you?

WS: Never! The New Testament and the Old Testament did much more than he did. Look, I try to acknowledge influences. If he did, the guy who influenced him influenced me more than Hemingway ever did, and that's Sherwood Anderson. I love Sherwood. I've written tributes to Sherwood, but I won't write a tribute to Hemingway as a writer, because first of all he'd like to feel that he influenced everybody. I think that's going too far, he didn't. Did he influence Steinbeck? Well, Steinbeck is a fairly ordinary writer insofar as usage of language is concerned, and Hemingway is a great, great stylist. That's all what you call a stylist. No, he didn't influence me. But also it would be dishonest not to say that I was unaware of his writing. Aware and respectful of its effectfulness. But I hated *For Whom the Bell Tolls,* I couldn't read it.

GB: Which writers have influenced your writing?

WS: Mark Twain and Walt Whitman. Guy de Maupassant really threw me into writing with full force. At technical high school in Fresno, learning to type so that I could be swift and efficient at writing not yet 14 years of age, in an anthology of short stories in the school library, I read a story called "The Bell" ("La Cloche") by Guy de Maupassant, that made me a writer. And he told me, tell a story, do not take sides. After that I was deeply moved by *The Adventures of Huckleberry Finn,* very deeply moved. Everything I read of Chekhov's, I liked. Plays and short stories. I liked also very much some of the comparatively insignificant writers of America who were only ahead of me by ten or twenty years. One was Sherwood Anderson, terrific. I like Ring Lardner. A very savage humorist. I liked Strindberg, the playwright. I liked Ibsen. I read plays as a kid. I liked to read plays and imagine them. I loved Shaw, George Bernard,

The Prefaces. One of the greatest influences on me was *Oliver Twist* by Charles Dickens, that's laughter, but in the midst of the most profound difficulties and sadness and isolation. I used to sell papers in the rain and go home and worry about Oliver Twist. I was in a worse condition than he was, but I used to worry about him. *Ayt kheghdj deghan, hima anor inch bidi badahi.* (That lovely boy, what is going to happen to him now?)

GB: In *Sam Ego's House* you've written the following: "Everything I write, everything I have written, is allegorical. This came to pass inevitably. I am a product of Asia Minor, hence the allegorical and the real are closely related in my mind. In fact all reality to me is allegorical." Let's talk a little about this.

WS: I accept every word of that. This afternoon you shared with me a luncheon and a wedding. Both were terribly real, were they not? And yet they are so rooted in allegory that they are a continuation of gatherings, of lifting glasses, of toasts, of honoring one another, of loving one another before we go to the grave. Remember, a lot of those people won't be here two years from now. The Bitlistzi will not be here in two years. I hate to say this but I know he is dying. Because his clamour, his clamour for acceptance, is death. These are allegorical. The wedding and our participation in it, even though we were only witnesses, yet we were sharing the whole adventure and the deepest implications of it. Everything is allegorical. How could it not be? It's especially allegorical if I think so and if I think so in my writing. You take [takes the book] *The William Saroyan Reader* I'll open this anywhere, here. "A Visitor in the Piano Warehouse"—allegorical.

GB: "Everything is allegorical" takes us back to the old times, to Asia Minor, the oral traditions of Armenia, to Armenian folklore. It seems that you *tell* your stories like famous storytellers of Armenia, you don't *write* them.

WS: Yes, but besides, my stories were told to me. Once I left the orphanage (just about the age of eight) I began to hear them from both my paternal and maternal grandmothers and from my mother's uncle, Garabed Saroyan, and from all my other relatives, old people. They all had stories.

GB: This also might explain your incredibly large output.

WS: There may be an explanation for what you refer to as incredibly large—is my my restless nature, and I want a day to be marked. The passing of a day has to be marked. I buy trash books. I make a drawing, and I put the date and everything, and twenty years later I look at it and study my mind of that time. Why did I draw like that? And it's interesting. I don't want any day to go by without something. That's been going on for more than forty years. Something must be done. I think it comes from the day when my father died. When I was a little kid and I had

nothing from him except six chairs. I didn't like the almost total effacement of my father, and I replied to that effacement: "Well, you are not
going to efface the son too. That will not be possible. I'll do something."
And before I chose writing, I studied the things that time cannot destroy.
They were statues, they were paintings, they were musical compositions,
and they were writing. Nothing else. Money did not enter into it.

GB: Is there anything that endures?

WS: The only thing that endures is relative truth and beauty. That
includes the world, the streets, the impertinences of the world; that is,
the railways and the ships and the airplanes and the towers, and the
stadiums and all the rest of it. For me, I tried to tell myself long ago:
"Remember hieroglyphics and words chiseled in stone, the Rosetta Stone
for instance, and when you write, think that it must go into stone, and
then you will say something." It can paralyze you, if you insist that this is
going to go into stone. You might not say anything for a long time.

GB: You have memory as well as imagination.

WS: Where is the question?

GB: It's a statement.

WS: Memory arrives early with pain, with deprivation, with denial. If
you are the center of a loving home and family, your memory will not be
quick, it will be delayed because you are in a great condition. If you are
deprived of your father by death and your mother by necessity, and you
are in a strange smelling place, like an institution, the first thing you're
going to remember is the separation of your mother. She's gone. You're
not three years old. She's gone and she says: "Now you're a big man, no
tears." So you stop. You say my mother knows. I am a big man. Then the
superintendent comes. He doesn't look right, he doesn't smell right. He
takes you by the hand and he speaks in a very jovial way and he puts you
down in a small boy's dormitory: "That's your bed." That will cause
memory to begin. If my father came home from work and took me by
the hand, he said, let's go take a walk, and let's go look at the vines, the
flowers, and hear the birds, I won't remember that, there's no trauma.
Memory is imagination. There's a kinship because what you see and what
you remember is never literally what it is. It's what it is to you. And that is
an order of imagination. I went to New York just before I was twenty and
was intrigued by the subway that I took, to go to work every morning. I
started at six in Washington Market, and the people on the subway to me
were everything else in the world as well as people. One was a potato, one
was an onion, one was a lizard, one was a snake, one was a canary, one
was a hog, one was an elephant. And I wanted to write a book, an
important novel called *The Subway*. Also *The Way of the Subconscious*, and I
never did it. But this refers to seeing people in great numbers, remem-

bering them, and vitalizing what we call the imagination. Now what is the imagination? Imagination is the real, recalled, it's all it is!

GB: In the "Armenian Writers" you say that your name is Zavzag. Are you a *zavzag* (idiot)?

WS: [laughs long and heartily] Oh yes! That story came out in the *Yale Review*. I had to write it. I knew it was a little bit uncharitable about certain friends of mine, certain people that I had met in the Armenian circles. But we are so charming in our sincerities and in our self-importance. The story touches on those things. It's a funny story.

GB: Are you mainly serious?

WS: By nature, by the fact of being, yes, I am very serious. How can I not be serious? I'm very serious. I don't want to be serious to the point of paralysis, of ineffectuality, of not being able to function, of looking and saying "It's hopeless."

I went to Calcutta and for six days I was there. This beautiful woman is sitting on the sidewalk in front of the rich hotel with her four children. They lived there. I look and say to myself: that woman is the most beautiful woman in the world, those children are beautiful, they LIVE there. Now you'd say what we are going to do about her? Nothing. Except write. That's all I can do. So you can't despair but you cannot fail to notice that on and on goes our terrible overpowering accumulation of the unresolvable story. I did a play in London called *Sam the Highest Jumper of Them All* in which there is a song:

> Too many people
> the wise men warn
> too many people
> who should never have been born
> too many people
> who take too long to die
> too many people
> not counting you and I

The grammar is wrong, but there aren't too many people to the people that are there. There's not enough for them. That's all. Too little: what is it that the people need? I don't know. Too little space? Too little rice? Too little shelter? Too little luck? Too little charity from the rest of us? But in Calcutta I saw a kind of human degradation and dignity that is hard to make use of. Someday I hope to write about that woman on the sidewalk, and those children and the people passing by. I hope someday to make something of that.

GB: Do you always try to make use of everything you see?

WS: Yes, I try to.

GB: You never forget that you are a writer?

WS: Never, never if possible. You will forget that you are alive. The man who gathers money never forgets that he's gathering money. The man who is trying to gather a usable procedure for himself, such as myself, never forgets that and a usable procedure is expressed in writing. That's my work.

GB: Don't you get fed up?

WS: No, I don't get fed up.

GB: Isn't it difficult not to get fed up?

WS: Let it be difficult. Why should it be easy? Of course it's difficult. What do I care about that. There's much more difficult things. A more difficult thing is to be deprived of my life: I spent three years as a private in the American army. I had only one enemy that more than anything killed me; that's the American army; thank Christ they didn't get me. But they would kill me. Nothing elso would kill me. You see, the thing that is difficult is escaping from these large orders of what I have to call historic rendering of the individual to helplessness . . .

GB: You talked a while ago about your song "Too many people", let's talk about music and Saroyan. You have written the lyrics and tunes of several songs; and one was an international hit, "Come on-a my house."

WS: [starts to sing]
Come on-a my house, in my house
I'm gonna give you candy
come on-a my house, in my house
I'm gonna give you apple plum
and apricot hey!
Come on-a my house, in my house
I'm gonna give you candy
come on-a my house in my house
I'm gonna give you everything

GB: "Everything I've done has been sort of song." Explain this.

WS: Ah! I have a book; my first play, *My Heart's in the Highlands*, is a song [he sings]

> my heart is in the highlands
> my heart is not here . . .

and so on. *The Time of Your Life* is all songs. Many songs are in there and then Reginald Beane the black boy, tried some on his piano and put it in; and Gene Kelly brought some of his own ballet and put it in, and we orchestrated the whole thing. It's like a kind of sonata. I have one book in which the structure unknown to the reader is symphonic. That is a book called *Rock Wagram*. You state the theme, you enlarge upon it and you resolve it. I have eleven themes in the front, eleven themes in the middle and eleven themes in the back, and they all work to one conclusion. The form is musical. How you'd say "What is the meaning of that?" The meaning of it is simply this: if there is a communication of form as language itself, form being the language, it's in music. With us it is not the form being the communication, it's the words that we put into the form. Now for instance, I find it and I won't permit anybody to belittle that man's talent, that nobody uses the piano like Chopin. Frederic Chopin is the man who made the piano speak everything. And if you listen to the ballads and the nocturnes and the preludes and the waltzes and the polonaises, and the two concerti, he speaks, he says virtually everything. He says comedy, he says laughter, he says madness, he says profound sorrow and he says melancholy. He says the whole range but with a deep, decent courtesy. You'd say why do you use the word courtesy? Because I say courtesy is the true kindness, is the true mark of the civilized human being. I can't see any culture in which courtesy is not central. If you don't have it, forget it. That is the mark of a real culture. The Armenian has it very strong. And strangely, I think he has it stronger with strangers than with his neighbors . . .

GB: Are you an Armenian Don Quixote?

WS: No; or I don't know enough about it; no, I'm not; Don Quixote is Don Quixote and I am an Armenian Saroyan, that's enough, I'm not like anybody else; *Yes Saroyan me;* I have written a play incidentally in English and I may have mentioned it to you that I am going to put it on tape in the Armenian language to be taken to Soviet Armenian and produced there. I'll call it *Ouzenk chouzenk hay enk* (Like or not, we are Armenians). I think it's an interesting play, it's a good play, it's unique for me.

GB: Have you ever thought of shaving your moustache?

WS: In the days when I was searching the world for a bride, the mother of the kids, the beautiful girl that was out there, I tried to take the moustache off. I look terrible without it. It isn't that I don't look terrible with it, but no, I wouldn't take it off. Recently I saw it was going out too far so I trimmed it; I even got a haircut too; these are concessions one makes to *hayotz parker: amot e, kich me gdre adi, kich me mazeret gdre, amot e* (Armenian pride: it's shameful, cut it a little, cut your hair a little, it's shameful). [laughs] They say, *darorinag ellank, paytz ayschap darorinag betz che ellank* (Let's be different, but not that different). We do wish to look well enough, I think we all do, we have the right to, it is better to look well, it is better to look healthful. I study people quickly, almost instantaneously. I can tell healthy people from their eyes, and I see many people where the eyes get rheumy, blood shot, and coals in the eyes; that old Bitliszi got them, I'm beginning to get them but not very much. I'm very pleased with myself about losing weight. I used to be fat; I was close to two hundred pounds and hundred-sixty-five is much better; it's not wrong to have vanity, be concerned about appearances. My mother was very fond of her sister's boy Zaven; my mother had a tremendous sense of humor and she was a great mimic, she could imitate everybody and Zav was a kid who was always in trouble; one day he is visiting my mother and she's giving him a good meal "*gloukh gakhetz geragou bidi ouder.*" And Zaven looks up and says: *Gides Takouhi, mart kich me al desk bedk e ounena;* if anybody doesn't have desk it's Zav. My mother says, *haba mart desk bedk e ounena, ayt kou kisbat desk e?* (He craps on your head, you give him dinner. And Zaven looks up and says: "Do you know, Takouhi, a man has to have a certain appearance; if anybody doesn't have that front, it's Zav. My mother says, "Of course a man has to have front, but is that your best front?" [laughs]

GB: It's time to talk about your so-called "vices."

WS: Like what?

GB: Drinking, gambling, debts . . .

WS: I share with every human being in the world an understandable wish not to be a fool. I also share with almost everybody in the world (perhaps there are some exceptions) of having been a fool, and being a fool. To pretend otherwise would be dishonest and I cannot pretend it. I would rather not be a fool I believe, but I do share the folly of all of us. It has modified my soul. I have under really inexcusable circumstances made an awful fool of myself (there's no lullaby in what I'm trying to say) and not having the right to do so. I have drunk to excess on many occasions and was once nearly an alcoholic in the sense that I needed alcohol to start the day. That wasn't for long and I didn't need to go to a psychiatrist or to a doctor to get over with it. I just needed to straighten myself up, which I was able to do.

GB: When was that?

WS: That was in 1952–53 when I was separated from my kids after the second marriage. I am not sure if ever I may have been basically at fault about understanding that wasn't the time; I think that was the time. I felt that those kids needed me more than they needed anybody in the world and that their being deprived of me was a terrible thing. Whereas the reality was probably, that they were having a much better life with me out of the way [laughs]. I could be very well guilty of an indulgence, of a misconception about my role there, but we, the Armenians tend to be fathers to everybody. I really was close to my kids, I loved them. I gave them everything; that is me, of myself, of my time. They haven't forgotten it. So that time I did become nearly an alcoholic.

GB: Then came gambling.

WS: Yet. We know Dostoyevsky was a gambler. We know his life; the compulsion that he apparently set to be in. Illusion so that he would go write his way back: by losing he would be driven into new writing. Do you understand what I mean? This sometimes happens to people; I wrote *The Human Comedy* because I had thrown away more than three thousand dollars in Las Vegas in one night. Now that's very little. I've thrown away much more than that; I've thrown away in one afternoon thirty minutes at a club, more than ten thousand dollars.

GB: Your debts?

WS: Well, the debts actually began during the three years I was in the army. Also my wife lived beyond my income; she was supposed to be independently rich, but it was a falsehood; and she was a terrible burden. I'm speaking impersonally; and also she had to have a lot of parties, and lots of people and everything was expensive. I was living way over my head. No writer should be asked to do such a social life. Also I canceled out the productiveness of my best three years of being in the army.

GB: When was that?

WS: That was from 1942 to 1945, during the war; I was here in Paris after the liberation and in London for many months and then in Luxembourg and Germany. I was hospitalized, sent back, and the war was over. So, the debts came from not writing and from not having a backlog of writing to offer to editors and publishers and from a spendthrift wife. Gambling was supposed to liberate me from all of this oppression and preoccupation with money and on the contrary it made it worse. One day I owed my bookie more than $42,000. I was so desperate that I said all right, I have no money, give me Grim Magic in the last race at Arlington in Chicago. I put my wife in the Cadillac and I turned on the radio to where we get the results and we were going to San Francisco up to the Cliffhouse he says "Arlington Park in Chicago, the winner in No. 4 is Grim Magic". I won sixty thousand dollars! So that's what you're hoping for; but of course that's fantasy, that's madness.

GB: And you generally lost?

WS: Well, you have to, if you gamble. The winning gambler is a cheat, he's a liar. He knows something there. No, I had sensational good luck, but if you win let's say two or three thousand dollars and you are not satisfied and you persist, you will lose, of course.

GB: You have said: I don't think my writing is sentimental, although it is a very sentimental thing to be human being. This is very well said, but it does not stop your writing from being regarded as sentimental by Anglo-Saxon criticism.

WS: We were speaking earlier about being Armenian. Homer Macauley in *The Human Comedy*, actually Homer Machelian, or Hrant Makelian or Haroutioun Michaelian or any Armenian name, is not speaking sentimentally. And yet when the Americans do my kind of thing, which is so natural to the Armenians, it comes out sentimental. Of course they don't even know how to act either these people; in the movie it was horrible, I was in the army when I saw it, I wanted to sue Metro-Goldwyn-Mayer, but you can't do that. Look, I will let time settle that account. I know many writers who are supposed to be tough hard, realistic writers, they are sentimental, I know them, I am not sentimental.

GB: Is Beckett sentimental?

WS: I need time. [long pause] Absolutely not. I'm referring more strongly not to the novels which you know (*Molloy* and all the others) but I don't, I'm referring only to the play about which I wrote for the Columbia long-playing disc. *Waiting for Godot* is one of the most incredible plays ever in the history of the theater. A play which is like a rock, and like sunlight and a landmark in view of others it might be called sentimental, but not in my view, No. Now you find some play of mine and say compare to that. Incidentally the theme of waiting came long before Godot, I have it in *The Time of Your Life* better than anybody else except for Beckett. Beckett like Joyce his master is a tremendous scholar! His scholarship is enormous. But I won't go into that because that's irrelevant.

GB: Is it right to find imitations or echoes of Beckett in your *The Cave Dwellers?*

WS: No! not in *The Cave Dwellers* but in another play, deliberately.

GB: Which one?

WS: *Life along the Wabash* and if it were ever published I would acknowledge that. No, *The Cave Dwellers* is mine, totally, it has nothing to do with Beckett. I am very honest. The other had. There I was actually thinking in terms of *Waiting for Godot: The Cave Dwellers,* if it is in any tradition, is a variation of *The Time of Your Life.* That's what is is [Two days later, W.S. sent me a letter, I find it appropriate to use here an excerpt from it.] ". . . sometime when you have a taped interview with Mr. Samuel Beckett you might find it permissible to ask him if he was influenced in the writing of *Waiting for Godot* by the scene between Joe and May L. in *The Time of Your Life* in which the very essence of *Waiting for Godot* is presented in a profoundly simple way, a play that was produced in New York in 1939 and published that year in America and the following year in London. No. Mr. Beckett's writing in any of its forms did not influence anything of mine, including the play I forced myself to imagine might have been the victim of such an influence, that is the play written and produced and directed in 1961, called *Life Along the Wabash.* And there is enormous sentimentality in *Waiting for Godot,* and I wonder that you didn't notice; far more, than in my most affirmative piece of writing, *The Human Comedy.*"

GB: There has been a prevailing regret in American criticism that you have not fully developed your extraordinary talent. What's your opinion?

WS: You will understand by now how respectful I am of the probable validity of almost anything that's said. There's probably some validity to this. I'll have to tell you a story: Max Baer was in the ring with Joe Louis; fighting; and Joe Louis wants the championship, and Max Baer doesn't like to get hurt; and after the first round he goes back to his corner and his second says "Champ, you're doin' great, you're doin' great, he didn't lay a glove on you" and they did that for three rounds and finally Max Baer says "Now look, I've been in there three rounds and every time I come back and sit here, you say "Champ, you're doin' great, he didn't lay a glove on you." For Christ's sake keep your eye on the referee, because somebody in there is kicking the hell out of me!" [laughter]. Now, somebody keep an eye on those critics, because for forty years I've been working very hard, and if I am not fulfilling, who the hell is? Then there is no such thing as fulfillment. You better keep your eyes on the critics then maybe they are wrong. I am not lazy. I was paralyzed, I was slowed down, and I was made sick and made mad by the three years in the army and two-three years after that (that's when I wrote the sick *Laughing Matter* because I was sick). After that I have been faithful to myself, I have been faithful to my talent to the best that I know; now, don't you see; I have many many friends who are very famous writers, and faded out completely: James T. Farrell, Steinbeck. I continue to be a real writer. I'm interested in everything.

GB: But your popularity faded out.

WS: Oh absolutely. The popularity, that's none of my business. No. I don't care about that. Somebody said: "You're not as famous as you used to be." I said: to you I am not, to me I am. I'm still very famous. I don't have to be famous in the external sense. I don't need to. I am famous to whoever it matters and it matters to me. But what the hell is popularity? To whom? I will not knock any contemporary, but at the same time I am obliged to make a statement: I'm now in my forty-first year as a published writer; of the published works only, not the unpublished, I am satisfied that it can stand beside anybody of anytime; if noticed, if read; I mean the whole. I am also able to believe about myself impersonally that now or at anytime there was never a writer like myself; and this is not the evidence or significance of myself alone, but it is certainly part of it. As long as reading is done, no writer has more reason to believe that he will be read more than myself. I believe these things. Now you'd say all of it? Hell no! nobody reads all of anybody; but some of it will always be there, and the specialists will study all of it, whoever the hell the specialist is. That's his work. No, I have no sense of rivalry, competition with anybody; I have enormous jealousy, I get very angry when other people

make a lot of money for instance; and get super famous and so on; but
that's my limitation, that's my character, and I don't mind it at all; I'm
amused by it. But at the same time there's nobody better than I am. No
writer is better than I am. I don't give a goddamn anybody you want to
mention, Beckett, Joyce or anybody. If there is anybody enormous in the
English language of our time it's Beckett's master, Joyce; *Finnigans Wake*
and *Ulysses,* but don't forget with punning and their enormous double
meanings and triple meanings and fun and criticism and interior dramas
and so forth; both are amusements for the snob and the expert, the rest
of us are excluded from it; we've to have guide books. *Chellar!* (impossible!) a guide book to read a book that is supposed to be for me? What the
hell do I need a guide book for! But still you can't take away from him
that he is an enormity, an enormity; preposterously, remember the man
who devoted all that time to his art. To know the enormity of this man,
read *Dubliners;* you know that he is the greatest in conventional writing
so why wouldn't he be the greatest in all the experimental writing, which
is so magnificent? But you can't read it. You can't read it the way I can
read the Russians in translation; also the way I can read Guy de Maupassant.

GB: In the background of the "high seriousness" and the pessimism of
American literature, your happy and good people could have brought a
new warmth to the reader. Why is even this merit taken as a charge
against you?

WS: [laughs long and heartily] Well, because critics are perverse. But
let's not put it that way. We don't know why. I suppose what I should say,
but I'm not going to . . . There is some flaw in everybody. But I will not
acknowledge that; I think I am misread. Walter Kerr wrote a review of a
revival at the City Center in New York of *The Time of Your Life;* he says,
"The other time around I thought this was a kind of sentimental, beery
play; no this is a savage play, a ruthless play; this is an unrelenting grim
play." Now, what is the significance of what I'm saying? The significance
of what I'm saying is that very thing that was charged as being sentimental can with time by the same man be seen as something else. *The Human
Comedy* is charged to be the most sentimental and so forth: a man dies
and the family feels the loss of him, his pal in the army who is an orphan
comes home to that family and he looks as if he might marry their
daughter. I think this is epic, I don't think it's sentimental. I think it's
allegorical; I think that it's slightly at worse if you could say about it is
childlike in the writer's deliberate choice, just as he says in the book
"Death, do not go to my town"; and that is myself also, don't hurt the
family too much, don't take away the kids of the family too much, in that
sense I'm guilty yes, of a certain longing of a certain deliberate chosen,

disciplined longing; you'd say well what about in your own life; I don't ask death not to come to my family, death not to come to me; I don't want that woman sitting on the sidewalk with her little kids! She is sitting there and she's not dead, she is alive, her kids are alive and they are beautiful; all five of them. Then in a certain kind of an arrogance, in a certain kind of annoyance, I'm gonna say: all right if the implication is necessary, by God, Saroyan you are sentimental; my reply is f... you! I am sentimental, I don't mind being sentimental, I'll be sentimental; you have to live with it, because besides being sentimental I am one of the greatest writers who ever lived, and you gonna have to put up with that aspect of me too; sentimental; *and* other things.

GB: Are you a careless writer?

WS: No! I am a swift writer but not careless. No, no, No!

GB: Do you revise?

WS: I didn't use to. I thought it was cheating at first. My first book has almost no revisions. But the second book begins, and then after that I revise. I'll tell you why: [pause] I decided that my responsibility is not to provide a casebook for the psychiatrist or the specialist or the scientist about William Saroyan. My responsibility is to provide the unknown reader with the best thing that I can give him without a betrayal of William Saroyan. Here is the book that you put beside me and I'm glad to see it [*The William Saroyan Reader*]; open it anywhere, it's all right, it's OK. Now for instance I open here to "The Man with the Heart in the Highlands." That's good writing! Over here "Corduroy Pants"; that's good; "The Pomegranate Trees," good writing; "The Poor and Burning Arab" [he says the title in Armenian: *kheghj ou Grag Arab*], that's great.

GB: Do you regret anything in the writing that you have done in the past forty years?

WS: I must confess that I do not regret any writing that I have written or published or that is not published; for this probable reason. [pause] The worst that I could write would be useful in comparing with the other. Somerset Maugham in giving out the *Traveller's Collection of Fiction* has "The Daring Young Man on the Flying Trapeze," and says Saroyan is an in-and-out writer. He will have eight out and one in. I accept that; that's all right with me, I'm not concerned about that; but I want the so-called "failed" stories as well; I don't mind; I don't think any of my stories are really bad.

GB: Did you revolutionize American writing?

WS: I think I did. I certainly broke down the door for all of the playrights who came after me and that includes Tennessee Williams and that includes that whole gang; yes. Albee and all of those guys could not do it except that I did it with *My Heart's in the Highlands* and *The Time of*

Your Life and then also *Love's Old Sweet Song,* and just before I went to the army, they drafted me from directing my play, how can I direct it they drafted me; that was the play called *Across the Board on Tomorrow Morning.*

GB: Is is right to say that your best output remain your plays and short stories and not the biographies and novels?

WS: I think that you have perhaps a preference. I would not distinguish. Saroyan is Saroyan. I hate to put it that way but that is so. I am the character whether I am in a short story as Mr. Spezzafly, or whether I am the kid in "The Daring Young Man on the Flying Trapeze," or the kid in *Fight Your Own War,* or the song and dance boy that Gene Kelly played in *The Time of Your Life.* It's all Saroyan. The autobiographical notes I consider in the long run probably as enduring as anything that I have. My favorite? If we want an addiction to form, then I would choose plays and stories rather than novels, although I am fond of one or two of my short novels and will not repudiate any of them. *Rock Wagram* is a good novel and it will come back. *The Laughing Matter* is too glum. I tend to be creatively, aesthetically embarrassed by the writing in which I don't laugh. And there is no laughter in that book. And that depresses me.

GB: From your short stories please name the three that you think are your best.

WS: Well, I can answer that, and I'll put first "The Daring Young Man on the Flying Trapeze," because it came first. "The Man with the Heart in the Highlands," second; and [pause] the third I want to get to something a little bit more away. The two I have named were away from the forms as they were doing them. They had an influence, those two. "The Daring Young Man," influenced a lot of people, so did "The Man with the Heart in the Highlands," the third one, I'm taking time, it's hard to choose, let's say that it probably would have to be something like that which came out in *Harper's,* the last two stories of mine in *Harper's* were "Isn't Today the Day?" that story, that's a landmark story and the other one is "Cowards." Those two would have to be third; take your choice in either one of those.

GB: Name your best play.

WS: I give it to my first, *My Heart's in the Highlands.*

GB: Again? First the story *The Man with the Heart in the Highlands* and now the play that you made out of the story?

WS: Well, no, you're right; that will have to be *The Time of Your Life.* That's true, you're right, you're right.

GB: And one novel.

WS: *Tracy's Tiger* I like very much; there's another one called *The Oldest Story in the World* which is neglected, is pretty good. But *Tracy's Tiger* of the short novels and of the large novels *Rock Wagram.*

GB: And one from your autobiography.

WS: *Not Dying.*

GB: What's the quality you like most in man?

WS: Well, there's an order of sincerity, both in the old and in the young, and puzzlement and pain that is heartbreaking and beautiful. And I cherish that very deeply. To get to the proper answer to your question, there is one irresistible, appealing and attractive quality in man that is being unstoppable. In the earliest films of Charlie Chaplin, he had that quality. He had nothing and he was pursued by the police and by bad faith. Faith was always giving him a bad time, but he was unstoppable. This is compulsion to survive. We Armenians certainly have that.

GB: What do you think of this interview?

WS: I'm pleased; you have it on tape, I'm not going to qualify anything; whatever it is that I said, it's part of me in relation to this occasion; the 25th of May today [1975]; and I only said of one work of mine something that I was obliged to say when you said "Is there any book that you regret?"; I don't regret it but I'm not pleased with *The Laughing Matter;* and the reason that I acknowledged that displeasure is that it doesn't have any laughter. I don't believe that even in the casket we should not laugh; that there is a right for us to notice the comedy of ourselves with love, with astonishment, with gratitude and with what the Mushetzis use in their expressing a feeling of change and loss: *inch eink, inch eghank* (What are we, what have we become?). [laughs]

Rites of Passage

ARAM SAROYAN

I got the telephone call on a morning in late June. It was from a law office somewhere—it sounded like a long-distance call, but I never made certain of that—and the man who spoke to me was making an inquiry on behalf of a lawyer, who no doubt had more pressing, first-person business somewhere else. It was an inquiry about a play of my late father's— the sort of call I get from time to time now. I referred him to the attorney for the William Saroyan Foundation. As the call was concluding, the man, whose vocal inflection sounded possibly Armenian, mentioned that he has just read my piece on my father in the July 1982 issue of *California* magazine. My interest picked up considerably. I hadn't seen the magazine yet; he had gotten an early copy by subscription.

"It's very interesting," he told me. Did I imagine he was hedging on a straight-forward compliment here?

"Yes," I said. I knew it was interesting myself.

He laughed, perhaps uneasily.

Then he added: "The title is 'Daddy Dearest.'"

My breathing did a sort of somersault that made me grateful I was on the phone and not facing the man. It took me a moment to restore a breathing pattern that would allow me to speak again.

"'Daddy Dearest?'" I asked, as levelly as possible.

"Yes," he said. "It's very interesting."

"I'll bet," I said, emboldened by the shock. He laughed again. We never got beyond that word—interesting. Now that I think about it, though, he wasn't the worst sort of person in the world to break the news that you have added a tiny item to the luggage of that swiftest and most indefatigable traveler of our time, mass media. "Daddy Dearest" . . . I see.

Sorry about that, Pop.

Not altogether unexpectedly, Fresno, wherein reside apparently a number of *California* readers and where there are certainly more than a number of William Saroyan fans, took the article personally. There was an editorial in the *Fresno Bee* denouncing me. The local columnist hit the ceiling. There were several Armenians on the television Evening News talking about the bad boy I was for writing the piece. There were also many distraught letters to the editor in the *Bee*.

First a Fresno TV News team was going to fly up to the San Francisco Bay Area to interview me on camera. On second thought, they decided to do it over the phone. We had a preliminary interview during which I detected more than an edge of hostility in the female reporter's line of questioning. My father's name is on a very large building in the downtown Arts Center in Fresno. The article, excerpted from my book, *Last Rites: The Death of William Saroyan*, portrayed my father as a person of mortal failings. However, at the same time all of this was happening, other people were phoning and writing me that they found the article compassionate and moving. (The title aside, I thought the editors of *California* did an excellent job of excerpting the book).

Aram Saroyan and his father at a television studio in Los Angeles, 1953. *(Courtesy of Aram Saroyan.)*

By the time I did the interview that was taped for broadcast, I had decided to take a gentle tack. I would tread softly and even apologetically. I realized, after all, that these people loved my father and, upset by the unfortunate title *California* had given my piece, they were rallying to his defense.

The reporter who conducted the taped interview, a man, went about it less fiercely than the woman had—but there was still an edge to his voice. He told me that a lot of people were accusing me of capitalizing on my father's famous name, of writing the book for money. Had I?

I said a few things about the book that were meant to be indirect replies to that question. I had written it in a white heat. I had never before had a book happen like this one. It had been as close to being an involuntary reflex as I could imagine writing a book ever could be. It had been written in three weeks.

Had I written it for money, the reporter wanted to know again. I sensed that he was under a certain pressure to ask that question a second time; that the force of community sentiment was looming behind him. It was his final question.

"No," I answered. I didn't say anything more.

The truth, of course, was less simple. For the first ten years of the twenty I've been a published writer, I wrote mostly poetry. Then, after marrying and starting a family, I branched out into prose. I wrote an autobiographical novel about the sixties, which I imagined was going to make a financial killing. My father had told me again and again over the years that if I wrote a novel, it would establish me. So, at last, I took his advice and wrote one. Then, for the following eight months, I tried to get either an agent or a publisher for it. Though many who read the book seemed to genuinely like it, I was told repeatedly that publishers just weren't interested in the 1960s anymore. It was the spring of 1973. I had a wife and a two-and-half-year-old daughter. And that fall we had our second daughter. And still there was nobody who wanted my book.

I fell back on my poetry and little-press background—"Don't kick down the ladder you stepped up," wrote the poet Louis Zukofsky—and the book was eventually brought out by a small outfit in the Berkshires. A nice job, but no money. However, my father now read the book, and liked it.

"It's their fault," he told me over the phone, referring to the publishers who had turned the manuscript down. Then he gave me what still strikes me—for the thoughtful room it leaves for future aspiration—as the best spot-review a young writer could get from an older writer: "It comes close to being great," he said of my book.

"Thanks, Pop," I replied, delighted.

Next I did a biography of a beat-generation poet, and helped along by the revival of interest in the beat generation, this one was published by a major New York house. I was given a modest advance, but it was still the most money I'd seen for a piece of writing. Then the book came out. And the critics hated it.

I had written the book as a kind of stylistic tribute to beat writing at the same time it told the story of the beat generation. Unexpectedly, however, it was reviewed the way Kerouac's own books had been reviewed when they appeared in the late fifties—with one exception. I didn't get the review in the daily *New York Times* that said this book was my generation's *The Sun Also Rises*. I really missed that one. But I got all of the others—the ones that were less reviews than they were character assassinations.

I developed a cough. I told my wife that the reviews didn't really affect me at all. But the cough wouldn't go away. I read about John Keats. He had gotten such a roasting from the critics on his first book that Shelley said it had killed him. My wife told me it was an honor to get such bad reviews—that only very good artists got them. We talked about the way the impressionists had been received at the beginning in France. It was me and Kerouac, me and Keats, me and Renoir. But my cough still wouldn't go away. It occured to me that I might have the initial symptoms of throat cancer. Perhaps I did. But thanks to the support of my wife, my family and friends, and of those readers who liked the book and wrote or told me so, after several months, I seemed to recover my balance—and the cough gradually went away.

However, I made the decision not to do another book. I'd learned my lesson. I didn't want to die. All I wanted was to make a living. I took up screenwriting. It was a new ball game. Let my friends scoff and accuse me of selling out; I'd cry all the way to the bank. I would stay young while they grew prematurely crotchety, guarding their dignity and integrity, yet committed to nothing so much as dispiriting poverty. But I was going to have a *life*. The first script was written in a breezy two months. One draft.

And only one problem. It wasn't, in the end, a very commercial script.

The next script—was different. It was a good idea, but it wasn't an easy script to write. At times, in fact, it seemed impossible. I did one draft. Then another. And then another after that. It's now in its eighth draft. And it's been optioned, but not yet bought. I've made a discovery. Screenwriting can be gruesomely hard work, and until a movie that one has written is made, one is not likely to be paid a lot of money for the work.

It was shortly after I'd finished the fifth draft of the screenplay that I got a call from my sister, Lucy, telling me that my father, from whom I'd been estranged for the previous three-and-a-half years, was dying of cancer. And the next day I got another call from Lucy, now in Fresno, reporting through her tears that my father didn't want to see her—or me.

Around ten days before, after finishing the fifth draft of the script, I happened to have started a diary—more or less to take up the slack each day now that I was off any writing assignment. With Lucy's second call, the diary turned into a marathon journal which I wrote eight, ten, and twelve hours a day as my father was dying. Since I had been told in no uncertain terms that he didn't want to see me, writing the journal became the means by which I tried to deal with the fact that he was dying without being able to know that reality at first-hand.

The initial entries after Lucy's call were written in anger. Suddenly, for the first time in my life, I was allowing myself to feel the depths of my own frustration as the son of a famous man whom I knew to be quite different from his public legend. As I wrote these first entries, I won't deny that visions of a six-figure book contract danced in my head (over toward the side, as it were). After all, I was telling a story that the world didn't know about a celebrity; indeed it even crossed my mind that this might be another *Mommie Dearest*.

But as the days went by, my mood changed, and so did the book. It became clear to me, once I had vented my anger, that there were good and deep reasons why my father was the man that he was. It also became clear that the way for me to deal with my frustration at being kept at a distance from him during the final days, was to go to see him—whatever the consequences.

The heart of *Last Rites* is the meeting I had with my father in his hospital room. The emotional culmination of the book was also the emotional culmination of our relationship, which had now spanned thirty-seven years. Had I not been writing the journal, I can't be sure I would have gone to see him at all. It was the deepening frustration in what I wrote that enabled me to see the necessity of my visiting him. My life and my journal interacted and, in conjunction, brought me to an entirely unexpected moment of healing with my father.

I never got the six-figure contract. There weren't, after all, any wire hangers in my story. It's true, *California* called the excerpt they ran "Daddy Dearest," but almost all of the readers I heard from said they thought the title had misrepresented the piece they read.

Then the book itself came out, and I steeled myself for another onslaught from reviewers. Remember, I had intended to give up writing books forever—to protectively gild myself with the big money in Hollywood. But then *Last Rites* happened, and once it happened, I knew from the outset that I wanted to publish it. This was so important, perhaps, because when one is born into a celebrity's family, one hears so often from other people what kind of person the celebrity is. Since I was now reporting something quite different from what had been reported *to* me all my life, an essential part of completing the arc the book began was to have it end up—not on shelf somewhere, but in that larger world which for so long had been telling me my father was another man than the one I knew.

But the reviews worried me. For if my biography of the beats had provoked such malevolent attacks, who dared imagine what might happen with a book that debunked my father's image as a sort of boisterous Santa Claus of American letters? It was worth it to me to suffer whatever slings and arrows might loom over the horizon in order to finally have my private truth made public, but it certainly made me uneasy.

But then the reviews began to come in and they turned out to be wonderful: the *New York Times Book Review,* the *San Francisco Chronicle,* the *Los Angeles Times,* the *Washington Post,* the *Philadelphia Inquirer,* the *Chicago Sun-Times,* the *Alabama Journal,* the *Dallas Morning News,* and many more—the reviews of a lifetime, certainly of *my* lifetime. And the letters that came from readers were, if anything, even more wonderful: lovely, deep, and caring letters that told me what was true of my father and me, was true, too, of the relationships many others struggled with in their own families. In fact, the book seemed to reach both critics and general readers, less on the level of a celebrity exposé than as the story of a father and as son, and of a passage in both their lives when, at the very eleventh hour, the two had finally broken through to one another.

Will the book ultimately diminish my father's name and reputation? In my opinion, no. It's true, he doesn't emerge from my pages as the bigger-than-life folk hero of his later persona, but it might be remembered that the public was never very drawn to that mustachioed legend in any case, as the neglect my father suffered during the last thirty years of his career testifies. Whereas the man in *Last Rites,* though both troubled and difficult, seems to me a deeper, more complex, and more compellingly *human* figure than his public image had ever allowed. I don't see how this could do him harm.

Likewise, the anger I released in the first part of *Last Rites* now seems to me to have been only the necessary, initial step in an extended, and ultimately healing emotional trajectory. For if, at the beginning, I myself entertained sly notions of "Daddy Dearest," in the end, knowing more of both myself and my father, I discovered I held him dear indeed.

How Like a Unicorn

GILLISANN HAROIAN

In the following interview, Lucy Saroyan, the younger of William Saroyan's two children, discusses his life, his work, and his fatherhood, from her childhood memories to adult recollections.

The thirty-seven-year-old Ms. Saroyan has recently moved back to New York. "It was a literary exchange," Saroyan explains, as she swapped her California apartment with the grandson of Maxwell Anderson, a contemporary of her father's. In Ms. Saroyan's tiny, informal studio, there are traces of her father, such as a small bowl filled with shells and water; when they were children, their father would always take Lucy and Aram on walks where he'd stop to pick up rocks, twigs, shells, pebbles, and bits of Nature he loved.

Back in New York, Ms. Saroyan plans to expand her career in acting and voice-overs. She attended Dalton High School and was then trained at Northwestern University, the Neighborhood Playhouse, and the Actors' Studio. Her first professional appearance in the theater was a London production of her father's *Hello Out There* and *Once Around the Block*. She has performed on Broadway in *Room Service* and off Broadway in *I Dreamt I Dwelt in Bloomingdale's*. She toured with Maureen Stapleton in *The Gingerbread Lady* and acted in *Barefoot in the Park* with Maureen O'Sullivan. She has also appeared at the Ford Theatre in Washington, D.C. in *Ah, Wilderness* and the Bucks County Playhouse in *The Prime of Miss Jean Brodie*.

Ms. Saroyan has also worked in television on "The Blue Knight," "Name of the Game," and "Mannix," and she has done commercial voice-overs for cosmetic products such as Clairol, Nice & Easy, and Love.

In the film industry, Saroyan acted in *Hopscotch, The Taking of Pelham 1-2-3*, and *Kotch* with her stepfather Walter Matthau. She also worked in *Lookin' to Get Out, Blue Collar, Prime Time, Greased Lightning, Maidstone, Some Kind of Nut,* and *Isadora*. She recently appeared with Katherine Hepburn and Nick Nolte in *The Ultimate Solution of Grace Quigley*.

G.H.: In a story, "The Unpublished Writer, the Rain, and his Daughter," your father writes a fond memory about you as a child. You kept telling him, "You buy me skate!" He was really upset that he couldn't buy them at that time. "What do I do? Steal some skates for my child?" Do you remember that? What is your earliest memory of him?

L.S.: My earliest memory of Papa was when he came to visit us in New York City and brought me a little, glass-blown cage with a tiny bird in it in a little box that was covered in newspaper from Portugal. We went back many years later, when I was about thirteen or fourteen, and tried to find the same. It was from a restaurant called "The Bird Cage." I just remember him that day arriving with his moustache and his hat and the bird cage, and I was so excited and pleased to see him . . . It's my first memory, of anything.

G.H.: In the "Freedom and Fun" story, do you remember that ride (from Malibu up the coast?)

L.S.: I remember many drives like that because he used to take us in summers and on vacations. Frequently we'd leave from Malibu. We'd go over to his house, spend the night, then take off for Fresno, usually, or up north, San Francisco.

On one of those drives, we stopped at a gas station. The man who ran the gas station, his house was part of the setup. In the back he had a cage with a brown bunny in it. I fell madly in love with this brown bunny. I wanted it very badly, so Papa tried to buy it from him. The man said, "That's not for sale. That's my granddaughter's rabbit." I said, "Oh no, Papa, I have to have this rabbit!" He said, "Well, you can't have this rabbit, but when we get to Fresno, I'm going to buy you ten rabbits." This seemed like an abundance of good fortune. I said, "O.K. All right," and I got back in the car.

We were visiting the Papazians, his sister Zabe, and we stopped at a rabbit store. He bought a mother and nine baby rabbits. We took them to Zabe's and we set them up. Of course, she was not delighted to have Aram, me, Papa and the ten rabbits as guests. We built hutches, and by the end of the summer we had about eighty rabbits. I had the biggest rabbit collection of anybody in the world! That was one of my great memories, because I was like a rabbit-keeper. Papa would say, "Have you looked after your rabbits today?" I was out there with the lettuce and the water. He always made everything seem like a great adventure.

We never knew on those rides what was going to happen, when we would take a side track, when we would meet some interesting person on the road, and get completely involved with their life and what they were doing. Papa would engage people in conversation—""Hello, how are you?"—the way we got to know that man and that it was his rabbit! We knew everything about that man before we left. He was sick that he couldn't give us the rabbit.

One of our favorite adventures with Papa was once in Europe we met a man named Cess Pelham who had this booming voice. He was one of our favorite characters. All through the rest of our lives, we would make references to Cess Pelham. We didn't know him well, but we remembered him well because Papa could imitate him. Papa had a booming voice as well.

We met a girl on a boat named Cha-Cha. Cha-Cha became a great friend of ours, and Papa wrote about her, too. We just met people, and he made friends with them . . . on those rides, when we stopped at gas stations, Papa was always asking everybody their history, "Where were you born? Where are you going? What did you do this morning, what are you doing this afternoon?"

G.H.: Another trip he writes about is that 1957 jaunt to Trieste, Belgrade, Naples, Venice. There's one touch he remembered in particular. In Athens, at Vougliamentis, you collected pebbles and he always kept those pebbles.

L.S.: The beach outside Athens? I do remember because there were rats on the waterfront. No, that was Gibraltar where I saw the rats. I remember . . . I liked the dancers in Barcelona. I almost got my famous Leopold Freckle, the donkey, Papa always promised me. We went to Barcelona, and rented a house. This was another of our famous adventures.

We were at the hotel in Barcelona, and we decided to drive to Seechus to stay there so he could buy me the donkey. We had a mad driver. He drove so fast I'm lucky to be alive today. We got there, and the man left us. We went to the residence that we had rented sight unseen. There was a great power outage that night. The toilet didn't flush. The water didn't run. There was no electricity whatsoever. We didn't have a candle between us. We had a couple of matches. We went out into Seechus.

There's something funny about a town that has no electricity. It's darker than you would imagine it would be because all the lights are out. So, on the streets people were gathered, and it was very gay and wonderful and everything was candlelit. It was beautiful. We laughed so hard. I'll never forget it. We laughed all night long. We finally located about two candles, and came back . . . the linens were all musty. The blankets were musty. It was an unmitigated disaster, but I never had a better time in my life.

The morning after the evening we arrived there . . . we must have been up until six in the morning and got a few hours sleep . . . we drove out. We drove back to Barcelona and continued our travels. Papa

Lucy and Aram, New York, 1956. *(Courtesy of Richard Avedon.)*

Lucy Saroyan. *(Courtesy of Aram Saroyan.)*

laughed and said, 'Well, it looks like you're not getting your donkey this year.'

I do remember that dancing in Barcelona and liking it very much. The costumes were very pretty. I was always interested in dancing myself. I do remember not liking the bullfights.

The first time I ever saw a bullfight was in Tijuana. Papa used to take us there on the weekend. We saw some very poor bullfights, which scared me. I never liked them in Tijuana and I didn't like them in Barcelona. It's morbid, and we saw a very sad accidental mutilation in Tijuana I never got over.

I remember going to all of these places. Sure, sure, I remember Athens. Papa was very popular in Greece, and they always gave him a press conference. I remember there were a lot of poor areas. And we visited a lot of Armenians. We went to the ruins, and we also took a boat ride to an island called Hydra. Once we had gotten there, there was a lady who was sort of showing us the layout of the island. The top of her bathing suit slipped down. It was me, Aram, and Papa in the boat, and the lady. Papa and Aram immediately were looking *way out to sea!* She didn't know it had slipped down. Papa was very shy about things like that. He was very well-mannered. He kept saying," *LOOK AT THAT!*" and it would be a seagull. He was trying to distract Aram. Aram went into a coma. He just didn't know what to make of it, and she had a very big bosom. I was so fascinated by the way they were behaving, because Papa was trying to do everything to distract the attention and Aram didn't know what to do.

G.H.: Your father mentions a trip to Tijuana in 1958.

L.S.: We have a picture where I have a hat on which says "Lolita" and Papa's says "Poncho Gonzalez." I have that picture. We went a lot to Tijuana. We would go to everything. We would go to the jai alai games, the dog races, the horse races, the bull-fights. Aram and Papa would go to the cockfights and I'd have to stand outside because they didn't allow little children and women. We would walk around and look at all the festivities. He did a lot of gambling, too.

G.H.: After that, he talks about 1959 and Paris. He said you all did a lot of drawings. He said he particularly liked yours because every one of yours was a self-portrait, not literally but they seemed to have you in them.

L.S.: I drew this one face. It was sort of a Modigliani type face. I thought it was based on his style, but Papa thought it was me. She did look a lot like me. She had big eyes and long, straight hair, and a long, long face. That was the basic theme there.

Pop just hated that drawing. I went from that sort of freedom that a very young person has in her drawings to somebody who was very literal.

Every petal of the flower was very precise, and very closed-in, like the leaves and the stem. He finally turned to me one day and said, "What is this, Lucy? This is terrible. What's happened to your painting! It's so specific. It doesn't have any freedom anymore. It doesn't have any joy!"

I didn't know what he was talking about since I hadn't really seen the transition that came over it, but I can see it now when I look back at my old artwork.

G.H.: He mentioned one time in Paris he had gone to the Aviation Club, and he gambled away a lot that night. The next day he took a walk with you on the Bois de Bologne. He said that you consoled him with, "What do we care? We've got everything."

L.S.: I do always remember vividly the morning after the nights that Papa lost heavily. He used to go into sort of suspended grief state. He would mourn. Somehow when he won a lot of money it would never affect him as when he lost. He would be very, very distressed. A lot of times it was the last money that we had for our summer. One summer we actually cut short our trip because he had lost.

I did feel that basically the concept of "we've got everything and it doesn't matter how much you've lost" is something that he taught me, but I would give it back to him when he would go into those sorrowful states the days after.

We lived near the Bois de Bologne. We were staying on Avenue Victor Hugo. I went for a walk with him. We were going to go for a walk anyway, and he made everything a joyous event. The only thing was that when he got very depressed or down, it was very disturbing to me. I never liked to see him unhappy. It took him about twenty-four hours to swing back from a big loss. His sense of joy and wonder at life . . . he'd be back at the typewriter writing a story or something that would make him cheer up. He'd always bounce back.

G.H.: In 1966 he writes about his renting a Whitelands Hall in Chelsea, London, for you. Later, Aram joined both of you. He said you talked for eight weeks, from nine at night until nearly dawn sometimes. His last line was, "Perhaps it helped. I don't know."

L.S.: Any time I spent with Papa, any sort of space, always helped. That was sort of my stepping off into my own life period, when I was living in London. It was a big help. Papa taught me . . . he was somewhat critical of me at the time because he thought I was permitting myself to be people's house guest and to receive their graciousness and generosity without really having the means to repay them. In many ways I think he was right. It was an indulgent period of mine, and I think he gave me perspective on how to hold my own. It always helped to spend time with him. He was a force to be reckoned with.

G.H.: Writer Alice Adams in *Roses, Rhodedendron* comments how everybody needs a second set of parents because the relations with the original set are too intense, and need dissipating. Would that be doubly applicable with William Saroyan as the father?

L.S.: That's interesting because I also had a second set of parents in the people I was staying with in London at that time, Karel and Betsy Reisz. Papa liked them very much, and I sort of became a member of their family. They had three young boys who were like little brothers to me. It was easier when it's not your own parents. Papa was very intense, and also very judgmental. When you're at a fragile stage in your life, criticism can be very tough to take. His criticism was so astute that he could stop you dead with a sentence. You're frozen in your tracks and you don't move for ten years. It's because you're paralyzed. I think in certain ways this happened to me, and it happened to Aram, too. We were both somewhat intimidated and awed.

But Papa came to appreciate my closeness and relationship with the Reiszes. In fact, he discovered Betsy. Betsy was Betsy Blair, who was originally married to Gene Kelly. Gene Kelly was in *The Time of Your Life*. He was madly in love with this woman, and said, "Bill, I want you to meet my fiancee." Bill said, "Bring her by the restaurant. I want to meet her." He brought Betsy in through the doorway, and before she sat down, Papa said, "Well, you're going to be the lead in my play *The Beautiful People*, Betsy, so sit down." She was in fact the lead of the play.

G.H.: Those are the main trips in his writing that he mentioned. Do you recall any other big ones?

L.S.: There were so many. Every summer I was with him except for two summers I went to Montana. He came to visit me there.

One thing I remember is that each day, every summer, he would shut himself in his room from eight in the morning to twelve to work. We were not to bother him. Even if the house was on fire, we were not supposed to knock on his door. We were to run out to safety. When the fire reached his door, then he would leave.

Everything he was working on was always his best one. That work would be his favorite. He would say, "This is better! Better!" I've never seen anyone work that hard. I think he wanted to be known through his work. That's why he was such a private man.

G.H.: Did your own desire for acting come out of exposure to your father's plays?

L.S.: Both my mother and father have theatrical backgrounds. I don't remember ever not wanting to be an actress. I wanted to be an actress before I'd ever been to a movie or a play. I used to put on little shows in the garage of our house in Pacific Palisades. Aram would get to do everything: costumes, props, curtain pulling, but I never let him on stage! I would give these one-woman shows, with Aram doing all the hard work. I guess I just had a show-offy personality. I wanted to be an actress—Papa was always sort of hoping that would change in my life. I think he was hoping I would be a writer. I think he really hoped that for both of us.

I did some writing but I was never pleased with it because I was so used to just first-rate writing. Papa would give us books—Guy deMaupassant, O. Henry, Willa Cather—to read. Salinger was my favorite. He encouraged us to read, and he read us his work. I read a lot of his work and it just seemed like an overwhelming task to compete with him, so I never got into that.

I remember in Greece they gave Papa a press conference. They very coolly asked me who my favorite was, to which I responded without missing a beat, "Salinger! J.D. Salinger!" Papa boomed out with a huge laugh and said, "You gotta be careful when you ask a Saroyan a question!" Everybody had expected me to say, "Oooohh, William Saroyan."

G.H.: You went to the Saroyan festival at Circle-in-the-Square (10/20/83). How did you feel to see the production of your father's writing, this immense revival of your father's works?

L.S.: I was tremendously pleased. It was packed, overflowing with standing room only. Everybody there had such a love for him.

I thought the program was very, very good. It had excerpts from a lot of his plays and some of his writings. But it was funny because the last two things on the program were songs that he did not write. They were inspired by his writing, but the lyrics are not Papa's, nor is the music. The minutes these songs started, I went, "These aren't Saroyan." The lyrics weren't right and the music wasn't right. As I understand it, when Jose Quintero and Carmen Capalbo said, "Let's make a musical out of *The Time of Your Life,*" he responded, "You can't. It has its own music." It wasn't his own music that I heard in those last couple of songs. I missed it. It's not the same flavor. They're very gifted songs, it's just that they seemed out of place.

G.H.: Do you have a favorite story of his?

L.S.: Definitely *Mama I Love You,* which he wrote for me, dedicated to me, put my picture on the back and was about me in essence. It wasn't literally about me. This story was made up, but it was a girl of my character and qualities. When we were little he would tell us stories of Fat Hushush who was always being thwarted by his little friends in the neighborhood. One year he said to us, "Listen, you guys are too old for me to keep telling stories. I'm going to write you each a book. I'll read you the book. That's it." Those were our special books. Aram's was *Papa You're Crazy.*

G.H.: In *Last Rites,* Aram says your father was so shy and private a man that the rare visits he made threatened his threshold for intimacy. Did you sense that?

L.S.: I didn't have any difficulty in achieving a certain intimacy and a language between us that was impenetrable to anybody on the outside. It was very uniquely ours. I think it was not hard to achieve an intimacy with Papa. He was shy, and he was thwarted by certain feelings he had about Aram in that Aram was his son. He was Armenian. He was old-fashioned in a way. He was very patriarchal. He had great aspirations and hopes for Aram, and I think that their communication was very different from ours. Ours was a little easier. The pressure wasn't on me as strongly as it was on Aram.

I didn't believe it was easy for outsiders to get to know Papa. The shyness . . . . Papa had a type of joyous, big, loud, friendly presentation, but if you tried to become very personal Papa would sort of thwart that. He would swing into another gear. I think that we had a sort of private, intimate side. It was not something I worked for or tried for in life. It was just there.

G.H.: In terms of trying to thwart . . .

L.S.: He would not try to thwart it deliberately. Papa was a loner. He was a maverick. He was one of a kind. He was not unlike a unicorn. There's only one. There's no way to reflect yourself back to yourself. He didn't have a lot of friends, a lot of male friends or female friends. He never had, like other parents, a whole gang to hang out with. He had family and basically that was it. Otherwise they were acquaintances, they were gambling buddies, they were professional associates. They weren't pals. The closest he ever came to having a pal was his best friend Ross Bagdassarian. That's his cousin. They grew up together. That was as close as he came to having a pal.

In this sense, you couldn't quite get to know him. You could be in his company and enjoy his good humor, without getting very close. He did love people. It's just that he didn't get to know them on a very intimate basis. He didn't play golf or tennis. His only recreational activity was gambling, and that doesn't make for long-term friendships. He came and went. He met people, thought of them as amazing and wonderful, then moved on. He was very isolated when he worked and wrote.

G.H.: Saroyan himself, he always thought about his own father a lot. In one story, he's writing with the portrait of his father above him. And you?

L.S.: I'm not sure how he grappled with Armenak, his father. I think he more grappled with the mystery of having lost him so early and having wondered about him as a man, as a writer, as a preacher. He didn't talk a lot about him except that he missed him and had always wished that he had known him.

He told a very sad story about how when he was in the orphanage he learned the reality of life. He was just in the orphanage. He must have been about three years old. He was the youngest in the orphanage. That Christmas . . . he hadn't had any Christmases that he remembered yet in his own family with Takoohi . . . they brought in this Santa Claus for all the children to get to talk to him. Each child got to go up to Santa Claus and say what he wanted for Christmas. When Papa got up to this big man who wanted him to sit on his lap, Papa didn't want to. He stood there. Santa said, "Well, what do you want, Willie?" His little name tag was on him. He said, "I want my father." Santa said, "Well, all right. I'll see what I can do."

Now Papa really believed that his father was going to show up on Christmas. He kept thinking, I don't see how that's possible. I don't understand how that's possible. He thought about it a great deal. Christmas came and they brought all the little kids into the room and each one had a little package for him. They took Papa over to his package and said, "That's your present Willie." He looked at the box and he said that he realized that his father couldn't possibly be in the box. He ran away from the orphanage that day. That was the first time he ran away from the Fred Finch Orphanage. He was totally disillusioned with all this Christmas con.

I remember that story so vividly because it broke my heart. It always seemed to me as good a story as anything that he wrote. It was a very Saroyanesque story. It was just a hideous, horrible, heart-breaking encounter. He never wrote it. He was just devastated by that experience. It's not the kind of story you forget.

In terms of grappling with the mystery of him as a father, yes I did and I do and I probably always will. He was an astonishing man. He was the most exciting, dazzling, vibrant, vital, and funny man that I ever knew, and mystifying, a very mystifying man. So, yes I grapple.

G.H.: He said in one of his stories that he told you and Aram that if you ever wanted to change your names to better than Aram and Lucy Saroyan, to feel free to do it, but so far you're still Aram and Lucy Saroyan.

L.S.: Actually, I remember when I was considering a career in the theater and I mentioned to him, "Papa, maybe I should change my name so that I don't take advantage of you being my father by having your famous name. Maybe I should make it on my own." He said, "Lucy, I worked my whole life to give you a name that might make something a little easier for you any step of the way. That is what my intention was.

Keep it if you want to rejoice in the efforts I've made or change it if you want to. But maybe trying things the hardest way isn't the best way. You are Lucy Saroyan. That's who you are. That's what you are. Go for it."

G.H.: And your debut?

L.S.: My debut in the theater was in London in 1965. I did *Hello Out There* and *Once Around the Block*. Papa and I were sharing that apartment in London. Somebody came to get permission to do *Hello Out There* and Papa said, "Well, you can do the play, but Lucy comes with it." He did some rewrites for me, and we did them and that was my first professional stage debut.

In a way it was easier for me because the material was so familiar. Papa had a sound and feel of his own that I'm very organically familiar with. On the other hand, trying to please your father for your debut performance can be very trying because if there was anything I wanted to do in my life it was to receive my father's approval. That was not always feasible. He had very high standards.

G.H.: As for your career in voice-overs, you seem to have that Saroyan voice.

L.S.: My mother says that we all shouted. The reason we shouted is that Papa had a childhood illness that left him half-deaf. One of his ears was completely deaf. He called it his bum ear. So we shouted. He shouted and we shouted. I was constantly being told by my mother to soften my voice. It turned out my voice has been very helpful to me.

G.H.: Last, Saroyan exposed a lot in his writings, but at the same time he was able to keep so much private, as you said. What last thing do you want to reveal about him as your father?

L.S.: I feel that I'm the luckiest person in the world to have this father who was the love of my life, the joy of my life. Any of the qualities in myself or my life that I feel happy about are things that he gave me and the way he nurtured my early years: a joy for life, a curiosity that's unabated, a kind of daring courage that a lot of women maybe don't have instilled in them by their families. There was never anything that I felt I couldn't do or at least attempt. He gave me a kind of courage that I don't think I would have had from any other father.

He was an extraordinary man. It's very hard to describe him because people have a public image of him as this friendly, outgoing, gregarious lover of life, which he was, but he also had a poetic, beautiful side to him. It's very hard to put into words how it manifested itself. It was tender, loving and . . . for example, we would walk down a New York City street. I remember when I was a senior in high school, he moved to New York because he felt that we would be out of his grasp when I was out of high school. Aram was already in college. Then I would be in college and I would go on with my own life, and we wouldn't have as much time.

He moved to New York and took an apartment for my senior year. He spent a lot of time with me in school, in hanging out with me, and we had a great time. We used to do things, like walk down a New York City street and Papa would pick up sticks, dead, empty twigs off the ground. I'd say, "Pop, stop it. Please stop picking up the garbage off the street. You look like a crackpot. Please don't embarrass me on the street." He'd say to me, "Lucy, Lucy, where's your imagination for heaven's sakes! Come back to my apartment in a week and you'll see what I do to these sticks." Sure enough he took the twigs and put them in a jar of water. A week later they would be blooming with little tiny green leaves jumping out of them.

He always had a "found jar", he called them, these very big jars where he put buttons, pennies, little toys. He always looked on the street and found a lot of stuff. He'd take it home and put it in his found jar. He had twigs that would grow into trees, old sticks that were now living, blooming plants, jars full of adventures. As kids we'd go crazy over them because they had wonderful little wings and buttons and doodads from the street.

He could make something out of anything. He saw the beauty out of anything. He saw the beauty in everything. That's what made him such a wonderful writer. He could take a piece of ordinary life and make it extraordinary. He once said to me apropos of *Hello Out There* that that was one of his worse plays. He said to me, "If you put a man in jail, lock him up, and you put a lonely girl on the stage with him, and you know the man is going to get lynched at the end of the play, the audience is already crying. You don't need to write the play. The situation is so sad that inherently it's a tear-jerker. It's melodrama. I'm not interested in melodrama. What is truly good writing is taking an ordinary situation and making it extraordinary, not taking an extraordinary situation and re-creating it. That's too easy!" He did in life what he did in his work. He took ordinary situations and made them magnificent, made them awe-inspiring and full of wonder.

I remember once the kind of thing that would frustrate Papa. I would find a stone, then I would paint it. He'd go, "Lucy! You missed the point completely! You don't paint a rock. A rock is a perfect beautiful thing!"

Addendum, November 1985:

Since the interview, Lucy Saroyan toured for six months, with director Mike Nichols and playwright Tom Stoppard, in *The Real Thing*. She has returned to New York, where she works in a shelter for disadvantaged children, taking them on the "adventures" her father once took her. She remarks that together they travel "down the same New York City streets,"

going to the park and, ironically, to Macy's where the children love to see
Santa Claus and ask for their biggest wishes.

Sometimes Ms. Saroyan recalls those special moments when she made
her father "soar": when he proudly hustled and cajoled people in off the
streets to see her art in an exhibit at her high school, Dalton, or when he
wept as she, long ago, read him seven short stores she had written in
seven days of youthful exuberance and agitation. Sometimes she dwells
on the larger inheritances from her father, such as honesty and di-
rectness, while at other times she glimpses him scribbling his writings on
napkins, or whatever was handy, a habit of his. In the end she comments,
"I still haven't met a man who thrills me the way Papa did—with his
intelligence, humor, and warmth."

On her father and the Armenians, she talks of a constant yearning.
Saroyan had visited Soviet Armenia three times and cherished the country, but from there he could only see Mount Ararat in the distance and
clouds. The majestic, towering side of *Maissis,* in Turkey, is blocked to
visitors because of its location near an American military base. Saroyan
had always wanted to go there, Lucy adds, "but he never could get to the
right side of the mountain."

The Daring Old Man on the Flying Trapeze

HERBERT GOLD

William Saroyan of Fresno and Paris, of San Francisco and the Great Northern Hotel in Manhattan, of Hollywood and lorn wanderings in theaters and on roadways, the Armenian messenger boy who outlived his hilarious and rambunctious early fame, announced in the spring of 1981 that he had always known he would live forever but now was dying and this was distressing to him.

And then, in fact, he died.

Since then, his son Aram has published two books about his father, both of them full of grief and loss, the pain of losing his father and the grief of never having had his father he needed. The estate is in turmoil, with large sums of money and millions of unpublished words left to the William Saroyan Foundation and no clear message about what is to be done with them. The man who preached simplicity, fun, bicycle-riding, French bread, a bit of wine, and a bit of love left havoc in his wake.

Lawrence Lee and Barry Gifford, in *Saroyan,* a biography stitched together with matter-of-fact history and passionate monologues by some of Saroyan's friends and family, document the progress of a turbulent life toward havoc. Creditable, convincing, and saddening as it is, it also omits the essence of the man.

The book is a useful chronicle. Lively monologues by Artie Shaw, Paul Gitlin [Carol's divorce lawyer], Carol Saroyan Matthau, Aram Saroyan—who comes through as a sad and loving and distraught son, more moving here than in his memoirs—and Lucy Saroyan, who comes through as a sweet and sensitive and wronged daughter, and the various Saroyan cousins and uncles and nephews, and Budd Schulberg and Irwin Shaw and other literary friends—are blended into the story of Saroyan's career. More of his swiftness would help; there is a blank space left in the frequent references to his laughter and fun, very little of the actual laughter included. The book is elegiac in tone. References to invention, play, and appetite do not evoke the enthralling presence of the man, any

179

more than references to his fame and success evoke the charm and energy of the writing. And of course the griefs of a long decline in public esteem, disasters of personal life, and the irony of his often writing better and newer than ever while many readers thought him dead—no sensible chronicle can master such material, although it suggests what remains to be done. What chiefly remains to be done for William Saroyan, of course, is to read him.

The beginning was an American legend for all of us outsiders who dreamed of telling the angels our words and thus finding salvation for ourselves, glory, glory, glory for everyone.

The semi-orphan from Fresno decided to be a literary genius and wrote a story a day, a book a month. "Our Willie is in one place, the world is in another," as his grandmother said. He was discovered with "The Daring Young Man on the Flying Trapeze" in his early twenties. He rushed off to New York, he wore his hat rakishly, he was a loud-mouthed sensation, proclaiming that he was the greatest writer ever. He was still a boy. He wrote plays in a few days, and refused the Pulitzer Prize because he gave himself all the prizes. He wrote a poem celebrating other victories for which he deserved a prize: "First to Climb Geggenheimer's Water Tank and Drop a Cat." He gambled, he chased women, he drank, he played, he made noise. He wrote a description of conventional the-ater: ". . . a little stuff, then a little more stuff, some acting, some personality, a lady with years of experience, a little more stuff and then Intermission. . . . The speech clear and full of innuendo, the air tense, the eyes wild, and then he says and then she says, and the guy across the aisle says. . . ."

Saroyan brought something new with *The Time of Your Life* and *My Heart's in the Highlands,* which have never ceased to be performed, almost every day someplace. Of course the victorious roll could not be sus-tained. Saroyan fled back to his family in California. The war happened and manic Saroyan was drafted. Love, marriage, and divorce happened and this was even worse than the war. The children suffered, Saroyan's reputation declined precipitously, Saroyan was no longer doing what he was expected to do. He suffered. He never stopped remembering, collecting, writing; and as old age and death approached, an odd thing happened. He suddenly began to grow again in depth and feeling. And hardly anyone took notice.

"With its revelations of ambition, anti-Semitism, and compulsive gam-bling," the publisher advertises, "*Saroyan* reads like a novel." It also reveals IRS disputes, nervous breakdown in the army, excessive drink-ing, sexual withdrawal, enraged jealousy, monomaniacal pursuit of the woman he married and divorced twice, and glimpses of the two children he alternately tormented and delighted. These "revelations" are curiously unnerving and incomplete. To take one example, anti-Semitism, to which I am more than usually sensitive: most of the non-Armenian friends cited in the book are Jews. "Some of his best friends were Jewish" is an absurd defense, but the wife was also Jewish, the children are half-Jewish. Yet there is plenty of Armenian ethnocentricity in Armenian culture, and one can easily imagine Saroyan lashing out at his pink and blond wife who had neglected to tell him she was a Jew. How can we judge the matter? Saroyan was a contemporary of Hemingway, Fitzgerald, T. S. Eliot, who sought assurance in assuming they were purer, better, nicer than Jews or blacks or any other. But Saroyan's writing was actively, sometimes even saccharinely, concerned with universal brotherhood. In my own friendship with him—I am named in this book as one of his "surrogate sons"—I found him curious about Jews, questing and amused, loving to trace genealogies and similarities, fully appreciative of difference. He loved to speculate on the strains of connection between the half-Jewish inheritance of my sons and his children.

Nevertheless, alas, it is believable that he shrieked hurtful rage at a wife—this is something husbands and wives do to each other. I can't square the accusations of his son and former wife with my experience of the man who carefully wrote down the names of my twin boys, Ethan and Ari, and discussed with them the importance of their heritage, one called for Ethan Allen on his mother's side, meaning "Strength, Fidelity, Trust," the other named with the Hebrew word for Lion, and his delight when I told him that the Bedouin whom Ari and I met in Israel informed me that my real name is Abu-Ari, Father of Ari, because he is by a few minutes my elder son.

And then, showing Ari his typewriter, his manuscripts, his teapot, his records, telling him how important it is to be a writer and to have a writer for a father, Bill began to talk about his own children, to explore how they got the names they have and why such things are *verrry interesting*. And to me, over and over again, he expressed his grief over the breach between his children and himself, for which he blamed, yes, them, and their mother, and also himself. He wrote of how he tormented Aram on an automobile trip. "The sound of his sickness sickened me. That's the thing that bothered me in 1958, and will go on bothering me the rest of my life. I only hope it isn't the last thing I remember."

Saroyan may not have been clean on the matters of love, Jews, family, and generosity—who is? He made many loud claims for himself, but so far as I know, saintliness was not one of them.

When the generation of Jack Kerouac came in, owing so much to Saroyan's freedom, flow, and spirit, it replaced the aging wanderer as a

Carol and Bill, San Francisco, 1947. *(Courtesy of Aram Saroyan.)*

public nuisance. He took his neglect with his customary good and bad humor. He may have wanted to continue his role as disturber and consoler, but he also had his secret agendas. The letters to his friends grew longer, packed with gossip and fantasy. His new plays were mostly not produced. Once, in the Brighton Express in North Beach, he decided to cast the cook and her husband and me in a play in which God would be played by a horse. None of us gave up our regular jobs because of our coming stardom.

He gathered rocks, splinters, scraps of paper, clumps of anything to hold onto each day, to keep each day in memory as he tried to do with the day's writing. He signed books with flourishes—"May life be at least satisfactory." He lived in a tract house in Fresno, with an adjacent one for memories; he kept rooms for souvenirs in his shabby flat in Paris. He carried more happiness and more sadness, more wholeness and more brokenness than a man can properly bear. To his children, there was more kindness and more cruelty than is decent. And of course, for children, the kindness can never redeem the cruelty. "Pop!" Aram cried after he passed him on the street and each had pretended not to see the other. [Editor's note: Saroyan submitted his version of this encounter (on New York City's Madison Avenue) to *Ararat,* but asked to have it withdrawn just as the issue was going to press. He never explained why. Presumably the original manuscript is among his effects in the University of California at Berkeley archive.]

"I am an old man. I have no reason to be glad," he said to one of his friends. How could this man who gave so much pleasure—made his fame by laughing and making people laugh, making them feel both joyful and full of natural truth—have brought so much pain into the world? His own pain gives the edge of depth to his late book, *Obituaries.* If we look too much at any writer's family, striving, aging, and death, will the colossal effort to be more than ordinary ever seem worthwhile? Through his long, strange, and surprisingly secret life, William Saroyan made a wager that it might be.

The great challenge for a biography of an artist is to justify. Why all this gossip, detail about agents and lawyers, movements and transfers? Why these quarrels and divorces, family agonies and devotions, awed recollections and derogations? (Walter Matthau, who married Carol after the second divorce, meeting Saroyan for the first time on the stairway when Bill came to take Aram out: "Gee, I thought you were much taller, I didn't know you were short.") Why are we reading this with such curiosity? What is wrong with us, or even better, what could be right to us?

A writer's biography should give a sense of the worth, depth, and power to which we have responded. This history of William Saroyan is responsible in its details, touching in places, deeply mournful in its implications. It only occasionally gives a whiff of the special charm that it asserts for Saroyan, the delight and pleasure he made manifest, and the depth of grief he finally achieved in *Obituaries*. Occasionally, when his rhythm is captured in a quotation, we can understand why we are reading.

The great literary biographies—say, Richard Ellmann's *James Joyce* or Henri Troyat's *Tolstoy*—reveal the chagrin and pain and pettiness while admitting that the writer moves on past personal failures to something more. Saroyan was not a giant like Tolstoy or Joyce, but in his moments and flickers, in his special glint of feeling, he deserves to be read for what he says and does. It might be put differently; perhaps we deserve to read him for his fun, depth, grief, regret, play, his ultimate confrontation of death in his own swift style of defiance and laughter.

The End of an Era

DAVID KHERDIAN

When William Saroyan died an artistic era ended.

He played to near perfection the role of the brash and flamboyant writer for whom writing was more than a calling; it was a way of life. Art could justify life, and if it can be said that the writers of the opening decades of this century represented anything, they represented this. To write the Great American Novel implied that one lived it as well, even if only in the writing. This kind of specialization is thankfully gone; a writer today cannot say, as Saroyan said in the 1930s: "I am a writer who will live a life." The possibilities in life today are so much greater than they are in art, that only a fool would pretend to want to sidestep life in order to serve it in art. That day has passed, and those who served and were sacrificed in this way—for the benefit of the slow evolution of the species—have also passed away, and now, with Saroyan, the last of them is gone.

But in his time he made us believe in art in this way. "Form is our highest truth," I heard him say more than once. Because it was, it took precedence over human relationships, which could be salvaged in print if lost in life. In book after book Saroyan salvaged his life, and in the end with no book to write he phoned in his story and died. When I asked the AP reporter, who (in turn) had phoned me for a statement, how he had delivered his epitaph, she said, "With a great roar of laughter." He would die as he had lived. It was a whole life, or, as Saroyan would have said, "Pure," his word for anything that didn't deviate from its own laws, but remained simply and stubbornly itself, even when it objectified something less than pleasing to others. It was a word he used with charity more often than scorn.

Saroyan had come home to die. The year was 1964. He didn't know when the end would be, but he wanted to be home when it happened.

185

He was also returning, no doubt, to complete the picture or story of his life. He had begun is Fresno, he would end there. He had begun by hating the place, but he would end by loving it, or—if that wasn't possible—embracing it with something like understanding and love.

The great love affair in more writers' lives is their home towns. ". . . I discovered the human race there. I discovered art there. And wherever you discover man and his high hope, this is your place, favorite or not."

But hate is the opposite end of that stick, and the reconciliation can only occur when we find our way to the middle, the place between these extremes. Was it reconciled for him, and could it be reconciled by his going home? It was the last great drama of his life, and he enacted it with the same energy that characterized his life.

About this time I was *leaving* home, a place I hated with the same intensity that Saroyan had once hated his hometown. It was in Racine that I read about Fresno, and long before I arrived there I fell in love with the place, because I had fallen in love with the writing of the man who was engaged in this life-death struggle of love-hate with the town in which he had first seen the light of day. For a writer, of course, this is all it takes. The place where you encounter reality will always be your place, because everything that happens after that happens in relation to this place. We carry its mortal wound to our grave.

But a writer leaves his home thinking he has been cheated by his birthplace of ever having the possibility of being a writer. I had identified with Saroyan on many counts, but the most important, as I was to find out (or piece together) much later on, was not so much that we were both Armenian—as well as writer and would-be-writer—but because we really suffered alike from the weight we felt had been put upon us from being made to feel inferior because of our heritage, and—and this was even more important—our own feelings of inferiority because we had gotten ourselves born into cities as forlorn and backward as Fresno and Racine. Writing was a way of getting out and free from our stifling environments, and becoming famous was our way of transcending the limitations imposed by prejudice.

When I left Racine I left, not only in search of Saroyan, but in search of the kind of experiencings that would permit me to be a writer worthy of the attention of the world.

To put it briefly, I found what I was searching for both in Saroyan and not in Saroyan (he wasn't even there—Fresno *or* San Francisco, when I arrived); and then (in the end) I found it both through Saroyan and in myself, because he was able to bring me back to myself, to the realization that for the purposes of art all experience is the same, and no life (or place) is unworthy of the attention of an able writer.

One day, standing together across from the Fresno State campus, he pointed in its direction and said, "When I was growing up in Fresno, the entire city was from here to there." And then, that external pointing done, he made another (incisive) point. "You're the only writer to come out of Racine, so you've got the place all to yourself." I didn't know at the time what a shock he had delivered, but as the years rolled along the image of the two of us standing there kept coming back to me, and his words grew over the years into a richness whose truth became a treasure.

By then I had been in Fresno for several years. And that afternoon I had shown Saroyan the first draft of *Homage to Adana,* poems that were filled with recollections of old country Armenians who haunted my childhood, and of the factories and foundries where they worked. They were men very different from the vineyard workers that Saroyan wrote about, yet the same. For the human drama is different only in its variables, not in its essence. But only through its variables can its essence be released and held fast in a work of art. And this is what Saroyan was telling me, by pointing in the direction in which I should look. Like all good teachers, he was merely pointing the way, showing me the path, and then leaving it to me to travel it or not.

Shortly thereafter I moved to Fresno to try my fortune there. I combined my efforts of compiling his bibliography, which I was working on at the time, with a program of study involving the places and people and even some of the events that Saroyan had used in constructing his hometown stories. I had arrived on the scene just in time, because the old Armenian town was still standing, with the churches and bakeries and dairies and assorted buildings that he had written about, still somehow intact. And not only were the streets still there, carrying their immortal names, but the courthouse was still standing, with the postal telegraph office facing it, just as I had found it in *The Human Comedy*. It was all there, and I went out to all of it, to unravel, if I could, the mystery of writing. Once a place has been certified, so to say, by art, it can never be again what it was before.

As I watched the coming and going of the people, I thought of their drama, that they had had enacted for them in the pages of Saroyan's books, and I moved out from the immortal multitude and began to seek the individual ones, that he had patterned his stories after. There was the uncle that planted pomegranate trees, and I met him; the uncle that had cosmic vibrations and holy tremors, the cousins, the Boxer, the Dentist, and all the others that had been capitalized, as the Writer had capitalized himself, to stand off as the witness, self-conscious perhaps, but unashamed to be the chronicler of this tiny fraction of humanity caught in the midst of the wholeness of creation.

"It is the dirt of the world with the sun shining on it that astonishes a poet when he is a boy," Saroyan wrote; for in becoming a writer he had merely changed the method by which he would do the cleaning up. Are all writers preoccupied with cleanliness and order, and wholeness and dignity and form and truth? But the order of the artist is not ordinary; is, in fact, uncommon, and in each case one of a kind. Visiting the tract home that Saroyan had come home to die in was like visiting an alchemist's cave. Out of it anything could come, and much did. Out of the fluid, suspended, intentional-haphazard disordered ordering of the contents of it, there was a great inhaling and exhaling of art as well as the substances used in its creation.

All of that could not have been done by one man, and yet it was. And then he died. But something *was* actualized, and, whether he knew it or not, something had been completed in his being, for he represented in his person a single needed movement of energy in the overall flow and function of Time.

What happens when someone with whom your life and destiny have been entwined dies? Saroyan went on remembering his father. On my last visit to his home, I remember two very large photos facing each other on opposing walls: one, Saroyan's father, the other his son. "They are the same man," I said, for truly they looked like each other. Their countenances spoke of defeat, and it was because of this defeat that their faces reflected a kind of saintly vulnerability. "Who are you then?" I wanted to ask, but didn't. He might have answered that he was the Holy Ghost, the neutralizer, the force to enter and effect a change, before the discontinuance resumed its continuing course. He must have felt in himself a little like that. He was like a father to his father, and to his son a stranger. It was not his destiny to be either. He was a Writer.

I realized then that it was because of this that there had been room for me in his life; a willingness to impart and encourage and advance someone not of his blood line but of that other line that was closer to his heart.

On an earlier occasion he had returned from Europe and phoned me upon his arrival. By now I was writing poetry, the first writing that was truly mine and done in my own voice; so different from Saroyan's, and yet in many ways seemingly the same.

When I arrived at his home, he came out to greet me. "Let's stand outside for a moment," he said. "The sun is up, and besides the mailman hasn't arrived yet. I don't want to miss him." I must have had a questioning look on my face, for his answer quickly followed. "We are all men of letters," he said. "We wait for the postman." He laughed after I did, for once again he had said something unexpected, both funny and true, and all without intention. On another occasion, in speaking to a gathering of Armenians about his son's one-word poems, he said: "There is this to be said about Aram's poetry: what meets the eye meets it instantly." There was a great roar of laughter, and again Saroyan looked puzzled until he realized the truth and humor and precision of his remark.

After the mailman arrived and we had gone inside, he began to tell me of his latest plans. He wanted to start a Saroyan Library, which is why, he said, he had bought two adjoining tract homes in the first place. And indeed the second home was already beginning to look like a museum: player piano, cash register (salvaged from one of the old Fresno saloons, a self-sculptured piece of drift wood that he had titled "The Violin," a momento from the recently demolished court house, and of course endless boxes of books and memorabilia. "How would you like the job?" he announced. "I need a secretary, and an all-around organizer."

I was delighted. It seemed heaven-sent. I accepted instantly and began launching into plans for the library right on the spot.

Again the unexpected, or the message on the forehead, as the Armenians like to say, for in not knowing why he had wanted to see me, I had come with an intention of my own—in the form of a sheaf of my poems that I had wanted him to read. I had recently married, and wandering around the backyard of our Fresno home I began to write these mysterious poemlike structures. I had no idea of their quality or worth, only that they seemed to be pouring out from me as if I were an untended faucet, turned on and then abandoned. Aside from my wife, I had shown them to no one.

Fortunately, when phoning me, he had given me no time to worry or fuss over which poems to take along.

"What did you bring?" he asked at his home, after we had finished our talk, for there between us were a sheaf of poems, burning a hole in his table.

"Poems—I think," I said. "Will you look at them?"

"Of course!" he exclaimed, sweeping them off the table. "Stay where you are, while I take these into the other room."

A slow reader, he would need time to "study" them, for he often said that he couldn't read anything that interested him without at the same time writing it himself. At last, he emerged and handed me my poems. "Let me put it in Armenian," he said. "These poems are A-1."

My destiny was fixed. I knew—in equal mixtures of joy and sorrow— that I would be a poet. Not a short story writer. Not a novelist. Not a playwright. But a poet. At least I knew. And for a long, long time that was enough.

Saroyan withdrew the secretary job almost immediately after reading my poems. "You have your own work," he said as we drove along a dusty back road between Fresno and Sanger, "and now you must do it. I hope you've done all your preliminary work, because it's too late now, you have no excuse but to write." As I sat there pondering his words as he drove, a bird flew by the windshield. "What was that?" Saroyan exclaimed.

"A flicker," I replied.

"Aha, you see, you know the *names* of things."

And that sealed it—at least for him. The suffering he left to me, as he in turn assumed his own suffering. Still, he was twenty-seven when he "hit it big." And here I was, at thirty-five just starting out. We had much in common. Or did we? We were Armenians, we were writers, and now we were almost equals; for hadn't the pupil just given his mentor the name of a bird, and hadn't he after all this time, delivered over a sheaf of poems? I didn't (nor could I have, at the time) wonder what he must have felt, with his almost-secretary suddenly become his first-and-only-pupil-poet. I hadn't thought of that, nor had I wondered then how different our destinies were. It was more than enough to be sitting beside him, driving down a dusty road in Fresno or Sanger—what matter which—and to have on the seat between us 10-15 of my first tentative poems, the nucleus of what would become my first book of poems, that he, Saroyan, would write an introduction for.

And so we drove along, giving names to things, in English and Armenian, in real and imaginary words, in prose and in poetry, laughing at the top of our lungs in English, roaring in Armenian.

Under Saroyan's Spell

PETE HAMILL

The year was 1956. I was a student in Mexico City, trying unsuccessfully to be a painter through the slender bounty of the GI Bill. One afternoon, near the end of the month, when we were all waiting for checks from the VA, and surviving on onion sandwiches and eight-cents-a-bottle Carta Blanca beer, I wandered into the Benjamin Franklin Library on Insurgentes Avenue. This wasn't the greatest library that had ever existed, but the books were in English, and the building was right out of the era of Don Porfirio Diaz, and most important, it was free. I was then twenty-one years old, and had read my way through Hemingway and Fitzgerald and Eliot; I thought it must be time for Steinbeck. And while looking through the shelves marked "S," I found Saroyan. The book was, of course, *The Daring Young Man on the Flying Trapeze*.

"Horizontally wakeful amid universal widths, practising laughter and mirth, satire, the end of all . . ."

This was something new to me, a new voice, a fresh tone, an unusual attitude. I took the book back to the apartment on Avenida Melchor Ocampo, and read on, feeling as if this crazy man, this California Armenian, this William Saroyan was doing my own writing for me. I'm not certain now what attracted me so much; part of it, I'm sure, must have been the powerful way Saroyan wrote about hunger, while maintaining a kind of tough optimism. In Mexico that year, living on $110 a month from the VA, we were almost always hungry. But it could have been something else: Saroyan and I were both children of immigrants, which meant we were burdened by inexplicable nostalgias; to this day, lost cities, distant countries, and the unexplained past are a critical part of my imaginative life. Ireland exists for me the way Armenia did for Saroyan, distant, obscure, inhabited by a people To Whom Things Had Been Done. And yet America is central to Saroyan's vision, and to mine.

The children of immigrants are separated from their parents by many things: language, baseball, street games, friendships; but young Americans are free in a way their parents will never be, even though the parents usually have left behind some form of despotism. Both generations, however, are joined in some deeper way; deep down there is a river of legend and myth flowing through the country of the imagination. Reading Saroyan for the first time in those months in Mexico, I touched his myths, and in some stumbling, uncertain way, discovered my own. When the year was over, I no longer wanted to be a painter. I wanted to write. I wanted to express something about the way time affected us all, and painting simply was not the medium. I would have to use words, like that daring, dying young man:

> Now tell me, she said; what can you do?
> He was embarrassed. I can write, he said pathetically.
> You mean your penmanship is good? Is that it? said the elderly maiden.
> Well, yes, he replied. But I mean that I can write.
> Write what? said the miss, almost with anger.
> Prose, he said simply.

Saroyan wrote prose all of his life, of course, and the astonishing thing is how good so much of it is. In the 1950s when I first began to read him, the critics had already turned against him; it was as if they could not forgive him for the sunniness of some of his stories, for his insistence in the face of postwar despair that this world did contain some good men and women. Saroyan also wrote about large things: love, and death, and the meaning of life. This was to be fatal to his reputation while he lived, even though he did it very well. Consider the beginning of that unjustly neglected novel *Rock Wagram* (1951):

> Every man is a good man in a bad world. No man changes the world. Every man himself changes from good to bad or from bad to good, back and forth, all his life, and then dies. But no matter how or why or when a man changes, he remains a good man in a bad world, as he himself knows. All his life a man fights death, and then at last loses the fight, always having known he would. Loneliness is every man's portion, and failure. The man who seeks to escape from loneliness is a lunatic. The man who does not know that all is failure is a fool. The man who does not laugh at these things is a bore, as each of them knows. Every man is innocent, and in the end a lonely lunatic, a lonely fool, or a lonely bore.
> But there is meaning to a man. There is meaning to the life every

man lives. It is a secret meaning, and pathetic if it weren't for the lies of art.

This is not the way many intellectuals felt after a disgusting war, after the horrors of Auschwitz and Hiroshima, after Hitler and Stalin. Saroyan was dismissed as a naif, a man whose cosmic optimism simply could not be verified by facts. But I think they were wrong. To be sure, Saroyan didn't follow the pack; he didn't take his philosophy off the rack, picking up a socialist suit one year and an existentialist suit the next. He saw the world with his own special vision, and he was true to it all of his life. But that vision was not merely some form of mindless California optimism; Saroyan had some bright colors on his palette, but more often they were dark. I think of the barber, in that astonishing story "Seventy Thousand Assyrians." He doesn't want to think about the old country, because "everything is washing up over there." But he can't get over what has been done to the Assyrians, as Saroyan and others never got over what had been done to the Armenians, and the Jews and the Irish and the Poles and the native Americans and the Cambodians will never get over history either.

"We went in for the wrong things," says Badal, the Assyrian barber. "We went in for the simple things, peace and quiet and families. We didn't go in for machinery and conquest and militarism. We didn't go in for diplomacy and deceit and the invention of machine-guns and poison gases. Well there is no use being disappointed. We had our day, I suppose . . . "

Saroyan broods about this conversation (and there is no way to do justice here to the complicated mood of the story) and about his own writing and about being Armenian. He has chosen, after all, to write about this Assyrian barber. He says:

"Why don't I make up plots and write beautiful love stories that can be made into motion pictures? Why don't I let these unimportant and boring matters go hang? Why don't I try to please the American reading public?

"Well, I am an Armenian . . . "

Which, to some extent, explains everything. Saroyan's optimism, such as it was, came directly from his tragic sense of life, and that came from being an Armenian. This was a man, after all, whose father died when he was three, who was dumped for a while in an orphanage, who was raised by various uncles and aunts, who scrambled around, read everything, listened to music, heard the sound of the story of the race, and became a writer to tell the world what he knew. In the end, he loved human beings the way Faulkner once said he loved Mississippi: in spite of, not because.

This is not the place, and I'm not the writer, to argue Saroyan's enduring value. Certainly his vast body of work deserves much closer attention from academics, and someone eventually must acknowledge his influence on other American writers. There appears to be a lot of Saroyan in Jack Kerouac and other beat writers, in Richard Brautigan and Charles Bukowski and William Kotzwinkle; a number of playwrights have eaten from the plump table of *The Time of Your Life*. The critics now ignore him. But my sense is that Saroyan's achievement will be recognized eventually for what it was: a large, almost Balzacian attempt to turn one man's experience of the world into literature.

As happens to all prolific writers, the casual or trivial work that Saroyan produced will vanish. But I can't imagine an America in which it's impossible to find a copy of *The Daring Young Man*, or *The Cave Dwellers*, or *The Man With the Heart in the Highlands*. My own life would be meaner without that wonderful little book, *Tracy's Tiger*, or such stories as "Citizens of the Third Grade," "The Summer of the Beautiful White Horse," "The Journey to Hanford," "The Assyrian," and dozens of others. I cherish the novels called *The Laughing Matter, Rock Wagram,* and *One Day in the Afternoon of the World*. I never cared much for his most famous novel, *The Human Comedy;* it seemed too glib, too easy, a form of wartime propaganda. But I think Saroyan would have enjoyed the stage version that Wilford Leach has directed for Joseph Papp's Public Theater; I certainly did, and if the play helps expand the audience for Saroyan's other work, then it will have accomplished something very fine.

In the memoirs written in his last years, Saroyan's tone began to shift; bitterness entered his language; and his son Aram's account of their terrible relationship indicates that the bitterness had soured other parts of his life too. But the earlier, more confident work remains, with its sense of joyful abundance, and the best of it will endure. If Saroyan's greatest literary invention was Saroyan himself, then Saroyan will continue to ask future generations those questions which haunted him all of his life:

"What does a man mean?" he asks in *Rock Wagram*. "What is the meaning of a man? What is he supposed to be? How is he supposed to be what he is supposed to be? What is the purpose of him? What is he supposed to do? How is he supposed to do it? Does he mean anything? Does his birth mean anything, his boyhood, his early manhood, his manhood, his work, his failure, his humor, his anger, his despair, his death, his actual death in his body? . . ."

There are answers to such questions, of course, tentative, uncertain, even wrong, and in Saroyan's case, they are all to be found in the work. His answers might not be ours. But I know this: Somewhere, in a library in a strange town, a young man is looking at the shelves of fiction. His eyes move slowly, he bends his neck to read the titles, and when he reaches "S," he sees Saroyan. Perhaps for the first time. And I envy him.

The Saroyan Self Remembered

ARTHUR SAINER

Two emotional role models beckoned to many university students in the forties. Our T. S. Eliot selves sauntered about like elegant survivors of some stupendous Western calamity that had been slowly nibbling at the collective will since the foggy regions of the fourteenth century. We (Western Civilization) had been rapidly going to the pits since Dante, and the Eliot self loved the concept. Opposing this baleful persona was the William Saroyan self, a model of such unremitting joy (if curiously tinged with sadness) that one was almost apologetically happy in the face of the doom-and-gloomers. The Saroyan self embraced everything in a kind of slowly accelerating ecstasy, its bearhug of indiscriminate pleasure cradled such phenomena as pomegranates, broken marriages, ferry-boats, and ailing typewriters. The Eliot self showed marked distaste for cities: cities were vulgar, ossified remnants of psychic wounds, and were unbearably loaded down with people. For the Saroyan self, cities were too empty; to the immeasurable disgust of the Eliot self, the Saroyan self wanted to rush into the streets or into meadows; in its very loneliness it sought out the lonely other, it fought its own sadness in order to partici-pate in silent paeans to the incorrigible loveliness of existence (I should add that there was a third self in those years, the Hemingway self, but he was too much of a loner, hardly given to human exchange).

At New York University, several of the Saroyan selves and their bud-dies began funneling their stories to an Armenian-American publication called *Hairenik Weekly*. (One of my published stories, I believe the title was "Brahms On a Summer's Day," had to do with young lovers whose sexual stirrings corresponded to the kind of urgencies Johannes Brahms was laying out musically as he yearned for Clara Schumann.) It was not that the NYU literary apprentices were necessarily of Armenian stock, but rather that *Hairenik* was a publishing home for the fiction of Saroyan. *Hairenik Weekly* (later to become *Hairenik Monthly*) also became a home for us; in some fashion, we were basking in the warmth of our elder statesman of joy. Added to that is the evident fact that if Saroyan reached out, without judgment, to all mankind, Hairenik's editor reached out with a gentle kind of judgment to all young writers.

The Saroyan side of myself helped ease me into the world of literature, and into the theater. In many ways, this easy entrance proved illusory—there were hard-nosed editors and wary producers down the road who would question the coin I'd used to get myself through the gate, and philosophical and psychological struggles waiting for me that I'd in no way imagined. But Saroyan also helped with precious gifts, among them an appetite for lustre, a sense of a subdued shimmer of sunlight that would envelop the stories of troubled souls. And he left me with a way of engaging the imagination, a way of entering the world of the play: by demonstrating that one needn't all but sink the play under a preponderance of realistic details; that "serious" dialogue needn't have a pedestrian ring to it, and that proclaiming beings uttering remarks normally associated with the dream life or Utopian fantasies do address some urgent impulse in the human psyche; and that the strict adherence to the principle of cause-and-effect is not the only way to understand the movement of events.

Saroyan once said, reflecting on the impoverishment he sensed in the drama of his time: the play has gone out of the play. My guess is that he was speaking about joy, and about a kind of fancy, or fancifulness. Theater critic Joseph Wood Krutch notes that Saroyan represented "everything uncharacteristic of a year [1939] which was just emerging from the gloom, anger, and dismay of the depression decade (*The American Drama Since 1918* [New York: George Braziller, 1957], p. 322). Nineteen Thirty-nine saw not the first but the first *two* Saroyan plays on Broadway, *My Heart's in the Highlands* and *The Time of Your Life*. "His skyrocket," Krutch tells us, "rose so suddenly into the theatrical firmament and then fell from it so suddenly that he seems to belong, not to a decade but to the single year 1939 . . ." As against the grim realism and sometime didacticism of much thirties drama, Saroyan was "gay, exuberant, romantically an individualist, and so convinced that the world was full of 'beautiful people' as well as of all manner of other delightful things that we should all be happy as kings if we would only relax and 'believe everything'" (Krutch, p. 322).

The fanciful in the Saroyan narrative is exemplified by the serendipitous manner in which people and events suddenly materialize, often without discernible cause, engage our attention for a moment, and then disappear. Unlike the picaresque novel, in which ordinary or grotesque beings are met in the course of the protagonist's ongoing engagement (even if the engagement is as loosely defined as "seeing the world"), the Saroyan narrative finds the leading character without concrete engagement; the world rather than a particular thing in it or a particular end engages him. Or rather, the end is not so much to witness the world on the way to one's developing some calling (often that of writer) but to embrace the world while the calling appears to be perfecting itself. And in the Saroyan narrative, suddenly materializing beings and events seem to impel themselves inward, as if breaking through a skylight into the interior structure of the story. Beings and events manifest themselves for nothing more nor less than the ongoing delight of the universe.

It is true that the old man with the bugle, in *My Heart's In the Highlands*, though he appears as if from nowhere, and blows his melody of freedom through the streets and into the firmament, is eventually tracked down by the conscientious caretakers from an old people's home. This transformation from generalized dispenser of joy to particularized escapee from a fretting social service is not only Saroyan's error (perhaps the tribute a novice playwright mistakenly felt was due to the Goddess Accountability), it is *our* error for quietly allowing the transformation. For *My Heart's in the Highlands* isn't essentially about a moment of breaking free from the confines of civilization's corrupting necessities, though there's always that thematic undercurrent; it's essentially about the life of free spirits. And some of these free spirits, for example, the father-poet, are wedded to and residing in their own perceptions of Paradise. The poet and the old bugler are like firm disciples of Jesus, having a kinetic understanding that ultimately the Lord provides. When asked to consider the question of earning one's bread, they consider instead the lilies of the field. In contrast, the poet's small boy, with all the warmth and charm in the world, is constitutionally a bit of a worrier. But the boy hardly worries without reason. It is his task each day to con the neighborhood grocer into extending a little more credit. And this small boy, this small worrier, reflects something in *us*. For we are forever asking, who will provide? That is, we are forever asking the wrong questions. It isn't that the questions aren't valid in a certain context, it's that the context and the emotional spirit of the questions are too confining, and finally are not real. What the poet and the bugler and even the boy in his nonworrying moments, and William Saroyan, the angelic father of this work, seem to understand is not that bread falls from trees but that we live in a world in which, for all the terrible loneliness generated, we are not beings who have been abandoned, that something benign and caring has never for an instant absented itself from us.

This is not to say that the Saroyan world is without the possibility of misfortune, without the possibility of natural or man-made disasters. It is to say that the world is essentially harmonious, that there is a quality in us and a quality in the possible connections between one another that allows for harmony and joy.

And it isn't to say that there is not an element in Saroyan that doesn't reflect the edginess of the worrier. Nor is a certain air of fretfulness absent from *Highlands*, from *The Time of Your Life*, from *Sam Ego's House*, from *Get Away, Old Man*, or from all those sundry plays, many of which may never have been produced to this day. And it isn't to say there is not an undercurrent of melancholy, of plaintiveness that collects in the work like bits of gum in the wings of an angel. But the battle is always won by an innocent wisdom, a wisdom that tells us the Eliot self is radically in error to recoil from life and the Saroyan self is radically in the truth to rush out into the streets. The old bugler in *Highlands* could play it safe by sticking close to the old people's home, by allowing the home to care for his needs. Like one of Sam Beckett's old men, he could nurse memories by a dim fire. But the bugler understands what death is about, he understands that braving nasty weather and the exigencies of life on the road (which includes the possibility of dying on the road) is preferable to dying "agreeably," as Rilke once put it, in a hospital or at the institution. The street, of course, presents other problems. We need our time alone, our distance—many of us grow fidgety in a crowd of true believers, whatever it is they happen to be believing that week—but even alone we need to understand that we are connected to one another, that we aren't discrete beings but are beings connected to that force that got us here in the first place.

A few years ago a Saroyan play was in rehearsal in some basement in Manhattan. One day there was a peremptory banging at the door. The banger—William Saroyan. He'd gotten wind of the fact that some reasonably impoverished theater people were mounting one of his plays. And he tracked them down because he was delighted that somebody somewhere was still working on Saroyan-style grace and joy and beauty, and he wanted to witness the workers and the work collaborating in that hymn to the benign human comedy. Perhaps today this lovely free spirit is still banging on some door somewhere. Thank you, Bill. And Bill—hello out there.

Bread and Butter Note

JOEL OPPENHEIMER

[Editor's note: This piece was written while Saroyan was still alive.]

William Saroyan came into my life in 1943. I was thirteen; my oldest brother was twenty-one. He had discovered Saroyan in college, and he gave me *The Human Comedy* for a birthday present. I raced through it, loving every minute, and then dipped into my allowance to get *My Name Is Aram* on my own.

I had no idea then, of course, that I was to spend the rest of my life trying desperately to be a "poet," but I knew already that I would always be a reader. Now I'm fifty-four. I've discovered, loved, and grown away from an awful lot of writers in that forty-one years. The only one who's stayed with me—who draws me as much now as then—is Saroyan. That's not to say that other writers haven't come to mean more to me, and certainly my relationship with several others has been more intense; but Saroyan still holds the same mystery and wonder and delight that he did when I was thirteen.

Now one of my sons is twelve. He saw me reading *Chance Meetings*, Bill's collection of memoirs, and asked me what it was. I told him, and when he found out that I was going to review it for *The New York Times*, he asked me about Saroyan, and if I had any books by him that he'd like. I dug out my old copies of *The Human Comedy* and *Aram* and turned him loose. I haven't gotten a report from him yet, but I noticed yesterday while making his bed that they were tucked down in the corner as his presleep reading. It was exactly the same glorious feeling as when we sat at Shea Stadium and watched Willie Mays together—there are, after all, not that many things one can pass on to one's son.

Saroyan is, for me, one of the great hidden writers of our time. No one ever talks about him as one of the literary stars these days, and yet he has been with us consistently for almost fifty-five years. He comes up accidently, I find, in conversations with other writers, after the greats have been discussed and dismissed. Everyone has a favorite Saroyan; my own is *Rock Wagram,* a too little known novel from the fifties. I found my copy for a dime in a used paperback stall, and it sits on my shelf, a little ragged, but still there.

Then there are the short stories, all the collections of them. The man is a genius at these small slices of space and time and people, an absolute genius. Stories I read years ago stay with me still. *I Could Say Bella Bella,* for one, and another about a fight in a bar over whether the light in the fishtank should be on or off. The stories are economical and beautiful, sparse and rich, and they are, in the best sense, "unimportant," in that they deal with the small victories and defeats that make up life, and do all of life, and all of the big things in life comes clear in them.

I have friends who have traveled all over the Eastern seaboard tracking down college or little theater productions of *The Time of Your Life*—it never dates for them, and they always come back aglow with it, lit up like the insane jukebox in it. In fact, in the mad sixties, I came within an inch of being involved in a plot to show Europe America through a repertory presentation of that play coupled with Eugene O'Neill's *The Iceman Cometh.* We were all hanging out in a literary bar at the time and it seemed to us that these two great plays, each set in a saloon, were the best we could offer to show others what we were like. I'm sorry now that it never happened.

I guess this piece is, in the end, just my own memoir of my "chance meeting" with this crazy Armenian who knew only one thing, he thought: how to tell a story. It's time I thanked him for that chance meeting, which has stayed with me and grown each time a new book comes out until now I feel like an old friend. It's a good feeling, and he's a good friend to have.

The Middle-aged Man on the Flying Trapeze

JACK TREVOR STORY

[Editor's note: This piece was written while Saroyan was still alive.]

My mother's mother Lucy was forever encouraging me to move through life with what she called "guyrot," which is a phonetic rendering of an Armenian word, or a word of Bitlis, or a word of the Saroyan family, or a word invented by my grandmother herself, which signified, apparently, these things; to assault the world with early morning swiftness and clarity of mind, with panning, with zest, with brilliance, with cunning, with eagerness and with skill.

This passage taken from Saroyan's *The Bicycle Rider In Beverley Hills* might equally well have come from any page in any of his many books of plays, stories, and pieces. What is this man, who once described himself as "the kindest fourteen-year-old boy in San Joaquin Valley," really saying, and why has he been saying it so long and why are so few people listening these days?

Fortunately, most of his readers are writers, for he is a writer's writer as ever was. For my money he is the greatest writer's writer that ever was, for he has nourished and sustained me for twenty-six years and never ever let me down. Without Saroyan I would be either an indifferent electronics engineer or a fairly efficient butcher on the point of retirement. I might even have been a policeman or else a dead war-time pilot.

William Saroyan, my hero, has kept me safe and alive and writing since 1944 when I first read his collection of stories, *Dear Baby,* and as a result sat down and wrote my first published story after fifteen years of solid rejection.

I began serious writing in 1931 in Cambridge. We lived in two rooms above a sweet shop in the Cambridge slums, in East Road. Across the road, forever now stuck on my inner eye, was Loker's newsagents shop (it's still there) in the rain; on its scarlet and black posters I had followed the rise and fall of the R101, the death of PC Gutteridge with a bullet in each eye, the flights of Jim Mollison and Amy Johnson, and the special GIVE-AWAY model aeroplane kit in *Modern Boy;* in other words, we had had the glamorous movements of the world emblazoned like a newsreel opposite the windows of our poverty. Then one day: NEW: THRILLER Magazine. £100 GIVE-AWAY ! ! ! !

The AP magazine, opening with the first Saint story, I believe, was offering £100 for a 30,000-word thriller from one of its readers.

I had been writing in a desultory fashion since I was eleven and now at the age of fourteen I was still not rich and famous; this £100 prize was the spur to serious endeavour. I wrote ten thousand words of that thriller in laborious long-hand between spending my days at the open-air school in Ascham Road and much of the rest of the time cooking for my mother, brothers, and sister who worked variously at Chivers' jam factory, the Pitt Club, and the Home and Colonial Stores.

From then on I wrote fairly steadily at the rate of about one short story a week, that is to say fifty stories a year for another thirteen years without getting so much as a letter or word written about them; they went out and they came back. I wasn't depressed by this (I expected nothing); it gave me a feeling of being a professional rejected writer and not simply a schoolboy, office boy, and errand boy.

After about ten years of this, I sent a sample story to the Regent School of Writing. They replied that my writing was so bad they could not even enroll me as a student. The chief physicist at Marconi's found me crying on my bench and asked my why. I explained to him about not being a writer, showed him the letter from the correspondence shool.

"What authors do you read?" he asked me.

I didn't read any authors, I didn't have time. Then either he or the chief engineer, who was also a good helpful man, told me that I could be a writer if I set my mind on it. I remember the chief engineer telling me two things about that time. "An engineer can do anything," was one thing. The other thing was: "Some people have to work in the world, Story, and some people can run barefoot across the grass." I have an idea he was trying to tell me to get stuck into my work. I was the only wartime Marconi employee taken to court for lateness; arraigned in front of the magistrates who refused to convict on the evidence of a robot clock card.

One day Ronnie Wolfe, who was then a fellow electronics man but is now a top comedy writer, asked me if I had ever read William Saroyan. He had already taken me through Gerald Kersh without any noticeable effect, but now I got my girl friend (wives and families never stopped me having girl friends) to buy me *Dear Baby,* a collection of Saroyan stories.

Dear Baby is a slim book, I read it straight through; it gave me goose pimples. When I get goose pimples something has happened to me.

I laid the book aside that same night and sat down and wrote a short story called "Peter Keeps a Secret," about this chap who got killed before his time and found there was no place in heaven for him so they sent him back. I put it under my son's name, Peter Lang (named after Eddie Lang the guitarist) and sent it to *John O'London's Weekly*. I had a letter back offering me six guineas for first British serial rights, whatever that meant, and a postscript from Wilson Midgeley, the editor (he introduced crossword puzzles to Britain) in his blue fountain pen saying: "I like this very much."

It was my first acceptance, the year was 1944, I was twenty-seven, and something called D-day was going on somewhere or other.

"I can see we shan't have you with us much longer," the chief engineer told me when he saw that I was out of my mind. And in the works magazine they called me Compton Mackenzie Story. Later, C. P. Snow who was in charge of our personnel, gave me a job as St. Albans editor of the house journal. "I write books too," he told me, when I went to see him in his Kingsway office. "Oh yes?" I said. "What name do you write under?" I was clutching my first book jacket pull (*The Trouble with Harry*) and there were only two writers in the world—me and Saroyan.

I wrote fifty-eight more stories that did the out-and-back bit then sold my second story to *Argosy,* then a third,and then I was a writer, thanks to some Armenian American called William Saroyan whom I had never met. Excuse me a moment at this late date:

"Thank you, William Saroyan. That telegram you got in 1944 was from me."

Now whenever I dry up or stop feeling like a writer I read Saroyan and I'm okay again. What is it about his writing that can turn a boy into a writer? It is this: Saroyan is saying simple things in a simple manner. He is out of fashion at the moment because he is saying them without rancour, anger, or bitterness and because, unlike the rest of the artistic world with very few exceptions (Robert Nathan might be another), he is a man who believes himself to be mortal.

Leaping to success with his *Daring Young Man on the Flying Trapeze* in the thirties when everybody was too concerned with making ends meet even to bother with the rise of Hitler, he is now supremely unconcerned with the power complexes of the present scene; he seems to say who cares about power, black, white, or atomic, when life is only three mortgages long? As for nudity, Saroyan has been nude all his life in the only way that makes for sanity—the good nakedness of unadorned art. Above all, and what divorces him from today's poets and minstrels with their borrowed philosophies and unsuffered traumas, William Saroyan is himself. This is as naked as you can get, and this is the brilliant trick that, once mastered, makes a writer.

When I first read Saroyan I was trying to be Dickens, William Blake, Charles Lamb, and Jonathan Swift and, occasionally and when I was in the mood, Peter Cheyney, James Thurber, and Mark Twain. The 800 stories I had written before being rescued from the rock of artistic oblivion by Saroyan often read like hideous parodies of the real thing. I used words like "procure" instead of "get" and strung clichés together like so many bowler hats and rolled umbrellas. From Saroyan I immediately learned that if you couldn't think of the right word you didn't look in a Thesaurus, you just simply said so (I know what I mean).

Saroyan doesn't pander to fashion, attitudes, or concern himself with topicalities, because he is too busy being Saroyan to be aware of these ephemeral things. Saroyan doesn't write for money, that is, he doesn't write films or TV scripts or make adaptations of his books, because he is not interested in the second-order arts except, maybe, as audience. Saroyan doesn't write swear words or obscenities or write about the act of sex because, I feel, they are too obvious for him. Saroyan doesn't very often write stories; he just writes. He is breathing (he is always glad to notice), he is walking about and sleeping and eating. He takes nothing for granted. If you are depressed or ill or broke, you pick him up and he does you good.

Why is William Saroyan underrated? Why is he now in partial eclipse—or even total eclipse in smart circles? If people once liked Saroyan, you will find they are now apologetic, even defensive about it. They feel that to admit liking or reading him now would date them; or that their liking for his writing was due to their immaturity (oh yes, I read him at college, of course). You get uncannily the same reaction if you mention Rupert Brooke to poetry lovers. Now Rupert Brooke is the only poet whose work has stimulated, inspired, and lasted me a lifetime—I need no other poet. Their common root, aside from their gift of words, lies in their belief in mortality, their lack of arrogance, their stripping away of human priorities over the more important priorities of animals and vegetables—in other words, their cosmic view. Both writers make you feel that you belong to the universe and not to the Labour party.

About someone else's novel, sent to him by a publisher, Saroyan says: "It wasn't bad, but it was about specific people in that peculiarly specific way which makes a novel meaningless."

When Saroyan writes about a car salesman, he is writing about every car salesman in the world starting from Henry Ford. In his short story "The Faraway Night," he is Everyman sitting in the long-distance bus next to Everygirl. And, like Rupert Brooke, when he is writing tragedy it

is comic and when comedy it is tragic—only even more tragic. These are
the metaphysics that make life bearable and death bearable and writing
great.

People who have "grown out" of William Saroyan are likely to have
grown out of the better side of their natures. In the world of Saroyan
there are no villains because, being only human himself, he prefers not
to see them:

> I do not think that in writing of them [his family] I ever lied, I
> merely chose to notice in them the things I cherish and preferred, and
> to refer to the things I didn't cherish with humour and charity. . . .

Now look through your newspaper today and see just how old-fashioned and out-dated and passé humour and charity is or are (I know
what I mean). Innocence, too, is a little shameful, isn't it? Saroyan is
surprised and intrigued by everything that happens, and if it happens
again tomorrow he will be equally astonished. This is another reason he
is a writer's writer, for writers must be perennial virgins, their recorded
experiences a continuous deflowering with a good exhilarating scream in
the right places; a shedding of new light, that's to say, on old things.

F. Scott Fitzgerald, dying of neglect (that writer's disease) in Hollywood, made various disparaging references to Saroyan. You can understand that Scott Fitzgerald, having made and lost a reputation with
his massively fashioned masterpieces, should now resent the sudden
rocketing to fame and fortune of a writer who just yacked about
breathing or chopping up onions or what his uncle did in Bitlis. Odd, to
my mind, though, that Scott should have disparaged Saroyan while
applauding Hemingway's posturings—masculine, American, and literary. Hemingway might have developed into a good writer had he begun
where he left off. Odd, because Scott Fitzgerald's judgment was generally sound.

What I set out to say somewhere back there is that the writers you love
most are likely to hate each other and have nothing whatever in common—except that mysterious unique something that turns *you* on. Because if my hero were not Saroyan it would be Scott Fitzgerald. I feel that
I know them both from their schooldays onward, though there is a
strangely contradictory thing about their writing which I'd like to mention.

Saroyan, who talks about nothing but himself, his family, his relations,
his life, tells us nothing about his marriages or his wives. You think he
does, but he doesn't. "My secretary ran away and married him," Al Hart
of New York Macmillan's told me once. You'll never find that in his
books. I have been reading him constantly for a quarter of a century: I

know his writing self from the telegraph office in Fresno to the hard-up backwaters of Paris, yet I find that I know nothing whatever—about Saroyan the man.

Fitzgerald, who is reticent and conventional and expresses himself only in terms of fiction and fairly nondomestic articles and essays, yet manages to give us his tragic wife Zelda and their life together down to the last heartbreaking detail. Work this out for yourself and you'll come up with my own conclusion: the highly personalized writing of Saroyan's is a brilliant phony. What looks like artless diary scribblings turns out to be art of the highest order; a synthesis of life that is so convincing it is mistaken for life itself.

Saroyan is in good company—Gainsborough had the same trouble with the critics. The lesson here is that you can reflect your life and times so accurately that your contemporaries think it's a snapshot—it may take 100 years to see the brush marks.

Letters from Bill

JULES ARCHER

My friend Arnie Bennett and I were nineteen when we discovered Bill Saroyan. The year was 1934, when the Dionne quintuplets survived and Chancellor Dollfuss of Austria didn't. Struggling for publication, we avidly read magazines like Whit Burnett's *Story,* a showcase for the best and brightest.

Lending me an issue, my friend said, "There's a story in it that will knock you out. Tell me what you think of it."

I read the whole issue. When we met again, I told him I was speechless. The story was fantastic. I'd never read anything like it, this side of Walt Whitman. The guy was a genius, and we had to do something to help him get famous.

When we began to discuss specifics, Bennett looked increasingly puzzled. "What the hell are you talking about?" he exclaimed. "There was nothing like that in the story."

It was my turn to look puzzled. "Well, what story did you mean? There was only one that was really amazing."

"The story by George Milburn, of course."

"Oh, that was good, but it couldn't hold a candle to that piece by a guy named William Saroyan, called "1 2 3 4 5 6 7 8." Didn't you think it was fantastic?"

"That was one of the stories I didn't read."

"Read it," I said, pressing the issue into his arms.

He read it. When we met again, his eyes glowed when he talked about it. "You're right, Jules. We've got to do something for him. The guy *is* a genius. I'm going to write him a letter telling him we're going to whoop it up for him as the most original voice in America today."

So Arnie wrote the first letter. I don't have a copy of it, but I have a copy of Saroyan's reply, written on cheap yellow second sheets, dated 12 June 1934.

"A thousand thanks, Bennett," he wrote. "It is splendid to know that one's work is liked by the young. I am very glad you saw 1 2 3 4 5 6 7 8: let me try to explain about the song: it is possible to write about almost anything, and if one works hard enough it is possible sometimes to write *greatly* about anything. The song is Meditation by Massenet, from the opera *Thais,* as recorded by Paul Ash and his Granada Orchestra: Brunswick, record number 2783-A. The record is rather old, I think; and you might be able to pick it up at some record exchange store, or you might be able to find it among the old and forgotten records of a friend. In the story of the young telegraph clerk and the music and the dream of an artful life I meant to show that endings take place in life more subtly than in art, and that if art is to grow and not continue to be repetition, the artist must make some attempt to get into his subject matter and force himself to say what is truthful, no matter how unconventional and unusual his work of art may turn out to be.

"But I hate to talk about such things: actually it is impossible to speak of what goes on within a writer while he is writing. Poe, in explaining his composition of "The Raven," was either spoofing or kidding himself: He explained everything but his genius, which is the only thing.

"Please forgive me for taking so long to answer your letter. One thing or another has kept me going and coming for several weeks, and this is the first chance I have had to take time out for a letter or two.

"My sincerest good wishes to each of you: Jules and yourself. I will tell you something: at your age or for that matter at any age life is just a trifle more important than letters: living is just a bit more important than writing. When you devise an artful style of living you devise also an artful style of writing. Most writers make the mistake of trying to perfect their writing before trying to perfect their living: the results are generally sad.

"Tennis is swell, Lately, though, I have had to give it up. I used to play quite a lot. What I liked about the game was its liveliness: the bouncing of a ball and one's being in opposition to a bouncing ball. Also its precision. In the story, though, I was mostly spoofing Hemingway.

"It is probably true: very often I do not write short stories. I do not have to: I can get by with murder almost. *The American Mercury* is printing another story soon, called "Ah-Ha." If the story is a story, then it is perhaps one of the most original to appear in America in years and years. It if it not a story, it certainly is remarkable prose, of some sort. The story is very short: a little over two pages of *Mercury* print, but it says more than two dozen of the usual run of stories. (Pardon me: I'm not bragging.)

"You didn't ask for advice, but I am going to make a few suggestions anyway. Live first: write afterwards. By living I do not mean taking a boat and going to China. I mean keeping your ears and eyes and heart open: getting it all into you. Refuse to become an artist: remain, that is, a man: someone alive, nothing more. Artists are bores. They are conceited and generally stupid. Take little seriously: I mean little that is outside of yourself. Take very seriously those experiences within yourself which you know to be vital and good.

"There is hardly anything more to say. In other words, be. Verb. You yourself. Being is doing. All right. Let it stand.

"When my story appears in *The American Mercury* will you drop the editor a very brief note, if you like the story. Make it very brief, though. If you feel like it, send me a picture of yourself and Jules: and, if you like, something each of you have written. But don't worry about writing, and don't be in a hurry. If you have something to say, and I believe you have, it will be said inevitably.

"Random House is publishing a book of my stories some time this year: *The Daring Young Man on the Flying Trapeze and Other Stories*. If you are in the money when the book is announced, I would appreciate it greatly if you would send to the publishers for a first edition. If the first edition is sold out soon enough after publication, I believe the book will sell fairly well. If you can make any other sort of fuss about the book, by all means do so: I mean it would probably help a lot. And when I get to New York I'll get in touch with you and we'll talk things over: if I ever get to New York again.

"Many thanks again, and good wishes to each of you."

If we had been enthusiastic about Saroyan before, that letter set us on fire. I took over the correspondence. On 20 June I wrote him a long, effusive letter that let all my emotions hang out to a "kinspirit," to use Christopher Morley's term. Saroyan's words had touched us to the core. We saw him as the purest, most honest spirit in modern letters.

"It is 11:15 and I ought to get to bed, but I would rather write to you," I wrote him. "I have just torn up a rough draft of a letter about four typewritten pages long. I tore it up because in it I told you how your letter to Arnie almost cost me my job, about my acquaintances— postmarked—in the literary field, about the dime I gave the bum at the opera house on account of you, and because I referred to Francis Thompson, Gertrude Stein, and Schnitzler. I couldn't decide whether or not I was showing off, so I tore it up.

"You are wrong about *The Philosophy of Composition*. There is no reason why Poe should have deceived his readers. I think you have twisted his genius to fit your own theory.

"Look, Saroyan—living is fine. I mean, you've got to live to write. But aren't books living? Isn't Dostoyevsky an adventure? Anyhow, Arnie says the chief distinction between someone like you and ourselves is that you begin with the premise that you have something to say and must say it, while we begin with the assumption that we want to write. When I think of you, Saroyan, I get literary constipation and write worse than usual.

"I told Arnie I was afraid to criticize you in my first letter because I was sure you wouldn't think me sympathetic. It's always easy to condemn something new on the grounds of precedent. You see, I was going to throw in your face Irving Babbit's theory that a genius which is nothing more than an outpouring of undisciplined emotion is not really great. It is personal, without craftsmanship, and therefore limited art. Also, that your type of story is easily duplicated—the fate of all work created with little effort—and therefore worth less than a story by George Milburn or Albert Halper. When I read what I have just written, it disgusts me. I hate to think that it might be true. I'm too crazy about your stuff to want to find fault. I've already spread the gospel by introducing '70,000 Assyrians' to five people, and mentioning it in my English class. They are all agreed that it is fine stuff, but cannot concur on a verdict of story or essay.

"Arnie and I will be among the first subscribers to 'The Daring Young Man,' in spite of the fact that we never buy new books. . . . The *Mercury* story will be boosted as innocently as we can manage, and any other break we can give you, you can depend upon us to do it. We are afraid, however, that you are a writer's writer, and you know what that means.

"Some questions: How much money have you left of all you've earned since 'The Daring Young Man?' What does 'Aspirin Joins the NRA' mean? What do you look like? What do you do for a social and sex life? (Arnie and I hoped you went out with whores, and in the next breath, hoped you didn't.) Do you honestly despite the literati? And what's wrong with *Arrowsmith?*

"I have a friend who's your age, Saroyan. He's a clever, talented young man of twenty-six, and he's had about the lousiest breaks of any writer I ever read about. We call him Midas, because everything he touches turns to brass. He is so soul-sick, he has utterly renounced good writing—after finishing a particularly fine story—and has declared his intentions of writing and selling only junk. He has been everything from as assistant stage manager with a group theater to a radio writer, and the net result is that he is hopelessly in debt to his mother, and completely despondent. Cornel De Jong, whose book 'Bella Fulla Straw' is a financial flop, must now either get a job or starve. Milburn, until the angels descended with a Guggenheim Fellowship, was up against it badly. Saroyan, why should a young man tear his guts open for the privilege of pouring perfume on a garden of weeds? Saroyan, why shouldn't I write conventional, readable

stories and eat regularly? Why shouldn't my friend? How many un-
heeded Saroyans are still starving and freezing in cities like San Francisco, and in towns and in the country? Saroyan, the rose that once has
blown, forever dies.

"In a week or so Arnie and I will forward pictures and a short story
each. Have you photographs you can spare?

"I will close this letter with a quotation, but I will not tell you where it is
from. I think it is beautiful: ". . . Keats, half chewed in the jaws of
London and spit dying on to Italy. . . ." It is 12:00 and I am tired, Good
night, Saroyan."

Forty-eight years later that letter would crimson my cheeks, but remembering that I was only nineteen and as honest as I could be at that
ambivalent age, I can make paternal allowances for the literary excesses
of youth. And so, verbatim.

On 26 June 1934, Saroyan replied with a letter that I often quote to
classes I teach on writing at the University of California, Santa Cruz,
Extension, because it has lost nothing of its validity in the intervening
years.

"Many thanks, Archer, for your fine letter," he replied.

"I wish you hadn't destroyed the other one. Unwitting I meant: in
regard to Poe. Certainly he didn't lie. But he failed to explain his genius.
I meant this. I think my story "Ah-Ha" comes closest in spirit to Poe than
anything printed in this country. Angoff [*Mercury* editor] describes it as
nightmarish. Well, that's all right, too. I didn't quite get how my letter to
your friend Bennett nearly cost you your job. Why? Also: don't be afraid
of showing off. Every man who ever got around to being great started by
showing off. Me, too. Max Baer, too. It's the overture. One outgrows it,
but it's necessary. If you think you are good, say it loudly, and often.
Living and writing are the same thing. Anything I say I say for myself:
there can be no arguments. I speak only for myself. You must feel free to
criticize my work as much as you feel the need to: your privilege. I assure
you I won't mind. I do a bit of criticising myself: of my own work.

"Tell me about your English class. What school? How do you like it.
How old are you?

"I have earned very little money writing. I have about a dollar and
thirty cents in cash at the moment. The title is "Aspirin Is a Member of
the NRA." It comes from the radio program, Bayer Aspirin is a Member
of the NRA. It means that contemporary management of public affairs is
basically evasive: pain is eased, but future pain is not avoided. I look like
hell. My social life is extremely simple: part of the time I talk with the
unemployed around Howard Street, and part of the time I visit the rich

at their homes: Fairmont Hotel, etc. For a whole picture. "The Poor and the Rich" is a recent story, not yet sent out. Most of my stuff hangs around until I feel like wasting postage. Sometimes a story never goes out. Years ago when I sat down to write, I sat down to write for myself: no thought of even wanting to be printed. It is a wise method. No headaches. My sex life is also simple: I take what I can get, provided I feel inclined. My relations with whores are generally platonic: I do not like to mix art with business and with whores the act is business, and when it isn't fake, so I stick to art. Whores are the loveliest of people when selected with care. See my story "Sleep in Unheavenly Peace." I honestly dislike those who think they are artists and nothing else. *Arrowsmith* I did not read; I saw a movie of it. I don't know what's wrong with it. What is? Sinclair Lewis, perhaps?

"Cleverness and talent mean nothing: everybody is clever, and talented. It is no easier to write and sell junk than it is to write and sell other kinds of writing. Your friend isn't going to have an easy time. Tell me about him. Writing should never be a profession. I mean this. I'll starve forever, but I won't be amazed. I knew this when I started out to write. There are worse things than not having lots of money. De Jong, I think, deserves to be given a decent break. I hope he has some luck: sorry to hear his book flopped. Now get this straight: mine will flop, too. It's in the cards. But I'm not worrying. Let it flop. If I am offered any sort of a prize or fellowship I shall have to ask those who hand out the doughnuts to eat them themselves. My sympathies are with the unknown writer; always. I think, in his way, he is doing the real writing of America. I am the unknown writer who got around to a bit of mediocre recognition by standing on his head and saying, 'Take a letter to America.' I need no introduction. I am unknown from coast to coast. There ought to be ten thousand good writers starving in America.

"My old man died when I was two and a half. I live with my mother and sister when I am in Fresno. Send along the photographs and stories. Return the photograph I am enclosing. Good wishes all around."

That letter just about flipped us out. Arnie Bennett and I lost no time in sending short stories to our idol. And we set about writing threatening letters to magazine editors, warning that any issues they put out without a Saroyan story would be ignored as beneath notice. When "Ah-ha Ah-ha" appeared in the *American Mercury,* I wrote editor Charles Angoff, "Is it possible the *Mercury,* zombie-like has come back to life?" He replied, "I agree with you that it is a superb job."

He showed my letter to Saxe Commins, a Random House editor, who wrote and told me about their forthcoming edition of Saroyan's first book, *The Daring Young Man on the Flying Trapeze,* a collection of his short stories. "We are confident in our prediction," he declared, "that his volume will win recognition from critics and public alike." I replied that he already had my order, and the orders of Arnie Bennett and another friend, waiting to be filled.

I wrote Saroyan in part, "'There ought to be ten thousand good writers starving in America' was inspiring enough to make me temporarily abandon a well-rounded plot for the S.E.P. in favor of something I've put off for two years; a story of life in a large law office and its effect upon adolescents. Slightly proletarian by suggestion. I know about this."

On 1 August he send me a card: "I meant to write to you and Bennett long ago, but one thing out here head [sic] to another. I went away for a while, and when I came back there was a lot of work to do, and consequently this delay. . . . I have read about half of your story: so please do not mind. The writing is good and the story holds one's interest. This is just to let you know I haven't forgotten you fellows and will write when I get a chance. Say howdy to Bennett. See the next issue of *Story:* and if you have cash, send for a copy of my book"

I replied, telling him that Arnie and I were doing to whoop it up for the book. On 12 August he wrote me, "You are a pal, and I'm damn grateful, though you have a right to feel that I am no such thing, which isn't so. I have actually been dizzy with all sorts of complications, and I have done hardly any work, hardly any letter-writing. . . . Please be patient, though. Getting a first book off the press is one of the toughest things I can think of, and when you get one off the press I think you will agree with me. A while back I managed to write some stories and sold one to *Vanity Fair,* called "Little Caruso": it is fine American humor, and it willl appear in a couple of months. Thanks for writing Angoff; his reply seems swell. And thanks for getting your third friend to send in an advance order, too: that is doing a fellow a favor. I'll do the same for you some day, and no fooling. You fellows will be coming along soon, I'm sure, and I feel pretty proud of knowing you beforehand: I mean, proud too that you know me beforehand. Say hello to Bennett, and write again. Good wishes."

Our little fan club continued bombarding magazine editors with letters hailing each new Saroyan story as it appeared. I wrote him recording our efforts, and editors' responses, along with my own evaluations of the stories. In my next letter I told him that no other modern writer had the power to stir me to my depths as he did.

On 2 October he send me a card: "I feel miserable: I haven't written you a decent letter. . . . Many thanks for your last letter: and for the ballyhoo on my behalf. I think I understand how you feel. All of us are still a bit young. Ten years or twenty from now I'll have an idea or two. Bill."

In October, when I read my autographed copy of *The Daring Young Man,* my astonishment, admiration, and enthusiasm knew no bounds. The impact of reading a whole book of his stories left me despairing of my own small talent. The emotion impelled me to write a sonnet called "To William Saroyan," which conveyed how Arnie and I felt about his genius:

> O true, we look and seem alike, but then
>> One star seems like its brothers in the sky,
>> A shameful cheat upon the naked eye
> For one may have the size and light of ten.
> Before I lived what crime did I commit,
>> What sacred beard did these hands tug that I
>> Should sit here now before some sheets and sigh?
> To feel the earth—and lack the simple wit
> To clothe my secret in a shining word?
>> While yonder walks a man whose meanest thought
>> Reveals itself with double meaning fraught
> And flies above the mind, sun-swift bird . . . .
> It strikes me as a little cheap and odd
> That favorites are played by even God.

As I said, I was only nineteen.

On 16 October a third friend, Herman Baron, felt impelled to write to Saroyan, and received this reply: "You three fellows are really whooping it up for me in a big way in the big city, and I'm much obliged to you: and what's more nothing could please me more than to know that young men, guys who are alive, find something in my stuff. This means plenty to me. So I feel proud of the letters from Arnold and Jules and you. Yesterday I returned that gangster photograph of myself, signed for you, but I didn't mean to be in such a hurry, though it actually was yesterday: therefore this note. I won't try to explain the two stories you didn't get because explanations are a nuisance: they do stand, though young fellow, and my saying this (of course) in no way is meant to ignore your own attitude toward them. So: don't be worried. Rhapsodic? Don't worry about that either. When you must be rhapsodic (and all young writers must or else don't deserve to be known as either young or writers), be rhapsi (tough word that:), be rhapsodic, that's all. Refer to Prelude to an American Symphony: New Masses: soon. Very rhapsodic, but what of it? Well, many thanks again for reading my stuff and writing to me: and very good wishes to you, to Jules, and to Arnold."

On 20 October Saroyan wrote me, "In much haste: many thanks for finding so much in the stories you have read. I am returning the gang-ster photograph, signed. . . . Please do not feel bad because I cannot take time out to talk about the stories you mailed me. They show much that is admirable, but some need of growth, technical: I mean, you and Bennett must learn to stand over your subject matter and make it behave: must be the boss."

When I wrote Saroyan again, I sent him copies of all the reviews of the book I could get, and discussed them. On 8 November he wrote me: "The reviews make me laugh. Thus & Thus & Thus: & the whole business comes to nada. I am answering the ones who are burned up because my book is going over quietly. (Quietly? Well, it's quiet where I am. I'm not in New York.) *The Nation* & *The New Republic* take vicious socks at my chin & make me laugh louder than ever & if they print my answers all of us will have a lot of fun. Which is one of the reasons why it is pleasant to have had a book printed. Send me any clippings (reviews) that come your way & any information you get about the book. I appreciate it very much. Bill."

I sent him some more reviews, and on 20 November he wrote me: "Many thanks for the letters & clippings. . . . I have no argument with any critics: they can think what they like. I just write and let it go at that. Sure Armenians are terrible, as per custom: along with all other people. Who cares? A good artist elevates them and embellishes their vices, alters them etcetera. Art, the general deceiver. (Not altogether of course.) Tell Bennett I can't write a letter just now. Working steadily etcetera. So long."

When Saroyan came to New York to make the rounds of the cocktail circuit, he phoned me. "Jules," he sighed, "I wanted to get together with you and Arnie and Herman, but do you know what's happened to me? They've turned me into a social lion. I perform at all these goddam literary affairs, and they've made me sicker than a dog. I can't even hold my head up. All I want to do is crawl into bed and sleep. But I had to call you and tell you I'm thinking of you guys, and maybe if I can get out of this rat race we can finally meet."

But we never did. Saroyan's star shot sky-high, and the demands on his time were overwhelming. I never stopped thinking of him, of course. Three years later I wrote him again at his 348 Carl Street address in San Francisco.

He replied, "I remember you. What's happened to that little gang? Now that you're 23 (and I suppose the other are about the same age) this is the time where you'll have a better chance to get going. That's how it was with me. Anyhow. Did I tell you I was dying of ptomaine that time we talked over the phone in N.Y.? Well, maybe that's what it was. Anyhow, I lived, I guess. I got a letter from your friend Pearl Gutfeld a while back and although lately I haven't been answering every letter I get I decided to answer hers, because there is always the chance that if I don't I'll be hurting somebody who shouldn't be, so if I can take time out I do and write an answer. My first book will always be an exciting when [*sic*], no matter when read. I looked it over again after the letter from Miss Gutfeld and was kind of impressed. That's what I meant when I said I read it for somebody young because even if you aren't young when you read it it somehow makes you go back to when you were young: that was what I meant to do, unconsciously anyhow, and it happened, which means I was very lucky, and I was. My new books are better, but different; they'd naturally have to be. In my opinion I am one of the most important writers in the world, which of course is going to make you laugh; it makes everybody else laugh when I tell them so, but it's the truth. The'll know as time goes on. I know now; that's the difference.

"I have two more books accepted, making six. The stuff is all very fine and practically the only stuff in print I care to read: that's how you can be sure of your reading, by writing it yourself; after four or five years what you wrote you wrote four or five years ago becomes especially fine because it becomes isolated, self-sustaining, by itself whole, and you know the years haven't been lost, though you yourself have grown and naturally changed; the change is subtle, sharply remembered things gradually becoming extremely dimly remembered, so that when you read, you live again. That probably explains some of what you ask in your letter. Hope you have a nice time in Europe; you're lucky to be going. I went all right; it was great; also worked in Hollywood a short while (read this issue *Story* about that). I note there are some more questions to answer, so I'll go over to a new page. I only write what I wrote, as the saying is. I never draw up a campaign. The others can do that and earn fame and fortune, which I don't need as badly as they do. When I write a novel it will be there: and a play too. I don't even promise to write another story; but it happens, as a rule. See "The Pomegranate Tree" in *The Atlantic Monthly* in the next issue or the one after. You ought to examine the book I published in Hollywood: *Three Times Three;* you can get it at one or another of the shops on Fifth Avenue. It's a good book for people who write. Dutton's has it, I'm sure. I remember seeing two copies there this August; it's a cinch they haven't sold them. Read "The Man with the Heart in the Highlands"; "The Living and The Dead"; read the whole book.

"I went around like this on my trip [answer to question]: London, Calais (no stop, though, just customs inspection) Paris, Vienna, Lemberg, Poland, Shepetovka, Russia, Kiev, Kharkov, Ordzonikidze, Tiflis, Erivan, back to Tiflis, by boat over the Black Sea to Sevastopol, up to Moscow, then to Leningrad, Helsingfors, by boat to Stockholm, by train to Oslo, Bergen, by boat across the North Sea, I think to Newcastle, up to Edinburgh, down to London, and home. That's a good trip. Any trip is good, though. Travel lowest class; it's fine. I did."

That was my last contact with Bill Saroyan. I made no further effort to continue our linkage. I liked to discover geniuses when they were unknown. Once their genius was recognized, and they were universally hailed, I lost interest and moved on to new discoveries. But Bill Saroyan continued to play a crucial part in my development as a writer. At least, the young, dynamic Saroyan did. Forgive my heresy, but I came to feel that his best work had been done in those unspoiled, go-to-hell years. In my opinion he was never able to top himself when young, an untrammeled spirit.

In the thirties my father, a man wise beyond his years, told me, "Jules, you'll never be another Saroyan—a genius. You'll be a fine, competent writer. But no genius. You know why? You've never known poverty, never suffered enough."

He was right. I published over sixty books, and more than a thousand magazine articles and stories. Fine. Competent. But definitely no works of genius. But what the hell, how many Saroyans are there in any generation?

Inhale and Exhale: A Letter to Henry Miller

JAMES LAUGHLIN

Every now and then a book comes along that changes the whole literary climate. It hits like lightning and then, after the rain, the air is clear for a new beginning in writing. Eliot's *The Waste Land* was such a book, and Delmore Schwartz's *In Dreams Begin Responsibilities*. And Saroyan's *Daring Young Man on the Flying Trapeze*.

That was in 1934. I didn't read the book on its publication because that year I had taken leave from Harvard and was studying with Pound at his Ezuversilty in Rapallo. When I got home I stopped by the Gotham Book Mart to see Frances Steloff, and as so often happened, she said, "Jamesie (she always called me that), here's something for you." And it was, oh how much it was, and to what a wonderful friendship it led. I had been writing stories, some of them published in *Story* and *The Harvard Advocate*, but I felt blocked because I couldn't do plots. Then here was the "daring young man" who showed me that you didn't need conventional plotting, that the structure of the story could be imagination and what the words did by themselves and excitement about life, people "inhaling and exhaling." It got me going again, though I knew I had to be careful not to sound like Saroyan. The real thing will not submit to imitation.

Our publishing relationship began with the second number of the New Directions anthology in 1937. Bill had run across the first number and sent me a batch of stories. To be exact, he sent me eleven stories, which was a small problem because, fine as they were, there just wasn't space for so many. But he didn't take offense, and we had "Everything," "The People, Yes and Then Again No," and "The Pool Game," in Number 2, and "The Journey and the Dream" and "Romance" were carried over to Number 3 in 1938.

But then there was a real problem and it was all my fault. Bill asked for the other stories back and I couldn't find them. This was no great wonder considering the chaotic operation that New Directions was in those days; sometimes I worked from the converted stable on my aunt's place in Connecticut, sometimes from the "office" in the living room of the Schwartz's apartment in Cambridge, and often enough out of my suitcase if I was off skiing in the winter or roaming around Europe in the summer. (One of Delmore's manuscripts was found after some weeks of agonized search under the floorboards of the mail truck that brought the mail up to Alta from the Salt Lake Valley.)

Naturally Bill decided that I was not a very reliable publisher. But we kept in touch over the years. Our first meeting was at Kenneth Rexroth's house on Potrero Hill in San Francisco. Life at the Alta Lodge, which I was trying to run that winter, was not culturally enriching, and when I had had enough of rousing drunken cooks from bed to get breakfast or explaining to irate guests that the hot water was quite hot enough for the likes of them, I would drive across the Nevada desert, stopping to shoot craps in deserted dream towns like Golconda and Winnemucca and Tonopah, to refresh my soul with the Rexroths.

Unfortunately, Bill arrived at Wisconsin Street on one of Kenneth's grouchy days. Kenneth could charm the birds but not if he didn't feel like it. I forget now what line of attack on Bill he took, but Marie gave me a sign, and Bill and I went off to a nice, rough bar on Market Street. I don't think I bothered to drink much because Bill was enough stimulation. It was a great day for me.

Perhaps I can best convey what Bill was like by quoting from some of his letters. It's all there. He could type himself right onto the page, as was true also of Henry Miller.

Bill was one of the most loyal, and vocal supporters that New Directions ever had. He would raise hell in bookstores that didn't carry our books; it was almost a personal affront to him, even though ND was not his publisher. He knew many of the ND authors and believed in them, in their right to have a showing in the welter of trash and pap. We corresponded about what he called "the New Directions War," the war against the status quo of mediocrity in book marketing. In November 1938 he wrote me:

> . . . Well, the poor bookstore keepers aren't really the enemy, although in a tragically silly way they are allies of the enemy; these poor people are trying to get a living out of *selling* books, and after a while the selling of the noblest thing in the world becomes a horrible activity; you have only to think of the women who sell it. . . . I used to get sore at the bookstore owners or managers for ordering only six copies of my books; now I ask them if they aren't afraid they'll get stuck; and sometimes I say let me know if you get stuck; I'll buy the copies you can't sell.
>
> I don't know who the real enemy is, Jim, unless it's ourselves; followed by our equals or superiors who read but don't write; it's a

cinch we don't stand a chance in the world with the people; they're busy with other things; we have an ally in youth, I believe, but as a rule youth reads, does not buy, books.

There is little interest in new directions in living, so it is natural that there shall be still less in N.D. in writing. . . . To us, no doubt, there can be no decent living without decent writing. . . . We ourselves, however, are several thousand light years from the truth, from a decent reality; a reality with dimension, order, reason, spontaneity, and dozens of other good things—and that's why I say that we ourselves are our own enemies. . . .

Some of our greatest writing has been great because it has been evil—evil is that which disintegrates the Man, that's all; good is that which integrates; the world disintegrated man first; we reported what the world had done, and because what it had done was so vast and tragic our reporting was, in one sense at least, great: James Joyce; poor Lawrence, trying to become integrated personally and thereby trying to save the whole race; many others along the way; and now Henry Miller. These men were or will be burned by the enormity of the task and will die, or have died, before they will have reached the light, and balanced the labor; given it dimension; inhaled and exhaled; and put the good over the evil . . .

I feel pretty certain of this, though; that you won't be knowing the real importance of New Directions for fifteen or twenty years. . . .

"Inhale and exhale," as Gary Snyder and Allen Ginsberg are telling us now, though I never heard Bill talk about Buddhism. But atman, as soul, he certainly had, and at his own level, in his own loving, Armenian way, his self was universal. So much of this comes out, bursts off the page, in a great letter that Bill wrote to Henry Miller in July 1936, when Henry was still in Paris. This letter came my way nearly ten years later. Henry showed it to me when I was visiting him on Partington Ridge in the Big Sur. I admired the letter so much that Henry, the perfect Chinese host, insisted on giving it to me.

The letter begins with Bill's report of an evening with the painter Hilaire Hiler in Berkeley. (Hiler was a Paris friend of Miller's, and the three of them—Miller, Hiler, and Saroyan—teamed up to write the symposium on modern art *Why Abstract?*, which New Directions published in 1945.) Then Bill jumps to the subject of the little magazines in which he published much of his work. He says to their editors:

All right, you sons of bitches are getting out a lousy little magazine and you can't pay for anything you print, so you are offered only lousy stuff and you print only lousy stuff, so here's something that itsn't lousy and maybe great, and you can have it free if you want it because a thing which is given must be a good thing, as a thing which is sold must

be a lousy thing. I mean, I give them all the breaks, and it is the same
when I gamble, or when I do anything else. I want them to have the
advantage because I know I don't need it. And then when I lose, I
haven't lost because I haven't sought to win, I have given. As a rule, of
course, Not always of course. The gamblers who know me think I'm
the best and worst gambler who ever gambled. Every time I walk into a
joint everybody gets happy because they remember my crazy and
generous and mirthful approach to the art and religion. Poker, horses,
or anything else. I am very often very lucky, for no other reason than
goodwill and amusement. And when I am unlucky, it is the same,
which amazes the gamblers and the others. They weep with the coming of disorder, unluck, and absence of universal smile. I have found
out a lot about the living in gambling joints and carried over into the
other joints this knowing. I have not yet said what I know I shall some
day say about this. Two Days Wasted in Kansas City is an introduction
to the theme. A note. Ah-ha, also. Our vices: man's child-like, innocent, vices: our desperate explorations of the scent and substance of
mortal magic in the female body, gay and bitter and comical; and
throughout the journey our sorrowful remembrance of days gone,
years gone, places ended or far away, faces lost, bodies swallowed by
the black of earth-river and night; eyes closed. And the world: its dull,
cold, hard, absurd presence, in and around us. And our drinking, and
the voyages to nowhere. Christ, man is innocent. Man's innocence is
endless. Evil, which is super-virtue, is beyond the powers of his being.
I am saddened and amused by the delightful and painful. And our
goofy ambition.

   My God damn Packard. What is it? Why have I got the contraption?
I am studying the path across the world: I know it as the walker; and
now at seventy miles an hour I am getting to know it as the swift rider;
rolling. It is a tremendous, a lovely and desolate, thing. I don't ride
often. I walk often; even now with the Packard. Which I never drive
around in the city, since it is no good for anything there. It is for the
highway There is something to find out about travel too; which goes
down very deeply; which is of reaching or the other of the two only
real events, birth and death; of reaching, of being on the way to, one
or the other; but mostly death, in our time. There is, at seventy miles
an hour, in an automobile, or sixty, in a train, or two hundred in an
airplane (perhaps only; I am not sure about the airplane) a sense of
deep inward relationship to an operation: to death, though one lives. I
think travelers, who are a special tribe, are happiest in motion because
deeply they (that depth) feel an increasing nearness to death, to end:
sleep. Maybe I'm wrong, but I sure as hell am right too. I don't give a
good God damn about the way they receive my stuff, although I'll
always tell them it's great stuff and burn hell out of them, especially
the lousy writers; they hate my guts; and all I do is keep on showing
them how it can be done; there are few great writers over here because
there are few great men. They sometimes ask me, the unpublished

ones, often much older than myself, how to do it; and when I tell them it has nothing to do with writing, they don't get it. When I tell them any writer's work has ultimately only one character, the writer himself, they don't get that. When I tell them to reach the first-rate in themselves, they don't get that. So I try to talk their language and tell them something about something they've written which is lousy and always will be. But the published ones are sore at me. I'm not sore at them because they're nothing and I can't waste the anger which is too valuable. That makes me a son of a bitch; they sense these things I'm telling you and it gripes them. They have my good wishes, as usual. I don't sell stuff; I haven't compromised; I don't write for anybody; I don't even write; I don't know anything about the things they know about; I get along all right with the language because it is no language for me until I have made it a language and then it is my language; it is my means of keeping the mood, gay or tragic, kindly or angry, alive. It is going to be one book or course; all of [it] together; very short ones; short ones; and if it happens, long ones; novel, or anything they wish to call it. That doesn't matter; technically the whole thing will be a novel; but the identification tag doesn't please me. I asked Hiler about you last night; about being in Paris. He told me what you've told me, and I get it. I can tell, from the language of your letters, that you are one of the great ones. "Now I am never alone. At the very worst I am with God" is plenty. I want very much to read your stuff. That long novel you are doing sounds great. . . .

Many thanks for being so generous about my stuff: I know you mean it. I'm not that good though; although I know I'm plenty good. I'm writing the book all right. I'll have written it some day; I hope it won't be before I'm seventy or eighty or ninety, because getting to be seventy or eighty or ninety is part of it. . . .

Good luck to you, Miller; and thinks for referring Fay [Frank Fay, the actor-director] to my stuff; he doesn't seem to like it, but he will; they all will; how can they get away from it? I've got them by the nuts, only they don't want to admit it. I look forward to seeing the books; and don't forget to turn on the machine-gun on Cerf; and let me know if I can tell him anything from this side. Yours truly, as they say:

:Bill Saroyan

Yes, inhaling and exhaling, Bill was crazy and generous and mirthful. He didn't always make life easy for himself but he was a damn fine writer, one of the real ones of his time.

Goodbye, Wild Bill

WILLIAM CHILDRESS

William Saroyan is dead, his ashes scattered equally between California and Armenia. But to me he'll always live in those three days when, after ten years of trying, I finally got to meet him in Fresno, California, in the autumn of 1973.

I suspect he invited me to his Fresno home because I was married at the time to the former Rosemarie Hanemian, a beautiful Armenian girl with big dark eyes. In 1973 Bill was closing fast on sixty-five. But the bull-like bellow that greeted me as I walked through the tangle he called a yard didn't sound like that of a man just eight years from death.

Saroyan was a bellower. His voice preceded him by a good mile on windfree days. As an Ozarkian, it delights me to know that if Bill hadn't made it as a writer, he would have done right well hog-calling. It wasn't that he had a hearing problem—he heard everything I asked him perfectly.

No, his loudness was simply part of the joy he brought to living—and living was what William Saroyan was all about. His life was a celebration of words, and his words were a celebration of life.

His last utterance, published posthumously at his request, showed the humor he found in life and death, which, to him, exemplified the human comedy. "Everybody has got to die," he said, "but I have always believed an exception would be made in my case."

The "Now what?" he added seems gratuitous. Even his last words needed editing, as much of his writing did. For all his greatness, Bill sometimes didn't know when to stop. He wrote like a bubbling cauldron—and cauldrons can overflow.

But his books brought joy to millions, which is what he wanted to do. "I'm too busy writing about people to philosophize about them," he once told me.

The day I met Saroyan, he wore a white pinstriped suit as rumpled as he was. His greying hair, swept back at the temples, struggled to escape

224

from under an ordinary straw hat of the kind farmers wear. The hat suited him. Bull-shouldered, stocky, a good three inches under six feet, he sported a white walrus mustache that went well with his noisy nature. He was a writer of the earth. Farmers were his people. He knew a lot of them around Fresno.

Sunflowers with stalks as big as a man's arm sentineled the narrow path. Saroyan bought two tract houses side by side—and promptly left them alone. The first, a weedgrown corner dwelling, stood empty at all times, his buffer against the world. The second was even worse—or better, if you shared Saroyan's view. Roof-high vegetation concealed him from prying neighbors.

"I see you out there in the weeds," he shouted from the door. "Come on in!"

The horticultural clutter included grapevines, apricot, fig and apple trees, and—on the ground—melon vines. Like green snakes, they twined with clumps of Thompson seedless grapes. Everything needed trimming, including Saroyan. I would learn that he got haircuts from his cousin Archie Minasian when he could.

"Ain't this some spot?" he roared, his brown, eyes twinkling. "Drives the Fresno city fathers crazy! They've threatened to mow my yard to make it conform to all the rest on the block. But 2729 West Griffith Way stays like it is! I'd fight 'em all the way to the Supreme Court if they touched a single sunflower."

For Saroyan's purpose—writing—the untended jungle was perfect. Anyone passing would think both houses were abandoned. "You'd be surprised," he said, ushering me inside, "at the number of peddlers who walk right by, never dreaming I'm hiding behind the bushes."

In the kitchen, he turned on a burner beneath a kettle from which he would serve us tea as we talked. The house had a large living room, stacked wall-to-wall with books in teetery piles. On a cluttered desk stood a shiny black portable typewriter. "I've had that machine over thirty years", he said, "and it still works like new." Frowning, he added: "They don't make anything near that quality anymore. Even that same maker has gone cheap and plastic."

Beside the desk stood an old-fashioned brass cash register. "Just for the hell of it, I chalk up every sale on that thing," he explained. Then he launched into his favorite topic—writers and writing.

"The duty of a writer is to write," he said. "If he's really a writer, and not just some faker talking about writing. As many hours as he can stand, day in, week out. The real ones go at it 14 to 16 hours a day, seven days a week." His voice, warming to the topic, was booming now. "They don't talk about writing. They don't belong to writers clubs—a silly notion since you can't write if you're sipping tea and nibbling cookies.

Saroyan with his lifelong friend from Palo Alto, Archie Minasian.

Saroyan talking to William Childress. *(Courtesy of William Childress.)*

No real writer does anything but WRITE. There are no union hours for real writers. . . ."

He ended with a gust of sound that seemed to sway the curtains. Among the Everest of books, I spotted stacks of hotel stationery and gew-gaws from foreign lands. Saroyan threw nothing away. In years to come I would receive letters on hotel stationery from Paris, Athens, and Rome. Once in a letter he sent me a wonderful drawing of himself peddling a bike in Bitlis, Armenia, his long beard flying in the wind. Saroyan was a fine sketch artist.

His drawings had a simple roughness as appealing as that of Grandma Moses. The sketch bore the inscription: *"Hello to William Childress from Armenia and the Old Man on the Bicycle Himself, March 3 1980."* It was signed "Bill Saroyan." Even then the cancer had begun its deadly work.

Bill disliked formality. His best friends called him Willy. Archie Minasian helped me meet Saroyan—and accompanied us on a romp through Saroyan's childhood in Fresno. My photographs show a man glad to be alive, but critical of the changes in Fresno since his boyhood.

"It's a damned city now," he said brusquely, as we looked at a bronze stallion in the civic center cast by Varaz Samuelian, a sculptor friend. "Cities have city fathers. Just look what they made the sculptor do before they would let him put his stallion here."

The stallion lacked what it took to make him a stallion.

During our drives, we visited a garage and gas station on Fresno's outskirts owned by a big, blue-eyed Armenian named Buck Makasian. "He's a throwback to the crusades!" hollered Saroyan. "See those blue eyes?" Buck, a quiet man, merely grinned.

Nothing would do but that Buck get in the station-wagon with Bill, Archie and me, and revisit Saroyan's childhood stomping grounds. "We must go by Selma and pick up Harry, too!" he shouted—and off we went to Harry's Toy Shop to pick up a small, dark-haired man with a cheerful face, whose last name I never learned. Saroyan was taking Buck and Harry away from their day's work, but they wasted no time getting in the car.

"Work can wait!" Saroyan boomed. "This is a holiday!"

He introduced me as a writer who was doing a story about him, adding "His name is William, too, and there have been some very fine writers with that name!"

Saroyan saved stationery and hotel trinkets from around the world, but he was not stingy. A more generous man never lived. He was lavish in his praise for other writers—but only if he liked them. He considered Will Rogers a fake, for example, and despised Louis B. Mayer and Sam

Saroyan with Childress. *(Courtesy of William Childress.)*

Saroyan plucking grapes. *(Courtesy of William Childress.)*

Goldwyn. But when the late James T. Farrell, author of the *Studs Lonigan* trilogy, hit hard times, Bill called publishers on Farrell's behalf.

The final day of my visit, we went on a gleaning expedition. Fresno farmers loved to have Bill come and pick fruits, melons, or vegetables when he was in town. One of them showed us raisins drying like zircons between rows of vines. Saroyan often took boxes of fruits and melons to his aging sister Rose in San Francisco. "Food," he remarked, "is something you can never have too much of." It was the poverty of his childhood speaking.

Saroyan's zeal for accepting anything free, especially food, stemmed from his years in an Oakland orphanage. That also explained his devotion to Rose, his oldest sister—blind and in her seventies at the time of my visit. Rose had cared for him in the orphanage. However, San Francisco held an especially warm spot in his heart. He would say after I had driven him there: "I did some real starving in this city. If you are hungry in a place, even if you don't like it, you remember it."

When Buck, Harry, and Archie begged other commitments, Bill and I spent more time talking about writing. He acted quite matter-of-fact about his five books in progress, and showed them to me.

"Let's just hope they amount to something," he said. He wrote as much for the act of writing as for money. Bill's task, he always implied, was to write the books. Let the publisher worry about publishing them. And true to his nature as a man with opinions, Bill had some about people who wanted to write.

"You know," he said, "when someone asks me to tell them how to write a book or a play or a story, I know they are just silly people who haven't any notion what writing is all about and never will. The writing business is full of fools. There are schools, contests, and anthologies waiting to take advantage of them. These people pay into these schools, contests, and anthologies just so they can see their name under something they have written. But that's not writing. That's preening. Real writers don't have to pay to be published; they will be discovered soon enough— usually when they have mastered their craft enough to be discovered. . . ."

Fixing me with keen brown eyes he continued: "Let me tell you how I write a book. I write books fast sometimes and not so fast other times. But I always make certain no day passes without at least one page being written. Anyone can find time to write just one page—even it if is a bad page that must later be changed. But the point is, at the end of a year you'll have a book, or most of one. This is not fresh advice. But it's the only advice I have about writing."

The next morning Saroyan, Archie, and I left for San Francisco. Throughout the drive Bill showed remarkable zest for everything he encountered. When the owner of a roadside restaurant recognized him, Saroyan said in a stage-whisper: "Tell everyone, but after I leave! I want them to buy my books."

Dropping Minasian at his home, I drove Bill to the home of his sister, Rose. It was lightly raining as we shook hands and said our goodbyes.

"This has been fun!" Saroyan roared, the bellow back in place and echoing in the narrow San Francisco street. As I left him standing in the mist that September night in 1973, I didn't know it was the last time I would ever see him.

When my story and color photos appeared in the April 1974 issue of *Westways*, editor Frances Ring wrote that Bill was pleased. Then came a letter from him, asking if I had any photographs left over. It marked the beginning of our correspondence. Over the next few weeks, Bill purchased many color photos of the day he frolicked in fields and orchards with his boyhood friends.

We wrote each other from 1973 to 1980.

His letters were invariably a *pot-au-feu* of opinions, wit, and humor. He could also get exasperated. "Please do me a big favor with our friend Frances Ring," he once wrote. "How is it that I haven't seen one issue of *Westways* in 8 months is it? and I have asked several times to have the magazine come to me: they can bill me: I'll pay! The same with *Smithsonian* and Ted Park: I especially want to see *Westways* because it is such a readable publication. And thank you for those color shots, they're fascinating."

But Fran Ring, after struggling against PR-interests determined to make *Westways* more corporate, would soon leave the AAA magazine in frustration. The PR types got their wish, and the seventy-year-old publication was reduced to being just another company organ.

"Buck Makasian fetched me home . . ." (Saroyan's letter went on) ". . . after visiting the art yard of Varaz Samuelian. Do you see Archie sometimes? The government is mentally arrested and all its people are necessarily ethical abortions—but the hell with it: let us pay up and think about large landscapes and easy open skies.—I am still thinking about David Park (artist brother of *Smithsonian* editor Ted Park)—is there a book about him, or a book reproduction of his staff: he was bold, swift, and very intelligent in his line and color. Thanks again for writing, and my best always to poet, prose writer, husband, father—that's a big job, but try to imagine how much harder the work of being would be if you weren't able to manage that big job? And think of all the poor sons-of-bitches who aren't able to.

"A very very rich man told me in San Francisco almost 40 years ago:

'Christ, I wish I had been born poor: I would now be a writer, a great writer.' (Is that so? comes the roared reply. Well, he thought it was, and I must say I wasn't sure it wasn't) . . .

William Butler Yeats was married to George (she ran the Cuala Press, Lower Baggett Street, and I bought a lot of the excellent books they got out 30 or 40 years ago) and I imagined she was his brother but she told me no her name just happened to be George. Years later I read in a biographical note about him that his wife said of him, Willy's silly. And Joyce's wife said of her husband, He's got a very dirty mind. This is all right and traditional. Kindly overlook the little Word for Today from Unity Village, Missouri—is that right? Do you ever see them on TV? Real crazy: so long: Bill."

On 21 February 1974, Saroyan wrote: "I have got to thank you for your fine February 12th letter full of good news and good doings and good plans—because I don't want to risk letting it go. I have got stuff on hand that I meant to answer right away, and all of a sudden I notice that four years have gone by. Great stuff you've written about Richard Gehman, but how is it that I never know about these writers dying? I swear I don't think he's dead. I keep running into his stuff. The money he earned—well, forget it. Does it really mean anything, at all? I doubt it. Aram interviewed Jack Kerouac for the *Paris Review* years ago, and Kerouac kept saying to Aram, Your father did it, he did it twice, he went broke, and then he started all over again, and made a million again. (Bullshit, but why Kerouac was obsessed with that is not so hard to figure out: Scott Fitzgerald lived by that philosophy, so to put it, isn't this America as they say). . . . Bill."

Saroyan was soon roaming the world again. I got letters from him postmarked Athens and Paris. He sent me a book in galleys that would become his latest. Back home in Fresno in May 1976, he wrote: "Dear Bill: Just back, and it's time I thanked you for your letters, and for the copy of *The Smith* which I hope to study soon . . .

The new book, properly titled *Sons of Bitches Come and Go, Mothers Hang in Forever,* was written last year in Paris while other stuff was also being written. This trip, a very short one, this visit that is, was four new 18-day works being written, but I haven't looked at them yet: I can only hope they aren't useless. Earlier this year in Fresno I wrote a book called *Nobody Wants to Die Old, Ugly and Not Feeling Well*—it is being typed in New York and Doubleday has first look at it, because their Paris editor Beverly Gordey is such a nice lady, and lets me have some of the books come to her in wholesale lots not just from Doubleday but from other houses. The basis of this book is that to me there is no such thing as a trash book—if I spend time with it, it is an immortal book. It would really amuse me I believe if the book turned out to be a success, but my experience has been that isn't the way it goes. And in my case that's another table entirely—I'm thinking of waiters in certain restaurants who are politely asked to bring a glass of water and reply, this isn't my table. So long, thanks, best always: Bill."

At the bottom of the letter in large scrawly letters was the question: "How much does *The Smith* pay for a story?" I passed on the information, and on 9 June 1976, Bill wrote:

"Thanks for the information about *The Smith;* it is quite a production and it is understandable that Harry Smith cannot pay much. I may someday send him something . . . what's wrong with $25 now and then? As for James T. Farrell, I wrote to Ken McCormick at Doubleday years ago and said: what is this, his books are rejected all over the place, he's a great American writer—and Ken took over and has certainly published some of Farrell's recent stuff. You speak of *California, Here I Come*—at the Fred Finch orphanage in Oakland one of my favorite songs was *I Love You, California,* and still is. Also, *Tenting Tonight* somehow meandered from the armies in the Civil War to the campfire songs of sleepy summertime (sleepy for a three-year-old at any rate). Yes, I agree, I ought to buy a 35mm camera, and by god I believe I will—but first things first; I want to find out how to write first (he said: and replied: You know there is no such thing as finding out, you write and that's the end of it, there is no how to it). All best always, Bill."

The last letter I received from Saroyan had a tinge of melancholy to it. I knew he'd had some ups and downs with his health—he was now seventy-one. And one by one, his old friends were dying.

Shorter than the others, the letter is 427 words long counting Bill's signature. It's dated Monday, 3 March 1980 4 PM, although Saroyan rarely counted the hours. Possibly he had some intuition that his life was nearly over. He was just fourteen months away from death.

"Dear Bill: How good to have a letter from you again: wasn't it perhaps six years ago that we made the rounds with my cousins. . . . I am glad you met Buck (Makasian), dead now three or four years. And Harry, retired from his toy shop in Selma and addicted to a daily visit to the YMCA and the company of other retirees. As for this old man I am deep in the midst of a new book which ought to be my best, or the best of my senile years, and I expect to be in at the Finis, ha ha ha, remember the movies that affected that word when they imagined it was upper class and cultured? I expect to have 300,000 words (or more) by the end of April. Then, I am scheduled to visit five countries partly under the sponsorship of the U.S. Information office. Then Moscow, perhaps Tashkent, Samarkand, Baku, Tiflis, Erivan, and back to Paris by way of Odessa and Athens. Or so I say, although it is not inconceivable that all of this may be simplified because I may find out that I don't feel like working that hard because summer is coming. . . . Here's the form (legal release) for *Friends Magazine,* but what's the matter with them? Surely they won't mind keeping me on the mailing list? . . . I really enjoy *Friends,* and if they want me to write something they need only ask, most likely. [Saroyan had written an earlier story for *Friends* when editor David Lawrence, who revered him, found that we corresponded and asked for Bill's address.] . . . . Thanks for introducing me to *Westways,* for Frances Ring is one of my favorite people even though I've not had the pleasure of meeting her. [He finally did meet her some months later.] Take care: Bill."

Over the years I sent Saroyan many pictures he hadn't seen of the dozens I took of him during those three summer days. Pictures of him teetering on railroad tracks, or filching figs, or staring through the fence at his childhood school in Fresno—seeing the ghosts of kids he'd played with more than half a century before.

I remember Bill as a man of joyful energy, reliving for a photojournalist he'd never met some of the crazy things he did as a boy. I'll remember my time with him as a celebration of life. Bill paid his dues and never stopped paying them. When young he roared, bellowed, and rebelled. When older, he roared, laughed and adjusted—more or less. Whatever pins he stuck in Hollywood "immortals" were doubtless deserved. Any barbs he tossed at other writers, they probably had coming—certainly as far as he was concerned.

William Saroyan was the only American writer I have ever really wanted to meet—a desire that went back to the first time I read *My Name Is Aram,* an Armenian *Tom Sawyer* if ever there was one. When I was a young college instructor assigning his books, Saroyan was a latter-day Mark Twain to me—but only time will tell if he will be ranked along with that great American author.

Saroyan was often called a genius—but most of all he was a *writer.* He never rested on one or two good books. They poured from his platen like sheaves, over fifty of them, some good, some not so good, all of them unmistakably Saroyan. "A writer's job is to write," he told me, and he meant it. He knew there is no other way to become a writer.

On the day, Bill died, 18 May 1981, I had written and sealed a letter to him, chiding him for taking to his bed—he who had run through Fresno fields picking melons and vegetables like a field-hand. Before I could mail it, a reporter from the *Los Angeles Times* phoned to say Bill was dead. Fran Ring had told him I knew Saroyan, and he wanted to know if I had anything to say. I said, "He'll be remembered when all the rest of us are forgotten."

Much of the letter is too personal to quote, but in part I wrote:

"Dear Bill: I called the hospital several times. They had you cordoned off with hundreds of relatives zealously keeping anyone from you, so this old *odar* [stranger] will write you instead. I hear you are alive. That's good. I have no use for dead Great Armenian Writers. I told the nurse, 'He is just being lazy. Go in and tell him to get up and write.' Bill, I have no way of knowing if she ever gave you the message, but she did giggle and say, 'I bet that will get him up if anything will.'"

The Unresolved Riddle

CLARK BLAISE

1

He seems so remote from us now, the dark, glamorous boy-o bearing stories of people who had never existed in American literature, an honest proletarian who still spoke of land and love and American values. He was the Armenian Huck Finn—brash and confident—but underneath it our most appealing archetype: a brilliant orphan, pert and ambitious, from the meanest streets a white man could travel. Even his name, someone quipped, made him his own acolyte. No wonder he shot to fame with a single story—he was made, like Capote, like Mailer, like Kerouac—for that kind of sudden success (but what a price the gods extracted)!. By his early thirties he was the most famous writer in America, the most famous Armenian who had ever lived. Six years after that story, he had published six volumes of stories, and his plays had won both the Pulitzer Prize and Drama Critics Circle Award. The competition must have wondered about a Faustian pact. With his good luck and swagger, his talent for nonstop merriment in the depths of the Depression, he could, if he chose, communicate with America through the gossip columns of Leonard Lyons and Walter Winchell.

We've had better writers, but few more productive and varied in their output. He was our best-known short-story writer in the great era of the story, and a major force in the theater—a unique combination, judged either by sheer bulk, or by influence and quality—but also an unstinting memorialist, autobiographer, ethnicist, essayist, film scripter, prefacer, letter-writer, and novelist. Only as a novelist did he consistently try, and fail. This judgment sees *The Human Comedy* as a serendipitous event: a young editor of genius, Robert Giroux, reading a film script and seeing a first novel within it.

Yet it is the perverse fate of Saroyan and his contemporaries, fifty-

book authors who knocked themselves out in blue-collar labor, to appear
to us insubstantial, fatally lacking the "big book." He felt with some of
them his lack of education, he missed the genteel respect, he seethed
with anger and passions he couldn't master, and it was drink, divorce,
and gambling, along with the war, the change in critical climate, and
perhaps the accumulating defeats he'd absorbed in just half a decade of
the late forties that diminished him. His story is told—with variations, of
course—a dozen times in the lives of Steinbeck, O'Hara, Farrell, Algren,
Marquand, and Cozzens. Who cares for them now, our fathers, these
children of Dreiser and Anderson and Lewis, mortar between the bricks
of their nemeses, Faulkner, Fitzgerald, and, always, Hemingway?
Saroyan was even assumed to be dead, literally dead, twenty years before
his actual death in 1981.

2

The Daring Young Man on the Flying Trapeze, his first and maybe his best
book, came out in 1934. Miraculous 1934: so did the first O'Hara, the
second Farrell, *Tropic of Cancer* (Saroyan considered Miller middle-class
and boring, though the parallels are tighter than he might have wished
to acknowledge), and there was Faulkner in 1934 between masterpieces,
Steinbeck a year away from *Tortilla Flat,* and Algren preparing his first
book, and Papa was writing stories. Kerouac, then twelve years old,
would soon discover Saroyan, and make him his early model. One story
in the right magazine could make a writer's fortune. Saroyan hit it with
his "Daring Young Man" in *Story* magazine. His conspicuous, brash
success even tripped the wires in Hemingway's cage. Papa offered to
push Saroyan's puss in.

Who, and what, was William Saroyan? An imperial personality, tyran-
nous and benevolent, and (if Gifford and Lee's oral biography or his son
Aram's two books can be trusted) ultimately unknowable. A figure like
Saroyan, nearly a politician in his ability to keep people fascinated and
distant, emerges from the attempts at biography as unrevealed as ever.
What we are told is that he was often (by which I mean more than most
of us) an evil, lying, shit-heeling son of a bitch of extraordinary pettiness,
violence, and prejudice—just as we learn from the special issue of *Ararat*
(Spring 1984) devoted to Saroyan that he was a concerned, generous,
endlessly fascinated spokesman for his chosen people.

We know only this with reasonable certainty: there were four traumas in his life (one of them a dispute with M-G-M, is too petty to recount here), against which his will and intelligence and maybe even his decency proved insufficient. The first was his father's death, when he was three, and his placement for five years in an Oakland orphanage.

For some observers, following closely the Freudian model, the child's personality was frozen at that moment, turning rigid and crystalline, and a mature ego never developed. In other words, there was a "Saroyan," a character and a personality, but never a mature human being. He was a libido and a superego, with a patchy turf of ego keeping them apart. One might also speculate that a certain supressed resentment toward his mother (who stashed him in the orphanage, who gave his father a drink of water though she might have known she was killing him), and thus to other women, enters into it, though, like Kerouac, he seems to have remained a classically mother-besotted figure most of his life.

Short of analysis, who can tell? The later years as a tamed, Fresno recluse, unsexed it would seem, author of a series of remarkable works of selective recall, could indeed be read as a "revenge" of the superego.

He survived orphanhood. By the age of eight he was back with the family, thanks to the financial success of his hated uncle, Aram. He fought as hard to be a writer as any author in our history—against a family (and a social climate) that expected him to push a mop, pick grapes, be a contributor. He was driven to success, there was literally no turning back, for surrendering the dream was retreating to death.

His father, a gentle minister, was also a poet in the Armenian language. The poems were displayed in the house during William's upbringing. Though the family invariably spoke well of Armenak, it is not without a certain immigrant derision—too gentle, too good. He died at thirty-six from a burst appendix, after drinking a glass of water given by his wife.

William never learned to read Armenian, though he spoke the language fluently. I agree with Gifford and Lee that the desire of the orphan-boy to leave a written record could derive, initially, from the presence of those poems; I wish only we had some indication of their content. Saroyan began publishing as a poet, in the Boston Armenian journal, *Hairenik*. They are not, apparently, poems of distinction, being English evocations of an unseen Anatolia—are they perhaps, memories of his father's poems read to him as a child? Anything more? Is there a reason, beyond the difficulty of the script and Saroyan's own anti-scholarly inclinations, for him never to have learned to read his mother tongue? Did he know his father's verse?

The other trauma can, perhaps, be related to the orphanage experience. In 1942, as a thirty-five-year-old bon-vivant, he was drafted into the Army and served three years under conditions that many would call absurdly favored. He stayed in hotels in London and luxury apartments in New York, he wrote films, speeches, and finally even a novel, he saw no action, and he made an absolute botch of it. His friends at the time— Irwin Shaw, with whom he shared assignments—acknowledged a simple truth that the army could not admit: he was not suited for regimented life of any kind. He was an anarchist, philosophically and psychologically, and he turned on the system, even in wartime, with the fury of a cornered beast. In the novel he wrote of the experience, *The Adventures of Wesley Jackson*, every petty complaint is magnified, no inconvenience goes unremarked, every insult to his own vast self-esteem is lovingly catalogued. The result, predictably, was not the sympathy he seemed to expect, but front-page *New York Times Book Review* scorn from his friend, Irwin Shaw:

> . . . Once more Saroyan is full of love for the entire world. He loves the Germans, he loves the Japs. . . . The only people he can find to hate are the Americans. He forgives the Germans Dachau and Belsen without blinking an eye, but he cannot forgive the sergeant who assigned him to KP in New York City. He goes through the entire American Army without finding a single officer who is worthy of any but the the most savage satire and derision. The only decent and pleasant officer in the entire book is the German officer who shoots Jackson's friend and takes Jackson prisoner. . . . Just why Saroyan feels that a world being murdered by fascism is merely "sad" and a world saved, even momentarily, from fascism is "hideous" is a matter between him and his conscience.

And Shaw was not unsympathetic to Saroyan's problems.

Time—working through different, less-good wars—tends to soften some of these judgments. In political matters Saroyan was innocent, but at least consistent. Individuals were good and bad (and that included Armenians—he was never short-sighted about his people, nor did he ever take the Turkish nation to task for the genocide); only governments (and lawyers) were invariably despicable.

The problem with Saroyan—in judging him, in feeling sympathy for him, and finally, in assessing the honest of some of his writing—lies far closer to home. His deepest failures were as a husband and possibly as a father (evidence from his children, especially his daughter, is ambiguous). His writing, however, is less equivocal. Novels like *Boys and Girls Together* and *Rock Wagram* try to rationalize his actions, and they, in a word, are embarrassing.

At the age of thirty-four, he married a seventeen-year-old Park Avenue debutante, Carol Marcus, whom he'd been courting for over a year

Carol and Bill, Fairmont Hotel, San Francisco, 1947. *(Courtesy of Aram Saroyan.)*

with all the ardor of a bachelor bull, but with the demand, extreme even by Old World standards, that she prove her worthiness by *first* getting pregnant. (Could it have been his fear of sterility, one wonders? He had been a steady consumer of paid sex from the moment he could afford it). [Editor's note: Saroyan denies this allegation in the interview with Garig Basmadjian.]

On the surface, she was entirely Saroyan's opposite. Dalton school, classmate of Oona O'Neill and Gloria Vanderbilt—pink, blonde, rich, and gorgeous. And, as her mother, Rosheen, put it—"a baby," "innocent," "spoiled." (The fact that she was, in truth, an orphan, that Charles Marcus was merely her step-father, that her mother had borne her out of wedlock at sixteen, that she never even knew her father's name, is the stuff of a Hollywood happy ending that simply refused to be written).

But she was as anxious for the marriage as Saroyan, and she bore their son, Aram, seven months after their marriage. The daughter, Lucy, came three years later. The marriage lasted six years, ending on the night Saroyan learned that his wife—his beautiful, blonde, pink, teen-aged bride—was Jewish. He leaped from their bed, left the apartment, and sailed for Europe. The cause of Saroyan's desertion had been secret until Aram gave us his version of it in *Last Rites*.

He was sensitive enough to public opinion never to state his justifica-
tion for leaving his family. He hinted at his reasons in various plays and
memoirs, suggesting betrayal, that his wife was dishonest (as, technically,
she was, since she had denied his bullying interrogation—"You're not
Jewish, are you?"—early in their courtship). Sympathetic readers of
Saroyan's later books had only his rage as an explanation: "I understood
instantly how a father might destroy his entire family and himself. I
couldn't look at the woman." (Even this, we learn from their remarriage,
and his frequent connubial visits between and after, is a lie. The far
more painful and moving truth is that he couldn't take his eyes off her.)

"She knew what she was," he wrote, and it served his self-mythologiz-
ing purposes to leave it at that: she was the rich, cunning little sophisti-
cate, he the innocent provincial. Above everything—and here, again, he
is unfortunately consistent—he despised "cleverness" in women. They
were to be patronized as warm-hearted prostitutes, or else tucked away
in marriage forever out of view.

After the six-month remarriage, and for his remaining twenty-nine
years, Saroyan appears never to have had a love affair, never again a
serious female relationship. The marriage can be termed an all-time
disaster, with a thing called "Armenian culture" coming in for much of
the blame. But clearly, it was a marriage fueled by madness. The obsession with Carol seems to have set up conflicts in Saroyan that tore his
defenses apart. There's one extraordinary picture of the pig-tailed and
pregnant Carol being carried across a mountain stream on Saroyan's
back that belongs on the cover of *Lolita,* though the plot and some of the
scenes should be patented by Neil Simon. Carol Marcus, of course, is
now Mrs. Walter Matthau.

Saroyan had another dark passion that ruined his life on numerous
occasions—gambling. So easy to see it now as the downside to his phenomenal luck (Aram suggests he *had* to have faith in divine intercession,
he would literally stake his life on "God's intervention"). When good
fortune didn't descend on him unbidden, he would court it in Vegas or
at the track, or in any pick-up poker game (he was, apparently, one of the
world's worst card players), condemned, it would seem, to reconstruct
the *Ur*-condition of anonymous orphanage. He told everyone he needed
a handicap in order to write—*reculer pour mieux sauter*—but he burdened
himself with too many losses. So long as he was married he could blame
his wife for not letting him gamble, or blame her for letting him go too
far. After the War and the marriage, the gambling, if anything, in-
creased.

It was, as many of his friends saw clearly, another of his sicknesses.
And like all of his sicknesses, he used it for his writing and used against
his family. He was, in a way our generation has almost lost sight of, a

Saroyan at a gathering in the home of Diana Der Hovanessian in Cambridge, Massachusetts. Facing the camera are Jack Antreassian, former editor of *Ararat*, and Linda Hamalian.

writer. A writer, even without audience or publisher. A writer like his unpublished, unread father, the Armenian minister. If ever there has been a literal meaning to writing being salvation, then the last thirty years of William Saroyan are its proof on earth.

3

The special issue of *Ararat* reveals Saroyan in an older voice, the communal conscience, the faithful correspondent, the concerned, alert, decent patriarch. No hint here of anti-Semitism (and one should be extremely cautious in causally labeling him with such a sickness. The marriage was his sickness, it drove every passive prejudice to the surface). In 1977 he writes to Leo Hamalian of being "thrilled that the Jews [in Iran] were taking Armenian names" for their protection. Saroyan, the lifelong bully (he heard tapes of his voice with his children and was appalled at his helpless inability to show love), writes to Antranik Zaroukian, "The greetings of the Armenians are amazing to me in the

Saroyan during a lecture. *(Courtesy of Layle Silbert.)*

intensity of the kindness and even compassion of them: *Give me your burden of sorrow,* for instance. It must surely need many centuries of experience for a people to make such a greeting, such an expression, part of the people's speech."

And this was not an old man's deathbed conversion. He had answered letters from youthful readers, Armenian or not, even in 1934 ("ministories" he called his youthful letter-writing, from his days of being able to write a story a day for months at a time, a play a week, and still carry on at parties all night—and he was right). To his daughter Lucy, an actress, "He was not unlike a unicorn. There's only one. . . . In terms of grappling with the mystery of him as a father, yes I did and I do and I probably always will. He was an astonishing man. He was the most exciting, dazzling, vibrant, vital and funny man that I ever knew, and mystifying, a very mystifying man. So, yes I grapple."

It seems enough for all of us. A unicorn, an Armenian, an author of fifty books and untold plays, with, we're told, at least as much still unpublished in manuscript in the two houses he kept in Fresno. The last book he saw published, *Obituaries,* though I would not call it a masterpiece as some have, is one of the great unfettered romps in American literature. It could only have been written by a man totally at peace with himself, and totally at odds with critical opinion. If there are more books like it in the archives of the Saroyan Foundation, they'll be reading him when my generation is long forgotten.

William Saroyan (1908–1981)

ARAM KEVORKIAN

One day in the spring of 1967 when my firm was in its first year, and we were located on rue Galilée in Paris, a middle-aged woman whose name I have mercifully forgotten was just leaving my office when a dark-haired man walked in whom I introduced as William Saroyan. "Oh, Mr. Saroyan," she babbled out, "I thought you were dead." Chuckling graciously but without losing a beat, Saroyan replied, "That's all right Madam, sometimes I feel that way myself."

Now Saroyan is dead—dead of a cancer that started in his prostate and spread around, not being cared for, as Bill was not a believer in medicine or hospitals, until even his battling brain could not ward off the inevitable, as the saying goes (to use one of his phrases).

Saroyan was a client of my firm and a friend ever since my arrival in Paris twenty years ago in April, except for a period beginning almost nine years ago when as with everyone who was ever close to him, relatives, children, agents, publishers, doctors, and accountants, he got mad at me, too. He kept away for six years and then, in what seemed out of the blue, wrote to me. When I visited the West Coast and called him to arrange a visit to Fresno, I learned that he was dying of cancer. On that day, 8 April, my first visit to the city that had seemed so incredibly suited for boyhood when described in *My Name Is Aram,* I finally saw the two tract houses on West Griffith Way, which Bill had bought in the 1960s when he unexpectedly, I say, because he had told me that he hated the place, particularly now that the builders and city planners had destroyed so many of his childhood haunts.

Thankful I am, nevertheless, for having made the visit, because Bill came to life during the afternoon. With Bob Damir, his San Francisco lawyer and a former Fresnoian, we ate *kharpoot kofte* at an Armenian restaurant, tried to buy a lemon cream pie at Rosa Karsh's bakery, a pie that Bill suddenly had a craving for, and then drove around Fresno and the neighboring farm communities, with Bill in the front seat pointing out landmarks of his childhood. Bill guided us to the place which had inspired one of his most poignant stories, "The Pomegranate Trees," a work of art that becomes even more astonishing when one contemplates the barren field where his impractical, inept, impoverished uncle imagined that he was going to grow pomegranate trees. Yet I could understand why his uncle had chosen this field, for lifting his eyes to the east he could perceive the distant highlands which reminded him of his native Bitlis in Armenia.

Appropriately enough this book was his last published work, *Obituaries,* a typically Saroyan tour de force, the form of which is built around 130 short chapters taking as theme the necrology list of *Variety* magazine for 1976. Most Americans with whom I had discussed Saroyan in recent years assumed that he had stopped writing. Saroyan never stopped writing, for writing was as necessary to him as breathing. What stopped was his being in style and being acceptable to the reviewers. To this obsolescence he certainly contributed greatly by being so intransigent in his business dealings, by refusing to use agents, by fighting with publishers, in a word, by not accepting the world of business that controls the artist's world. Back in 1939 when Bill was awarded the Pulitzer Prize for *The Time of Your Life*—a play, incidentally that he wrote in six days—he ostentatiously turned down the prize on the ground that "business should not subsidize art." He once told me that he would refuse the Nobel Prize if it were offered.

For years I had been predicting that Saroyan's death would bring forth a Saroyan renaissance. I consider Saroyan to be one of the great writers of our time, one of the few who excelled in three genres: the short story, the novel, and the drama. How many contemporary writers can you name who have his range? To do justice to Saroyan's works the critics are going to have to reread him with a fresh eye and get rid of some of the clichés that used to infuriate him: that he was sentimental, fuzzy, and a mere lover of humanity. Saroyan was as much a hater as he was a lover. His wraths and resentments were volcanic. He never forgave the world for taking away his father when Bill was three, nor his mother for putting him in an orphanage, nor the Army for drafting him at the height of his creative powers, nor the fates that broke up his marriage and estranged him from his children, Aram and Lucy, when they grew up. No, a new vocabulary is necessary to deal adequately with Saroyan the writer.

In all my years I have never met anyone who was as alive, as vibrant, as hilarious, as seeing, and as sensitve as Bill Saroyan. In 1966 when problems in the firm where I was working lead me to contemplate leaving and establishing my own office, Bill told me: "Aram, there is no need to be anxious. When the time comes to make the move, go with joy

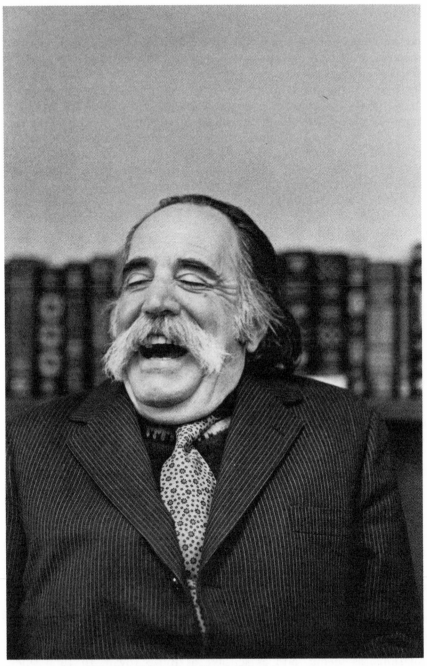

Saroyan in his seventies. *(Courtesy of Layle Silbert.)*

in your heart." Those words had an electric effect: they kindled my soul. I knew immediately that he was right, that the courage to make the big step must be mingled with joy.

In the last letter I wrote to Bill, I could think of no more fitting words to wish him courage on his last voyage than to remind him of what he had told me: "When the time comes to make the move, go with joy in your heart."

I know that Bill got the message. He replied on 20 April with a handwritten note that may well be the last thing he ever wrote, for he was found unconscious the following morning. His final words were "With deepest thanks and love."

Selected Books by William Saroyan

LINDA HAMALIAN

The Daring Young Man on the Flying Trapeze and Other Stories. New York: Random House, 1934; London: Faber & Faber, 1935.

Inhale and Exhale. New York: Random House, 1936; London: Faber & Faber, 1936.

Three Times Three. Los Angeles: Conference Press, 1936.

Little Children. New York: Harcourt, Brace, 1937; London: Faber & Faber, 1937.

Love, Here Is My Hat. New York: Modern Age, 1938; London: Faber & Faber, 1938.

The Trouble with Tigers. New York: Harcourt, Brace, 1938; London: Faber & Faber, 1939.

Peace, It's Wonderful. New York: Modern Age, 1939; New York: The Starling Press, 1939; London: Faber & Faber, 1940.

My Heart's in the Highlands. New York: Harcourt, Brace, 1939.

The Time of Your Life. New York: Harcourt, Brace, 1939.

Three Plays: My Heart's in the Highlands, The Time of Your Life, Love's Old Sweet Song. New York: Harcourt, Brace, 1940.

Harlem as Seen By Hirschfeld New York: The Hyperion Press 1941.

Hilltop Russians in San Francisco San Francisco: James Dellein, 1941.

My Name is Aram. New York: Harcourt, Brace, 1940; London: Faber & Faber, 1941; Cleveland: World Publishing, 1944.

Jim Dandy. Cincinnati: Little Man Press, 1941. Republished as *Jim Dandy: Fat Man in a Famine.* New York: Harcourt Brace, 1947; London: Faber & Faber, 1948.

Three Plays: The Beautiful People, Sweeney in the Trees, Across the Board on Tomorrow Morning. New York: Harcourt, Brace, 1941.

Saroyan's Fables. New York: Harcourt, Brace, 1941.

The Time of Your Life and Two Other Plays. London: Faber & Faber, 1942.

Razzle-Dazzle. New York: Harcourt, Brace, 1942. Revised. London: Faber & Faber, 1945.

The Human Comedy. New York: Harcourt, Brace, 1943; London: Faber & Faber, 1943; Cleveland: The World Publishing Company, 1954.

Get Away Old Man. New York: Harcourt, Brace, 1944; London: Faber & Faber, 1946.

Dear Baby. New York: Harcourt, Brace, 1944; London: Faber & Faber, 1945.

The Adventures of Wesley Jackson. New York: Harcourt, Brace, 1946; London: Faber & Faber, 1947.

The Saroyan Special. New York: Harcourt, Brace, 1948.

Don't Go Away Mad and Two Other Plays. New York: Harcourt, Brace, 1949; London: Faber & Faber, 1951.

The Assyrian and Other Stories. New York: Harcourt, Brace, 1950; London: Faber & Faber, 1955.

The Twin Adventures. New York: Harcourt, Brace, 1950.

Rock Wagram. Garden City: Doubleday, 1951; London: Faber & Faber, 1952; New York: New American Library.

Tracy's Tiger. Garden City: Doubleday, 1951; London: Faber & Faber, 1952.

The Bicycle Rider in Beverly Hills. New York: Scribners, 1952; London: Faber & Faber, 1953.

The Laughing Matter. Garden City: Doubleday, 1953; New York: Popular Library, 1953; London: Faber & Faber, 1954.

Mama I Love You. Boston and Toronto: Little, Brown/Atlantic Monthly, 1956; London: Faber & Faber, 1957.

The Whole Voyald and Other Stories. Boston and Toronto: Little, Brown/Atlantic Monthly, 1956; London: Faber & Faber, 1957.

Papa You're Crazy. Boston and Toronto: Little, Brown/Atlantic Monthly, 1957; London: Faber & Faber, 1958.

The Cave Dwellers. New York: Putnam's, 1958; London: Faber & Faber, 1958.

The William Saroyan Reader. New York: Braziller, 1958.

Sam, the Highest Jumper of Them All, or The London Comedy. London: Faber & Faber, 1961.

Here Comes, There Goes, You Know Who. New York: Simon & Schuster/Trident, 1961; London: Davies, 1962.

Boys and Girls Together. New York: Harcourt, Brace & World, 1963; London: Davies, 1963.

Me. New York: Crowell-Collier, 1963; London: Collier-Macmillan, 1963.

Not Dying. New York: Harcourt, Brace & World, 1963; London: Cassell, 1966.

One Day in the Afternoon of the World. New York: Harcourt, Brace & World, 1964; London: Cassell, 1965.

After Thirty Years: The Daring Young Man on the Flying Trapeze. New York:

Harcourt, Brace & World, 1964.

Horsey Gorsey and the Frog. Chippewa Falls, Wis.: Hale, 1965.

My Kind of Crazy and Wonderful People. New York: Harcourt, Brace & World, 1966.

Short Drive, Sweet Chariot. New York: Phaedra, 1966; New York: Pocket Books, 1967.

Look at Us: Us? US? With Arthur Rothstein. New York: Cowles, 1967.

I Used to Believe I Had Forever, Now I'm Not So Sure. New York: Cowles, 1968.

Letters from 74 Rue Taitbout, or Don't Go, But If You Must, Say Hello to Everybody. New York and Cleveland: World, 1969.

The Dog or, The Panic Comedy and Two Other Plays. New York: Phaedra, 1969.

Three New Dramatic Works and 19 Other Short Plays. New York: Phaedra, 1969.

Days of Life and Death and Escape to the Moon. New York: Dial, 1970; London: Joseph, 1971.

Words and Paragraphs. Chicago: Follett, 1970.

Places Where I've Done Time. New York: Praeger, 1972; London: Davis-Poynter, 1973.

The Tooth and My Father. Garden City: Doubleday, 1974.

Sons Come and Go, Mothers Hang in Forever. New York: McGraw-Hill, 1976.

An Act or Two of Foolish Kindness. Lincoln, Mass.; Penmaen Press & Design, 1976.

Morris Hirshfield. New York: Rizzoli International, 1976.

Chance Meetings. New York: Norton, 1978.

Two Short Paris Plays of 1974: Assassinations and *Jim, Sam and Anna.* Northridge: California State University Library, Santa Susana Press, 1979.

Obituaries. Berkeley, Calif.: Creative Art Books, 1979.

Births. Berkeley, Calif.: Creative Art Books, 1983.

For a full list of Saroyan's publications up to 1964, see David Kherdian, *A Bibliography of William Saroyan.*

Notes on Contributors

JULES ARCHER is the author of more than sixty books, his latest *Winners and Losers* (Harcourt Brace). He teaches writing at the University of California at Santa Cruz.

GARIG BASMADJIAN writes poetry, translates, and runs the Gorky Gallery in Paris.

CLARK BLAISE is a novelist, essayist, and short-story writer. His autobiography, *Resident Alien,* was published by Penguin in 1986. He has taught creative writing at Bennington College and McGill, Emory, and Columbia Universities.

WILLIAM CHILDRESS is a free-lance writer who lives in the foothills of the Ozarks. His poetry appeared in *Down at the Santa Fe Station,* edited by David Kherdian.

BRIAN DARWENT lives in Cheshire, England, and edited *The New Saroyan Reader* (Berkeley, Calif.: Creative Arts, 1984).

EDWARD FOSTER teaches at Stevens Institute of Technology in Hoboken, New Jersey, and is the author of *William Saroyan* (Boise, Idaho: Western Writers Series, 1984).

HERBERT GOLD, novelist and critic, has written an introduction to the new edition of *The Daring Young Man on the Flying Trapeze* (1984).

EDWARD HAGOPIAN is a playwright who lives in Bloxham, England, and California.

LEO HAMALIAN teaches at The City College of New York. He edited the Saroyan issue of *Ararat* (Spring 1984) and has been given a grant to study Saroyan's letters.

LINDA HAMALIAN teaches at William Paterson College and is writing a biography of Kenneth Rexroth for Norton.

PETE HAMILL, journalist and novelist, divides his time between West-hampton Beach and various points on the globe.

GILLISANN HAROIAN is completing a doctorate at The City University of New York while working as a free-lance writer and college teacher.

PENNFIELD JENSEN is a writer who lives in El Cerrito, California. He has been associated with the Creative Arts Press, publishers of *The New Saroyan Reader*.

ALFRED KAZIN teaches at The City University of New York. His appreciation is a shorter version of a piece that first appeared in *New Republic* 1 (March 1943).

ARAM KEVORKIAN is an attorney whose practice requires him to commute between New York and Paris, where he lives. He is on the editorial board of *Passion*.

HARRY KEYISHIAN is preparing a book of Saroyan criticism and a study of revenge tragedies of the Elizabethan era. He teaches at Fairleigh Dickinson University.

DAVID KHERDIAN has recently completed the third volume of his spiritual autobiography and moved back East with his wife Nonny, the nationally known artist.

DIKRAN KOUYMJIAN lives in Paris and Fresno (he teaches at California State University). He served as advisor to the Saroyan Foundation and teaches a seminar on his writing.

JAMES LAUGHLIN is a poet and the publisher of New Directions Press.

DANIEL LEARY, who teaches at The City College of New York, is a Shaw scholar and a specialist in modern drama. He lives in New York with his wife Judith Jobin, a free-lance writer.

EDWARD LOOMIS is a novelist who teaches at the University of California at Santa Barbara.

R. C. MacINTYRE teaches in Everett, Washington, and served in the army with Saroyan.

BRENDA NAJIMIAN-MAGARITY lives in Fresno, where she teaches in the public schools.

JOEL OPPENHEIMER is a New York poet presently teaching at the College of New England in Henniker, New Hampshire.

S. A. ROBBINS lives in Oakland, California, and is writing a book about his acquaintance with Saroyan of the orphanage days.

ARTHUR SAINER is a playwright and theater critic (*Village Voice* et al.) who is presently working as a free-lance writer in New York.

ARAM SAROYAN lives in Ridgefield, Connecticutt, with his three children and his wife Gailyn, an artist. He has just completed a novel.

PETER SOURIAN is chairman of the English Department at Bard College. He lives in New York with his wife Eva, a professor of French, and their two children. His latest novel is ready for publication.

JACK STORY, an English writer, is the author of *The Trouble with Harry*, made into a film by Alfred Hitchcock.

JAMES TASHJIAN is the editor of *My Name is Saroyan* (Harcourt Brace, 1983), a collection of Saroyan's early writing in *Hairenik*, of which Tashjian was the editor.

JACK WARNER, now retired from a long career in the motion picture industry and the Army Reserve, is a full-time writer. His novel *Bijou Dream*, appeared in 1982.

Index